Infrastructure Monitoring with Amazon CloudWatch

Effectively monitor your AWS infrastructure to optimize resource allocation, detect anomalies, and set automated actions

Ewere Diagboya

BIRMINGHAM—MUMBAI

Infrastructure Monitoring with Amazon CloudWatch

Group Product Manager: Wilson D'souza
Publishing Product Manager: Shrilekha Inani
Senior Editor: Shazeen Iqbal
Content Development Editor: Romy Dias
Technical Editor: Shruthi Shetty
Copy Editor: Safis Editing
Project Coordinator: Neil Dmello
Proofreader: Safis Editing
Indexer: Manju Arasan
Production Designer: Shankar Kalbhor

First published: March 2021

Production reference: 1160321

Published by Packt Publishing Ltd.
Livery Place
35 Livery Street
Birmingham
B3 2PB, UK.

ISBN 978-1-80056-605-7

www.packt.com

This book to dedicated to my late father, Mr. Patrick Nwose Diagboya, who was my mentor in knowledge acquisition.

Contributors

About the author

Ewere Diagboya is a technology lover at heart who started his journey into technology back in 2003. At an early age, he finished mastering Windows 98 applications. He learned coding in Visual Basic 6.0 with the help of his brother.

Afterward, he mastered other programming languages, building both desktop and web applications. Ewere moved into cloud computing and DevOps and has been practicing, training, and mentoring for close to a decade now.

He worked closely with other like minds to start the AWS User Group in Nigeria and fostered DevOps Nigeria Group vibrancy. In 2020 he was awarded the first AWS Community Hero award in Africa. Ewere also runs a training institute and has a blog on Medium where he writes about cloud computing and DevOps.

About the reviewer

Michael J. Lewis is currently a Principal in the cloud enablement practice at Slalom Consulting in Atlanta, Georgia, specializing in AWS, and DevSecOps. A computer science major and a US naval submarine veteran with over 25 years' experience in the computer industry, he has been at the forefront of emerging technologies, from the internet boom of the 90s to the latest trends in serverless and cloud computing. He and his wife Julie reside in Georgia with their three wonderful children.

Table of Contents

2
CloudWatch Events and Alarms

3
CloudWatch Logs, Metrics, and Dashboards

Section 2:
AWS Services and Amazon CloudWatch

4
Monitoring AWS Compute Services

5

Setting Up Container Insights on Amazon CloudWatch

6

Performance Insights for Database Services

7

Monitoring Serverless Applications

8

Using CloudWatch for Maintaining Highly Available Big Data Services

11

Best Practices and Conclusion

Assessments

Other Books You May Enjoy

Index

Preface

Monitoring, in my experience, is usually seen as the last step of the software development life cycle. It is, in most cases, the last of the DevOps life cycle under the *operate* section. This has made monitoring be on the back burner of the **software development life cycle (SDLC)**. Monitoring is only mentioned when systems start having problems, such as availability and reliability. Then the monitoring infrastructure is questioned in terms of its viability and its availability.

This should not be the case – when an application is being planned, monitoring should be a part of it. This is the role observability plays, taking monitoring to a whole new level. Observability is now built into an application that is being developed to allow internal traceability of the flow of transactions within the system.

This is kind of mindset and new method to monitoring, we will be able to draw good insights into the workings of applications as they are running and also be able to predict issues before they escalate to eventually become incidents.

A great deal of this book has been spent looking at monitoring from the angle of core and common AWS services used by organizations all over the world. This book will also teach best practices that can and should be employed as part of the availability, reliability, and survival of your application. Continually evolving your monitoring solution and ensuring even the smallest types of monitoring, as basic as endpoint monitoring, can make a big difference in your applications.

If you are just hearing about monitoring for the first time, this book is also for you. It will leave you with a solid foundation of the basic principles of monitoring and how monitoring started and grew to where it is now, and then take you through how monitoring works for different services in the AWS ecosystem.

Who this book is for

Monitoring can be a difficult concept to grasp for people just getting into the cloud. Having a structured part understand the fundamentals of monitoring can be daunting. This book helps those starting off in cloud computing and AWS to get a succinct explanation of what monitoring is about.

This book is also beneficial for those who are cloud computing users but do not have a broad and deep perspective of the concepts of monitoring, logging, metrics, and observability. This book will help to shape that understanding and help in understanding the role monitoring plays in the software development life cycle of any system or application.

What this book covers

Chapter 1, Introduction to Monitoring, covers the definition, history, and basic concepts of monitoring and the monitoring of systems, and an introduction to Amazon CloudWatch.

Chapter 2, CloudWatch Events and Alarms, explains how CloudWatch events can be configured for different scenarios and how to configure alarms.

Chapter 3, CloudWatch Logs, Metrics, and Dashboards, looks at the meaning of logs and metrics and how to create metrics from logs and a dashboard from metrics.

Chapter 4, Monitoring AWS Compute Services, introduces AWS compute services and how they integrate with Amazon CloudWatch for monitoring.

Chapter 5, Setting Up Container Insights on Amazon CloudWatch, explains concepts such as Docker, Kubernetes, ECS, and how Container Insights helps in monitoring containers.

Chapter 6, Performance Insights for Database Services, covers the concepts of different types of databases, AWS database services, and configuring monitoring on these services.

Chapter 7, Monitoring Serverless Applications, introduces the concept of the server and using Lambda Insights to get a clearer understanding of Lambda applications.

Chapter 8, Using CloudWatch for Maintaining Highly Available Big Data Services, explains basic big data concepts and AWS big data services and the monitoring of these services.

Chapter 9, Monitoring Storage Services with Amazon CloudWatch, introduces AWS storage services, the different types, and their functionalities, and how to monitor on them.

Chapter 10, Monitoring Network Services, introduces the fundamentals of computer networking, networking in AWS services, and their integration with CloudWatch.

Chapter 11, Best Practices and Conclusion, mentions some best practices with respect to monitoring and gives a summary for all the chapters.

To get the most out of this book

You should have a basic understanding of computers and how to use any operating system (Windows, Linux, or macOS).

You should be a cloud computing enthusiast working towards being an expert.

If you are a cloud/DevOps/software engineer who wants to broaden their scope of monitoring and see the power of Amazon CloudWatch in action then this book is for you.

Software/Hardware covered in the book	OS Requirements
Any type of Browser	Windows, macOS X, and Linux (Any)
Linux/Unix Terminal	Windows, macOS X, and Linux (Any)
An AWS account (Free tier suffices)	Windows, macOS X, and Linux (Any)

You need to install Terraform on your computer, whatever the operating system. **If you are using the digital version of this book, we advise you to type the code yourself or access the code via the GitHub repository (link available in the next section). Doing so will help you avoid any potential errors related to the copying and pasting of code.**

Download the example code files

You can download the example code files for this book from GitHub at `https://github.com/PacktPublishing/Infrastructure-Monitoring-with-Amazon-CloudWatch`. In case there's an update to the code, it will be updated on the existing GitHub repository.

We also have other code bundles from our rich catalog of books and videos available at `https://github.com/PacktPublishing/`. Check them out!

Code in Action

Code in Action videos for this book can be viewed at `http://bit.ly/3vgjYuk`.

Download the color images

We also provide a PDF file that has color images of the screenshots/diagrams used in this book. You can download it here: `http://www.packtpub.com/sites/default/files/downloads/9781800566057_ColorImages.pdf`.

Conventions used

There are a number of text conventions used throughout this book.

`Code in text`: Indicates code words in text, database table names, folder names, filenames, file extensions, pathnames, dummy URLs, user input, and Twitter handles. Here is an example: "Mount the downloaded `WebStorm-10*.dmg` disk image file as another disk in your system."

A block of code is set as follows:

```
[general]
state_file = /var/lib/awslogs/agent-state
[applications_logs]
region = eu-west-1
```

When we wish to draw your attention to a particular part of a code block, the relevant lines or items are set in bold:

```
buffer_duration = 5000
log_stream_name = {instance_id}
initial_position = start_of_file
log_group_name = server_logs
```

Any command-line input or output is written as follows:

```
yum install amazon-cloudwatch-agent
```

Bold: Indicates a new term, an important word, or words that you see onscreen. For example, words in menus or dialog boxes appear in the text like this. Here is an example: "To do this, click on the **Create rule** button in blue at the bottom right of the screen."

> **Tips or important notes**
> Appear like this.

Get in touch

Feedback from our readers is always welcome.

General feedback: If you have questions about any aspect of this book, mention the book title in the subject of your message and email us at customercare@packtpub.com.

Errata: Although we have taken every care to ensure the accuracy of our content, mistakes do happen. If you have found a mistake in this book, we would be grateful if you would report this to us. Please visit www.packtpub.com/support/errata, selecting your book, clicking on the Errata Submission Form link, and entering the details.

Piracy: If you come across any illegal copies of our works in any form on the Internet, we would be grateful if you would provide us with the location address or website name. Please contact us at copyright@packt.com with a link to the material.

If you are interested in becoming an author: If there is a topic that you have expertise in and you are interested in either writing or contributing to a book, please visit authors.packtpub.com.

Reviews

Please leave a review. Once you have read and used this book, why not leave a review on the site that you purchased it from? Potential readers can then see and use your unbiased opinion to make purchase decisions, we at Packt can understand what you think about our products, and our authors can see your feedback on their book. Thank you!

For more information about Packt, please visit packt.com.

Section 1: Introduction to Monitoring and Amazon CloudWatch

This part is focused on introducing the concepts of monitoring, logging, metrics, and alerts in a monitoring system. It will also explain the importance of monitoring infrastructure and applications and the advantages of using CloudWatch as a managed service for collecting metrics and alerting.

The following chapters are included in this section:

- *Chapter 1, Introduction to Monitoring*
- *Chapter 2, CloudWatch Events and Alarms*
- *Chapter 3, CloudWatch Logs, Metrics, and Dashboards*

1
Introduction to Monitoring

Monitoring is a broad topic that covers different human endeavors. Ignorance of monitoring ideals and concepts can adversely affect how to handle and manage engineering and computer systems effectively. Systems are usually not 100% efficient, and there are times they break down or do not work optimally as intended. The only way to understand and predict a breakdown is by monitoring the system. When a system is monitored, its pattern of behavior can be better understood, and this can help to predict a failure before it eventually happens. A proper maintenance process based on what has been monitored can be used to minimize failure of the system.

To help start the journey into monitoring, we will begin with understanding what monitoring is and the building blocks of every monitoring setup and infrastructure. We will explore the techniques used to monitor any infrastructure and for which scenario both of them are designed, and the relationship that exists between different monitoring components. Then, I will explain the importance of monitoring using real-life scenarios to help to emphasize and better your understanding of each importance mentioned. To crown it all, I will explain how the **AWS Well-Architected** framework portrays monitoring as a very important aspect of your **AWS workload**, using the principles of the **pillar** to galvanize what we have already talked about in terms of importance and how it makes the architecture of any **Cloud workload** complete. The purpose of this chapter is to help you understand what monitoring is, provide a little historical background of monitoring, explain the different ways software applications can be monitored, and shed light on the importance of monitoring and software applications.

In this chapter, we are going to cover the following topics:

- Introducing monitoring
- Discovering the types of monitoring
- Understanding the components of monitoring
- Getting to know Amazon CloudWatch
- Introducing the relationship between Amazon CloudWatch and Well-Architected

Technical requirements

To be able to engage in the technical section of this chapter, it is required that you already have an AWS account. If you do not have one, you can quickly sign up for the free tier.

Check out the following link to see how to sign up for an AWS account:

https://aws.amazon.com/premiumsupport/knowledge-center/create-and-activate-aws-account/

Introducing monitoring

Man has always found a way to take note of everything. In ancient times, man invented a way to create letters and characters. A combination of letters and characters made a word and then a sentence and then paragraphs. This information was stored in scrolls. Man also observed and monitored his environment and continued to document findings and draw insights based on this collected information. In some cases, this information might be in a raw form with too many details that might not be relevant or might have been processed into another form that removed irrelevant information, to allow for better understanding and insight.

This means the data was collected as historic data after an activity occurred. This could be a memorable coronation ceremony, a grand wedding occasion, or even a festival or a period of war or hunger and starvation. Whatever that activity is in time, it is documented for various purposes. One of the purposes is to look at the way things were done in the past and look for ways it can either be stopped or made better. There is a saying that goes as follows:

"If you cannot measure it, you cannot improve it."

– Lord Kelvin (1824-1907)

So, being able to make records of events is not only valuable in helping to draw insights but can also spur the next line of action based on the insight that has been drawn from the data.

Borrowing from this understanding of how man has been recording, documenting, and making records, we can list two major reasons for monitoring data —to draw insights from the data collected and to act based on the insights received. This can be taken into consideration with a system that we build too. For every system man has developed, from the time of the pyramids of Egypt, where massive engineering was needed to draw, architect, and build the pyramids and other iconic structures, documentation of historic works has been very essential. It helped the engineers in those days to understand the flaws in earlier designs and structures, to figure out ways the new structures could be designed, and to eventually fix the flaws that were identified. It is usually a continuous process to keep evaluating what was done before to get better and better with time using these past experiences and results. Documented information is also very helpful when the new project to be embarked on is bigger than the earlier one. This gives foundational knowledge and understanding of what can be done for a new and bigger project due to the historical metrics that have been acquired.

Applying new methods go beyond just the data that has been collected—there is also the culture and mindset of understanding that change is constant and always being positioned to learn from earlier implementations. Building new systems should be about applying what has been learned and building something better and, in some cases, improving the existing system based on close observation:

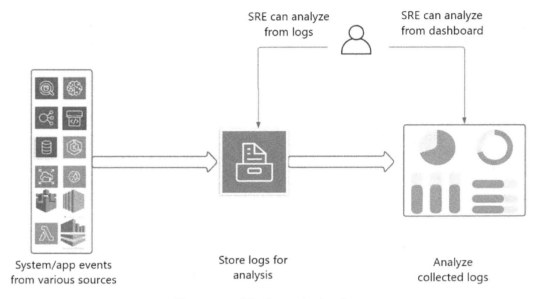

Figure 1.1 – A basic monitoring flow

What we have been explaining so far is monitoring. **Monitoring** is the act or process of collecting, analyzing, and drawing insights from data that has been collected from the system. In software systems and infrastructure, this includes analyzing and drawing insights from the data that has been collected from systems performing specific tasks or multiple tasks. Every system or application is made up of a series of activities, which we also call events. Systems in this context can mean mechanical systems (cars, industrial machines, or trucks), electrical systems (home appliances, transformers, industrial electronics machines, or mobile phones), or computer systems (laptops, desktops, or web or mobile applications).

Algorithms are the bedrock of how complex systems are built, a step-by-step approach to solving a problem. When a complex system is built, each of these step-by-step processes that have been built in to solve a specific problem or set of problems can be called an event.

Consider the following example of the process of making a bottle of beer:

1. Malted barley or sorghum is put in huge tanks and blended.

2. Yeast is added to the mixture to allow the fermentation process to occur to generate alcohol.

3. After fermentation, sugar is added to the mixture to sweeten it.

4. The beer is stored in huge drums.

5. An old bottle undergoes a mechanical process that washes and disinfects the bottle.

6. The washed bottle is taken through a conveyor belt to be filled up with beer.

7. After being filled up, the bottle is corked under high pressure with CO_2.

8. The bottle is then inserted into a crate with other bottles.

In this algorithm of preparing beer, there are various stages; each stage has various touchpoints, and each of these touchpoints is a potential for failure. The failure can be within a process itself or during interaction with other processes. For example, the process of fermentation might not be properly done if the right amount of yeast is not added to the sorghum or if the case of yeast and millet is not air-tight enough, because air is not needed for the fermentation process. Challenges could also arise from the machine that sends the bottle to be crated after corking—there's the possibility of the conveyor belt failing or, during corking, the bottle might explode. These are possibilities and touchpoints that needs close monitoring.

In a nutshell, when a system is designed to perform a specific task or a group of systems are integrated to achieve a common goal, there are always touchpoints both internally and externally that need to be understood. Understanding these touchpoints includes metrics that can be derived from each step of the operation, what normal or good working conditions looks like for both internal and an integration of two systems, and globally acceptable standards. All of this information helps in detecting and finding anomalies when they occur. The only way to detect an activity or metric is an anomaly is by monitoring the system, then collecting and analyzing the data and comparing it with perfect working conditions.

Since we have defined monitoring, the next step thing is to do a sneak peek into the history of monitoring and how it has evolved over time, down to present-day monitoring tools and techniques.

The history of monitoring

We can say for certain that monitoring is as old as man. As mentioned earlier, it is as old as when man started building systems and reviewing what had been done to find faults and fix them and find ways to improve when building a new system. But this book is focused on software monitoring, so we will stick to that.

A computer is made of up of different components, such as the memory, CPU, hard disk, and operating system software. The ability to know what is going on with any of the components goes back to your operating system **events logs**. The Windows operating system developed the Event Viewer in 1993 as part of the **Windows NT** system. This internal application takes note of every event in the system, which together forms a list of **logs**. These logs help to track both core operating system activities that keep the system running and the events of other applications that are installed in the operating system. The **Event Viewer** can log both normal activities and system failures. The following screenshot shows the Event Viewer:

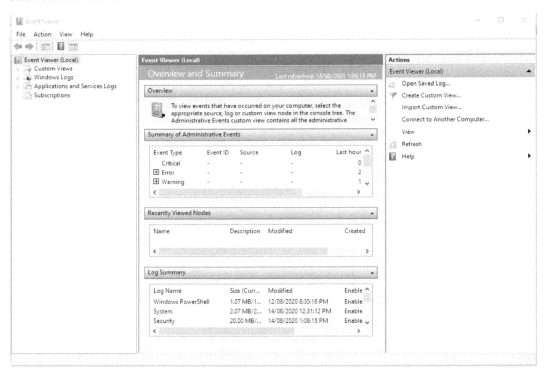

Figure 1.2 – Windows Event Viewer

Windows Event Viewer categorizes events into three groups, as shown in *Figure 1.2*: **Custom Views**, **Windows Logs**, and **Application and Services Logs**. The events captured are also divided into the following categories:

- **Error**: This means that the event did not occur and this gives details about the event that failed with other relevant information.

- **Warning**: This is a signal about an anomaly that could lead to an eventual error and requires attention.

- **Information**: This explains the notification of a successful event.

- **Audit Success**: This means that audit of an event was successful.

- **Audit Failure**: This means that audit of an event was unsuccessful.

The logs in the Windows Event Viewer look like this:

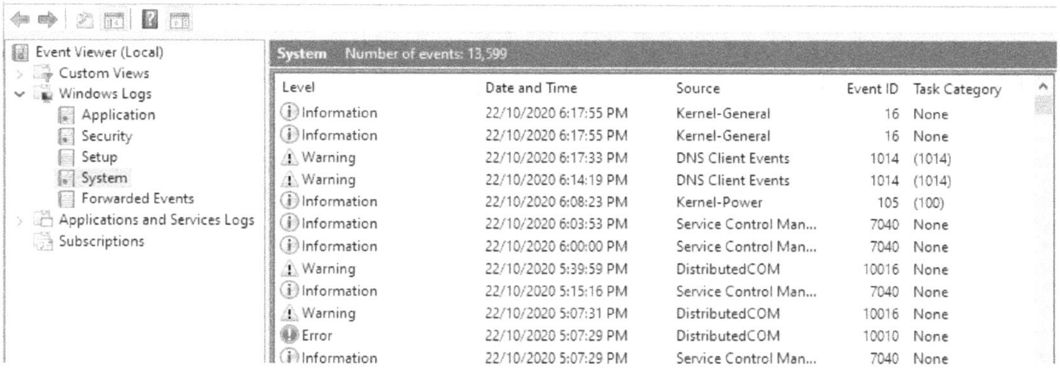

Figure 1.3 – Event Viewer logs

Figure 1.3 shows a list of events, which eventually forms a log.

Over time, monitoring systems have grown and evolved. Due to the importance of monitoring in applications, different organizations have designed purpose-built monitoring systems. There is a whole industry around application and system monitoring, and it has gone from just events and logging to alerting and graph **visualization** of log data. The list of monitoring tools and services goes on and on. Here is a summarized list:

- Datadog

- Nagios Core

- ManageEngine OpManager

- Zabbix

- Netdata
- Uptime Robot
- Pingdom
- Amazon CloudWatch

Now that we have been able to show the meaning and a brief history of how monitoring started, we understand that monitoring is about making records of events, and the categorization of events can have labels as warnings of something to come or something that has happened and needs resolution. Bearing that in mind, let's go deeper into the types of monitoring that are available based on the way we respond to the type of metrics and the information from logs of events.

Discovering the types of monitoring

We now have an understanding of what monitoring is and a brief history of its evolution in terms of techniques and tooling over time. In terms of the techniques of monitoring, there are some concepts that we should keep in mind when designing and architecting monitoring solutions. These concepts encompass any monitoring tool or service that we want to implement, even the one we will be deploying in this book. Let's now take a look at the types of monitoring and the techniques peculiar to each of them, including the pros and cons associated with both.

Proactive monitoring

Before anything goes bad, there are usually warning signs and signals given. In the earlier section, where we defined monitoring, and the Windows Event Viewer, we talked about a category of event called *Warning*. It is a warning signal that helps you to prepare for a failure, and in most cases, when the warning is too intermittent, it can eventually lead to a failure of that part of the system or it might affect another part of the system. **Proactive monitoring** helps you to prepare for the possibility of failure with warning signs, such as notifications and alarms, which can be in form of **mobile push notifications**, emails, or chat messages that hold details of the warning.

Acting based on these warning signs can help to avert the failure that warning sign is giving. An example is an application that used to be fast, and after a while, it starts to slow down and users start complaining about the speed. A monitoring tool can pick up that metric and show that the response time (the time it takes for a website, API, or web application) is high. A quick investigation into what makes it slow can be done, and when found, the issue can be resolved, restoring the application or service back to being faster and more responsive.

Another example of a good reactive monitoring scenario is knowing the percentage of disk space left in a server. The monitoring tool is configured to send warning alerts when the free disk space is utilized 70% and above. This will ensure that the **Site Reliability Engineer** or the **System Administrator** who is in charge to take action and empty out the disk for more space because, if that is not done, and the disk is filled up, the server where the application is deployed will no longer be available because the disk is full.

There are many scenarios where proactive monitoring can be used to predict failure, and it is immensely helpful to avoid a system from a total failure or shutdown. It requires that an action is taken as soon as signal is received. In certain scenarios, the notification can be tied to another event that is triggered to help to salvage the system from an interruption.

Proactive monitoring works with metrics and logs or historical data to be able to understand the nature of the system it is managing. When a series of events have occurred, those events are captured in the form of logs, which are then used to estimate the behavior of the system and give feedback based on that. An example is collecting logs from an nginx application server. Each request made to an nginx application server all combine to form logs on the nginx server. The logs can be aggregated, and an alert can be configured to check the number of 404 errors received within a five-minute interval. If it satisfies the threshold to be met, say, less than 20 and greater than 10 404 error messages are allowed within a 5-minute interval, an alert is triggered. This is a warning sign that the website is not fully available for users to gain access to, which is a symptom of a bigger problem that requires some investigation to find out the reason for that high number of *404 errors*, within that short period of time.

> **Important Note**
> 404 is a HTTP keyword for a page that does not exist.

Reactive monitoring

This type of monitoring is more of an aftermath monitoring. This is the type of monitoring that alerts you when a major incident has occurred. **Reactive monitoring** happens usually when the warnings of the proactive monitors are not heeded, and actions are not taken to resolve all symptoms presented. This will lead to an eventual failure of the full system or some part of it, depending on the architecture of the system, whether it is **monolith** or a **microservice** architecture. A basic example of reactive monitoring is to create a ping that continues to ping your application **URL** continuously and check for the **HTTP** status code for success, which is code 200. If it continues to get this response, it means the service is running fine and it is up. In any situation where it does not get a 200 or 2xx response, or 3xx response, it means the service is no longer available or the service is down.

> **Important Note**
>
> The 2xx response code means anything from 200 to 205, which means a service is OK. A 3xx response code is for redirecting; it could be permanent or temporary redirect. Reponses that indicate failure include 4xx, which are application errors, and 5xx, which are server-side errors.

This is what the monitoring tool checks and it sends a notification or alert immediately if it does not get a 200-status code. This is usually used for APIs, web applications, websites, and any application that has a URL that makes requests over the **HTTP/TCP** protocol.

Since this monitoring throws an alert after the failure, it is termed reactive monitoring. It is after the alert you find out something has gone wrong and then go in to restore the service and investigate what caused the failure and how to fix the issue. In most cases, you have to do root cause analysis, which will involve using techniques from proactive monitoring and look at logs and events that have occurred in the system to understand what led to the failure of the system.

> **Important Note**
>
> Root cause analysis is a method of problem solving that involves deep investigation into the main cause or the trigger to the cause of a system mal-function or failure. It involves analyzing different touch points of the system and corroborating all findings to come to a final conclusion to the cause of the failure. It is also called RCA for short.

Endpoint monitoring services are used for reactive monitoring such as Amazon CloudWatch **Synthetics Canary**, which we will be talking about later in this book. We will not only use simple endpoint pinging to get status codes but much more than that because Synthetics Canary can be configured to do more than just ping endpoints for monitoring.

Understanding the components of monitoring

Now that we understand the types of monitoring and how they can be applied in different scenarios, the next thing is to look at the components that monitoring needs to be possible. Every monitoring architecture or setup works with some base components, when implementing any of the types of monitoring in the previous section. They are as follows:

- Alerts/notifications
- Events
- Logging

- Metrics
- System availability
- Incidence

Alerts/notifications

An **alert/notification** is an event that is triggered to inform the system administrator or site reliability engineer about a potential issue or an issue that has already happened. Alerts are configured with a certain metric in mind. When configuring an alert or notification, there is a metric that is being evaluated and validated against. When that condition is met, the alert is triggered to send a notification.

Notifications can be sent using different media. Alerts can be sent using **SMS (Simple Messaging Service)**, email, mobile app push notifications, **HTTP Push Events**, and many more. The message that is sent via this different media contains information about the incident that has occurred or the metric constraint that has been met. Alerts can be used for both proactive monitoring, to warn sysadmins about a high network I/O and for reactive monitoring, to notify an **Site Reliability Engineer (SRE)** that an **API endpoint** is down. An AWS service that is specialized in this area is **Amazon SNS**. The notifications we shall configure in this book will use Amazon SNS to send notifications.

> **Important Note**
>
> Amazon SNS is a fully-managed messaging service that is used for sending notification using SMS, push notification, HTTP call, and email as the medium. SNS does not require you to set up any servers or manage any **SMTP** or **SMPP** servers for sending emails or SMS. AWS manages all of that for you and gives you an interactive UI, CLI, or API to manage the SNS service and use all of these media to send notifications.

Most users only use the SNS email service to just get notifications when something in a system goes down or goes wrong or they want to get a warning about something. The SNS HTTP call topic can be used to trigger another service such as an **EventBus** to start another process such as a background process to clean temporary files in the server, or create a backup based on the warning signal that has been received. The SRE can tie automated runbooks to **HTTP** endpoints, which **SNS topic** can trigger as a notification.

> **Important Note**
>
> An SRE is someone who is in charge of making sure that applications and services maintain the highest uptime possible. Uptime is usually measured in percentage. Uptime states that the system hardly goes down or is unavailable for customers to use. A good uptime for a website is 99.9%. A good tool to measure uptime is `https://uptime.is`.

Events

Any action or activity or series of activities that occur in a system is called an **event**. In computer systems, there are various events and activities that go on in the background to keep the computer running. A very simple example of an event is the clock. It is a background process that ensures the clock continues to tick to ensure time is kept. Each tick of the clock can be called an event. In the hardware that makes up a PC, there are components such as the **CPU, memory**, and **hard disk**. They all have series of events that they perform from time to time. The disk is the memory storage of data in the computer, and it usually performs two basic operations or events—either reading data that has been written to it or trying to write in new data. We can also call these operations events of the disk.

In software programs, every function or method can be called an event. Software programs are made up of hundreds to thousands of methods or functions. Each of these functions has a unique operation they perform to be able to solve a specific problem. The ability to track each of these events is very important in monitoring software systems and applications.

Logging

A **log** is a historical record of an event. A log does not only have the events and details of the event; it also contains the time that event occurred. Mostly, they are called logs. This means that a series of events form logs. Every programming language, when used to develop, generates logs. It is through logs that developers are able to spot **bugs** in code. When a log is generated by the **interpreter**, it is read and articulated, which informs the developer about what the bug could be and allows the developer to know what needs to be tweaked to be able to fix the particular bug that has been identified.

We also showed the Microsoft Event Viewer in the previous section, which contains a list of events. This list of events eventually forms what is called logs. They are events that have taken place with the description of the events, the status of the event, and the date and time the event occurred.

The following screenshot shows an example of a list of events that forms logs:

Level	Date and Time	Source	Event ID	Task Category
System Number of events: 12,510				
(i) Information	9/2/2020 10:37:24 AM	Kernel-General	16	None
(i) Information	9/2/2020 10:07:37 AM	Service Contr...	7040	None
⚠ Warning	9/2/2020 9:51:17 AM	DNS Client Ev...	1014	(1014)
⚠ Warning	9/2/2020 9:50:30 AM	DNS Client Ev...	1014	(1014)
⚠ Warning	9/2/2020 9:50:05 AM	DNS Client Ev...	1014	(1014)
⚠ Warning	9/2/2020 9:48:35 AM	DNS Client Ev...	1014	(1014)
(i) Information	9/2/2020 9:47:47 AM	Kernel-General	1	(5)
(i) Information	9/2/2020 9:47:47 AM	Time-Service	158	None
(i) Information	9/2/2020 9:47:47 AM	Time-Service	35	None
(i) Information	9/2/2020 9:47:47 AM	Time-Service	37	None
⚠ Warning	9/2/2020 9:47:43 AM	Time-Service	134	None
⚠ Warning	9/2/2020 9:47:43 AM	DNS Client Ev...	1014	(1014)
(i) Information	9/2/2020 9:46:48 AM	Service Contr...	7040	None
⚠ Warning	9/2/2020 9:44:17 AM	DNS Client Ev...	1014	(1014)
(i) Information	9/2/2020 9:44:11 AM	Service Contr...	7045	None
(i) Information	9/2/2020 9:43:42 AM	UserModePo...	22	(18)
(i) Information	9/2/2020 9:42:34 AM	Kernel-General	16	None

Figure 1.4 – List of events forms logs

Logs are the heart of monitoring because they give raw data that can be analyzed to draw insights from the behavior of the system. In many organizations, logs are kept for a specific period of time for the purpose of system audit, security analysis/audits and compliance inspection. In some cases, logs can contain sensitive information about an organization, which can be a potential vulnerability that hackers and crackers can use to attack and exploit the system.

Mostly, logs are stored in filesystems where the application is running, but logs can grow so large that storing them in a filesystem might not be very efficient. There are other places logs can be stored that **scale** infinitely in size of storage for log files. These will be revealed more as we go deeper in this book:

```
196.58.5.97 - - [19/Aug/2020:10:06:12 +0000] "GET / HTTP/1.1" 200 396 "-"
"Mozilla/5.0 (Windows NT 10.0; Win64; x64) AppleWebKit/537.36 (KHTML, like Gecko)
Chrome/84.0.4147.125 Safari/537.36
196.58.5.97 - - [19/Aug/2020:10:06:15 +0000] "GET /favicon.ico HTTP/1.1" 404 197
"http://45.33.21.227/" "Mozilla/5.0 (Windows NT 10.0; Win64; x64)
AppleWebKit/537.36 (KHTML, like Gecko) Chrome/84.0.4147.125 Safari/537.36
```

Figure 1.5 – A sample of an nginx log

Figure 1.5 is another example of events that form an **nginx** log. This is taken from the access log file of a nginx server.

Metrics

A **metric** is the smallest of unit of insight that is obtained from a log. Metrics give meaning to logs that have been collected from a system. They indicate a standard of measurement for different system components. In a huge collection of logs, what is usually needed is a single explanation for all of the information that has been captured. It could be the estimated disk space that is left or the percentage of memory that is being consumed. This single piece of information helps the SRE or sysadmin to know how to react. In some cases, the metric is fed into a more automated system that responds according to the data received

A simple example is the auto-scaling feature in AWS. This feature helps to create or spin up a new server when something goes wrong with the existing server. One metric that can be used to trigger this is the CPU consumption of the current running server. If the CPU consumption is above 90%, this could mean that, within a few minutes or hours, that server will no longer be reachable or available. Therefore, a remedy needs to be provided for that before the CPU consumption exceeds 90%. That information can be used to create a new server to either replace the existing server or added as part of the load balancer to ensure that the application or service does not have downtime.

The following diagram illustrates how auto-scaling works:

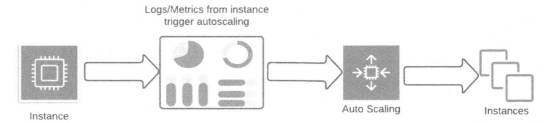

Figure 1.6 – Autoscaling based on instance metrics

Another use of a metric is in detecting malicious network activities. When the network activity of your cloud resources is closely monitored, there might be an anomaly in a metric such as the *NetworkIn* (which is a metric that measures the number of bytes of data that is transferred inside the network infrastructure). Anomalies could mean very high traffic at a particular time; this could mean that the resources on that network are being hit by unnecessary **DDoS** requests that could lead to a lot of different scenarios that are negative to the application.

The metric is key to understanding summarized information of what is going on and attach a label to huge events and logs of information that is received from various systems and take action based on this intelligence.

System availability

Availability in simple context means that something or someone is accessible. **System availability** in that same context means that a system is available for use, by users or customers who require it. In software systems, the availability of your website, application, or API means that it is accessible to whoever needs it and whenever they need to use it. It could be that shopping website that customer needs to access to purchase those Nike sneakers or a developer who needs to integrate a payment service API to their system to enable users to make payments. If the customer or **developer** is not able to access it anytime they need it, then that service is termed not highly available.

To understand the availability of any system, monitoring plays a very key role. The ability to know when the system is up or the system is down can be aggregated to get the system availability within a period of time. This is generally called **system uptime** or just **uptime**. The system uptime of any system can be calculated as follows:

$$\text{Availability} = \frac{\text{Uptime}}{\text{Uptime} + \text{Downtime}}$$

Figure 1.7 – Formula for calculating availability

In the preceding formula, we have the following:

- Total **Uptime**: How long the system has been available to the user or customer in hours.

- Total **Downtime**: How long the system has been unavailable to the user customer in hours.

- **Availability**: The final system availability as a decimal fraction. Which is then multiplied with 100 to get the percentage availability.

Another scenario in applying this is, say, we want to calculate the availability of an API application serving third-party customers who integrate with it for *Forex Indices*. Let's say within a month, the API was available for a total of 300 hours. Within that same month, there was a huge surge of traffic on the API due to some announcement in the news, which led to the API being unavailable for about 3 hours. Then, the development team also had to do a new update, which involved changes in the API functionality due to the surge of users on the API. The release of this update cost another 4 hours of downtime in the system. This brings the total downtime of the system within the month to 7 hours. Within that same month, the security team needed to look at the logs for roughly 1 hour during monthly system maintenance. This led to another 1 hour 30 mins of downtime.

We can calculate the availability of this system as follows:

- Total Uptime = 300 hours

- Downtime1 = 3 hours

- Downtime2 = 4 hours

- Downtime3 = 1 hour 30 mins = 1.5 hours

- Total Downtime = 3+4+1.5=8.5 hours

- Total Uptime + Total Downtime = 300 + 8.5 = 308.5 hours

- Availability = 300 / 308.5 = 0.9724

- Availability as a percentage = 97.24%

But it is not about this number—how do we actually interpret the meaning of 97.24% availability? There is a chart that will help us to understand the meaning of this number. We might say it is a good number because it is quite close to 100%, right? But it is actually more than that:

Availability (%)	Downtime
90	■ **Daily:** 2h 24m 0s ■ **Weekly:** 16h 48m 0s ■ **Monthly:** 3d 1h 2m 54s ■ **Yearly:** 36d 12h 34m 55s
95	■ **Daily:** 1h 12m 0s ■ **Weekly:** 8h 24m 0s ■ **Monthly:** 1d 12h 31m 27s ■ **Yearly:** 18d 6h 17m 27s
99	■ **Daily:** 14m 24s ■ **Weekly:** 1h 40m 48s ■ **Monthly:** 7h 18m 17s ■ **Yearly:** 3d 15h 39m 29s
99.9	■ **Daily:** 1m 26s ■ **Weekly:** 10m 4s ■ **Monthly:** 43m 49s ■ **Yearly:** 8h 45m 56s

99.99	▪ **Daily:** 8s ▪ **Weekly:** 1m 0s ▪ **Monthly:** 4m 22s ▪ **Yearly:** 52m 35s
99.9999999	▪ **Daily:** 0s ▪ **Weekly:** 0s ▪ **Monthly:** 0s ▪ **Yearly:** 0s

Table 1.1 – Uptime chart

If we are to approximate the uptime of our system based on the calculation, it will round down to 97%. Taking this value and checking it on the preceding chart, we can see that this value means the following:

- 10.96 days of downtime in a year

- 21.92 hours of downtime in a month

- 5.04 hours of downtime in a week

- 43.02 minutes of downtime in a day

The fact that monitoring can help us to understand the availability of our system is one step. But this system being monitored is used by our customers. Customers expect our system to be up and running 24/7. They are hardly concerned about any excuses you might have to give for any downtime. In some cases, it could mean losing them to your competition. Organizations do well to communicate and promise their customers system availability. This gives the customer a level of expectation of the **Quality of Service (QoS)** to be received by the organization. It also helps to boost customer confidence and gives the business a benchmark to meet.

This indicator or metric is called an SLA. **SLA** is an acronym for **Service Level Agreement**. According to Wikipedia, SLA is a commitment between a service provider and a client. In simple terms, an SLA is the percentage of uptime a service provider gives to the customer—anything below that number, and the customer is allowed to lay claims and receive compensation. The onus is on the service provider to ensure they do not go below that SLA that has been communicated to the customer.

Dashboard

For every event, log, or metric that is measured or collected, there is always a better way to represent the data being collected. Dashboards are a way to present logs and metric data in a graphically appealing manner. Dashboards are a combination of different graphical representations of data, which could be in the form of bar charts, line graphs, bar graphs, histograms, scattered plots, or pie charts. These representations give the user a summarized version of the logs, which makes it easy to spot things such as trends in a graph.

When there is a rise in **Disk I/O**, in the number of bytes of data written per second, one of the fastest ways to represent this is through a line graph, which will have a directly proportional slope showing the gradual rise traffic from one point to another. If, during the night, there was some sudden spike in the memory consumption of one of the servers, due to high customer usage of the service, a line graph can be easily used to spot the time of the day the spike happened and see when it came back down.

These, and many more are the values of having a dashboard, which gives a graphical representation of the data collection from the logs of the system. Metrics are also represented in graphs for much easier interpretation. Amazon CloudWatch has a built-in dashboard where different types of graphs can be created and hence added to the dashboard based on certain specifications, or to group related data for easy understanding of the logs and making better meaning of the log data collected:

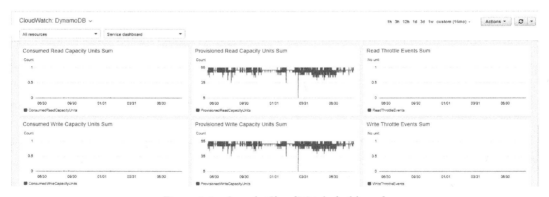

Figure 1.8 – Sample CloudWatch dashboard

Next, we will understand what an incident is.

Incidents

An **incident** is an event, condition, or situation that causes a disruption to the normal operation of a system or an organization. Incidents are negative to a system and are related to reactive monitoring. Incidents make a website, API, or application slow or unavailable to a user. Different things can trigger or cause an incident. It could range from a bug in the application that led to the application being totally unavailable, to a security incident where an attacker collected sensitive user or customer information. They are all termed incidents. Some of these incidents can actually be captured by the monitoring tool to show when the incident occurred and can form part of the incident report that is documented in your organization.

It is advisable for every organization to have an **Incident Management Framework**. This framework defines how failures, or any form of incident reported, is managed by the SRE/sysadmin team. Incidents are usually captured by the monitoring tool. When an attacker performs a brute force attack on a Linux server and gains access, this activity can be picked up by monitoring tools and an alert is sent over to the team. This will help the security team to investigate the issue and ensure it never occurs again. The incident framework guides every team within the organization on how to react in the event of an incident. There are usually levels of incidents labeled according to their levels of severity. In most cases, these are **SEV1**, **SEV2**, or **SEV3**, which means severity 1, severity 2, and severity 3, respectively. The numbers indicate the priority or intensity of the severity.

Phewww! While that was quite a lot of information, these components are at the heart of monitoring architecture and infrastructure. We have seen how dashboards help with proactive monitoring and understanding the infrastructure even before disaster strikes. The next thing is to look at the importance of monitoring, and how these components form up different aspects of the importance of monitoring.

When it comes to the value monitoring gives, there are major items that make it at the very core of every system that is designed and implemented. As far as it is a system that has been designed and is bound to have unforeseen circumstances, then the importance of monitoring the system can never be undermined. Disregarding the importance of monitoring means that the lifetime of a system is not put into consideration. We can also say, fine, we want to monitor this system or that system, but what are the core values that can be derived when engaging in monitoring activities, be it a pro-active monitoring approach or the reactive monitoring? There are key reasons to monitor a system:

- Realizing when things go south
- Ability to debug
- Gaining insights

- Sending data/notifications to other systems
- Controlling **Capital Expenditure (CapEx)** to run cloud infrastructure

We have been able to list some reasons to ensure monitoring is part of your infrastructure and application deployments. Let's expatiate on these with examples to help to drive home the essence on each point mentioned in the preceding.

Realizing when things go south

Organizations that do not have any kind of monitoring service suffer from customers being the ones to inform them of a downtime. The ability to know this before customers raise it is very important. It paints a bad picture when users go to social media to share negative opinions of a system downtime before the company finds out there is/was a downtime. Reactive monitoring is the technique that helps with this. Using simple endpoint monitoring that pings your endpoints and services from time to time to give feedback is very important. There are times an application might be running but customers are not able to reach it for various reasons. Endpoint monitoring can help to send email alerts or SMS notifications to the SRE team to notify them of a downtime before the customer makes any kind of complaint. The issue can quickly be resolved to improve overall service availability and **MTTR**.

> **Important Note**
> **MTTR** is an acronym for **Mean Time to Recover**. It is the measure of how quickly a system recovers from failure.

Ability to debug

When an application has a bug, be it a functional or non-functional bug, the developer needs logs or a way to trace the round-trip of the application to be able to understand where in the flow the bottleneck is present. Without logs or a way to have a bird's-eye view of the behavior, it is almost impossible to debug the application and come up with a solution after the problem is understood. In this scenario, reactive monitoring is the technique to be applied here. Logs from the application server or **web server** will lead to the bug in the system.

Gaining insight

Insights to the behavior of your system is critical to the progress or retrogression of your application. Insights that can be gained from any application is quite broad. These insights can range from the internal server components to the behavior of the network over time. These insights might not be to actually fix a problem but rather to be able to understand the state of the system from time to time. The ability to spot trends in the system, viewing intermittent behavior, planning capacity for infrastructure, and improving cost optimization are some of the activities that can be carried out to make the system better based on the insights that have been obtained. When there is monitoring of the environment, a rogue NAT gateway that is not needed for an architecture can be deleted, which could save huge costs, considering what Amazon VPC NAT gateways cost, especially when they are not actively in use.

Sending data/notifications to other systems

Monitoring is not just about watching events and generating logs and traces of these events. It also involves taking action based on the logs and metrics that have been generated. With the data obtained from monitoring systems or a notification, an automated recovery operation can be tied to that metric, which can recover the system without any manual intervention from the SREs or sysadmins. **Amazon EventBridge** is a service that can also send events to third-party **SaaS** solutions, CloudWatch can be configured to send triggers to Amazon EventBridge to carry operations on other systems that are not within the AWS infrastructure.

Controlling CapEX to run cloud infrastructure

CapEx can be managed when things are monitored. In using different AWS services, there is always the possibility of not keeping track of the resources being provisioned and overspend. The capital expense is what it costs to run a particular cloud service. Monitoring with a budget and billing alarm can be a life saver to alert you when you are spending above the budget that has been set for that particular month. This means the bill is being monitored, and when the services running go over the budget, an email alert is sent to notify you of it. There are also alarms that notify at the beginning of every month, to notify you of the possible forecast for that month.

We have understood the meaning of monitoring and its historical background from the days of Microsoft Windows **Event Viewer** to new tools that have evolved from that singular basic understanding. Then, we discussed the types of monitoring that can be employed and the strategies of those types of monitoring. We also identified the major components that must be considered when setting up or configuring any monitoring infrastructure. Finally, we have understood the importance of monitoring, drawing from the types and components and strategies we learned and the value each of these bring to the importance of monitoring as a whole. The next stage is to introduce the monitoring service that this book is based on, which is *Amazon CloudWatch*.

Getting to know Amazon CloudWatch

Amazon CloudWatch is a service designed by AWS. It is an all-encompassing and complete end-to-end monitoring solution, used for monitoring applications, servers, serverless applications, **on-premises** systems, cloud-native applications, storage services, networking services database services, and many more. CloudWatch has the ability to collect and store logs of applications deployed in any environment. You do not have to worry about any servers to set up, configure, or manage for your logs' storage and management. CloudWatch stores petabytes of logs that for AWS users. It is embedded with tools that make it easy to loop through and interpret log data that has been collected.

CloudWatch does not only store logs, it also has its own CloudWatch dashboard, which is used to draw different types of mathematical graphs used for data interpretation. With its built-in **CloudWatch Events**, which is gradually being migrated into Amazon EventBridge, it is able to respond to events based on specific conditions, and those events can further trigger other specific operations that have been configured with it. CloudWatch Event rules can be configured to trigger a specific CloudWatch Event to occur. A simple example could be configuring the CloudWatch Event to shut down an **EC2 instance** by 7 p.m. when the business closes down, and start it up by 7 a.m. when everyone is back at work.

Important Note

A CloudWatch Event rule is a functionality that is part of Amazon CloudWatch, which is used to schedule the time an operation should be performed. It is usually associated with Amazon CloudWatch Events.

One very important feature of every monitoring tool is also in CloudWatch, which is alerts. CloudWatch has a rich alerting system that works in connection with **Amazon SNS**. Alerts can be configured to trigger based on specific metrics identified in logs received into CloudWatch. Mathematical symbols can be used to configure granular metrics and specific time intervals to determine when an alert will be sent and for what particular reason that particular alert was sent. In some cases, the alerts can be used as the first point of call to solve the issue that has been identified, one of which is rebooting an EC2 instance that refused to start up for any reason.

CloudWatch also has a feature called Synthetics, which makes it possible for CloudWatch to send intermittent pings to an endpoint, a website, an API, or a web application to check for the status and when it is down, and it can send a notification. This means that CloudWatch can be used for both proactive and reactive monitoring.

This book will show how to set up, configure, and manage different types of infrastructure from the monitoring perspective. From *Chapter 3*, *CloudWatch Logs, Metrics and Dashboard*, through to *Chapter 9*, *Monitoring Storage Services with Amazon CloudWatch*, we will be configuring the monitoring of different AWS services and resources. This will be after a brief introduction to the service and its components.

Introducing the relationship between Amazon CloudWatch and Well-Architected

The **AWS Well-Architected framework** is a set of principles that can be used to govern how an application is architected, developed, deployed, and scaled in the cloud. It is a compilation of the experience of hundreds of AWS solution architects with decades of experience across various industries who have designed, managed, and scaled various types of systems. All of this knowledge and experience has all been put together to form the summarized principles that go into the AWS Well-Architected framework. This Well-Architected framework is made up of five pillars:

- Security
- Cost Optimization
- Performance Efficiency
- Operational Excellence
- Reliability

Each of these pillars covers a wide range of tenets for different aspects of infrastructure setup scaling, security, and deployment. But we will be looking at the monitoring aspect of the Well-Architected framework.

The **Reliability pillar** focuses on building systems that are reliable, stand the test of time, and are always available to do what they have been designed to do. This will require close monitoring of the system from time to time. It also refers to managing service quotas for different AWS resources as you continue to use the different AWS services.

> **Important Note**
>
> AWS provides an OnDemand scale for server resources and application services. This is managed using service quotas, which is a regulatory technique used by AWS to manage the maximum value of resources, actions and items in your AWS account (https://docs.aws.amazon.com/servicequotas/latest/userguide/intro.html).

CloudWatch alarms can be configured for these quotas so that alerts can be received when you are almost hitting the limit of the service allocation. This can be used to protect against a possible workload failure in situations when a service is needed and the limit has been exceeded.

With **Performance Efficiency**, the focus is more on ensuring that the application is performing well at all times. Two of the ways to ensure the system performs well are always having insights and understanding the behavior of the workloads and application. Rigorous testing of the application using various methods such as **load testing** can be very helpful in seeing the behavior of the system under load. When the load test is carried out, metrics and logs are collected. These logs are further studied to understand and gain insights into the behavior of the system. This can be done for the staging or test setup of the application, and it can help SREs understand what to get when the application is eventually released to customers.

The fear of bills is what chases a lot of first-time cloud users. The **Cost Optimization pillar** in the Well-Architected framework is focused on optimizing your AWS bill by using cost-effective services and designs when deploying workloads in your AWS infrastructure. But the part of CloudWatch that is connected to your cost is the **auto-scaling** feature, which can be very helpful in reducing the cost of your overall **workload**. CloudWatch metrics can be used to trigger the scaling up or scaling down of your infrastructure based on thresholds that have been configured. This can go a long way to save costs so that when the **server** resources being consumed are low, CloudWatch reduces the number of servers being used, but when the number goes higher, CloudWatch can still identify that and trigger a scale-up to add more servers and balance the load hitting the application.

Summary

Monitoring is quite a large topic; a lot can be said about it. But what we have done in this chapter is to consider monitoring a natural human attitude and characteristic. The fact that anything that is built can fail means that there is a natural instinct to ensure that things are monitored, understood, and augmented to work better with time. We applied this concept to computing and explained that computing brings automation into this natural human process of monitoring, and we talked about the different components of monitoring computer systems. We covered logs, metrics, dashboards, and incidents and explained the meaning of each of these components. Next, we explained the importance of monitoring, pinpointing specific key reasons to monitor your application workload and infrastructure. Then, we moved on to explain Amazon CloudWatch, the AWS managed end-to-end monitoring service that is built with all of the features that any monitoring infrastructure or service will require. Lastly, the icing on the cake was the AWS Well-Architected framework, which serves as a boilerplate for everything cloud-native and monitoring is not left out.

This has given us a solid foundation to understand the fundamentals and components of monitoring and the importance of monitoring in the day-to-day activity of an SRE. We have also seen that CloudWatch is a managed service that takes away the operational expense of running our own cloud infrastructure. This foundational knowledge will be beneficial as we go deeper into this book.

In the next chapter, we will take our first step into Amazon CloudWatch to understand the components, events, and alarms.

Questions

1. Which pillars of the AWS Well-Architected framework are focused on monitoring?

2. Which protocol is mostly used to send alert notifications?

3. Being able to know and forecast when things are going to have a problem is an important part of monitoring. What is this type of monitoring called?

4. What is the smallest unit of insight that helps to make all of the logs and data collected from applications and infrastructure meaningful called?

Further reading

Refer to the following links for more information on topics covered in this chapter:

- AWS Monitoring Overview: `https://www.packtpub.com/product/aws-masterclass-monitoring-and-devops-with-aws-cloudwatch-video/9781788999533`

- Monitoring Fundamentals: `https://www.packtpub.com/product/hands-on-infrastructure-monitoring-with-prometheus/9781789612349`

2
CloudWatch Events and Alarms

We spent the whole of the previous chapter talking a lot about the fundamental principles of monitoring. We also spent time talking about the components that make up monitoring. There are other components of monitoring systems and ways of understanding system behaviors that were not discussed. These components will be discussed as we progress, and practical demonstrations will be done. We will be exploring these components and the principles that guide how they are applied. The goal is to explain as much as possible how day-to-day scenarios connect with the **Amazon CloudWatch** services and architecture in ensuring high availability and better system performance.

CloudWatch has various components that make up the service. Two of the major components are the events that are converting every metric into an actionable item and the alarms configured based on a specific metric or threshold. Alarms send notifications when that threshold is met and can be based on various configurations.

Here are the main topics that will be covered in the chapter:

- Introducing CloudWatch Events and Amazon EventBridge
- Understanding the components of an event
- Configuring a basic CloudWatch event
- Introducing alarms
- Configuring a basic alarm

Technical requirements

To be able to engage in the technical sections of this chapter, it is required that you already have an AWS account. If you do not have an AWS account, you can quickly sign up for the free tier.

Check out the following link to see how to sign up for an AWS account:

`https://aws.amazon.com/premiumsupport/knowledge-center/create-and-activate-aws-account/`

Check out the following link to see the Code in Action video:

`https://bit.ly/3bB32H2`

Introducing CloudWatch Events and Amazon EventBridge

Events have been previously defined as every activity that goes on in a system, events can also be the attached as a response to another event thereby triggering this event. **CloudWatch Events** is designed to be able to respond to changes in the different **AWS** resources and services. Using some rules that determine the specific action or activity that took place, CloudWatch events can be configured to respond according to that particular event that has occurred. CloudWatch Events is not available for all AWS services but a bunch of them that we will be exploring in the *Components of a CloudWatch event* section. The event triggered by CloudWatch can be sent over to other AWS resources to act on the event that has been triggered by the previous service.

An instance could be an event from **Amazon CodePipeline** that indicates that a build pipeline process has been triggered. This event can be tracked by Amazon CloudWatch Events, which reads the pattern of the event and feeds it into another service such as Amazon SNS. The specified topic in Amazon SNS then notifies a user or group of users that a particular build has commenced. Another example is with ECS task events. ECS is an AWS proprietary service for container orchestration. ECS has various components for container orchestration, which include **task**, **service**, and **container**. Tasks are used to define the different components of a container, such as networking and storage. A task has a series of events that it triggers during its life cycle of container management. These events can be tagged as state changes in ECS. Amazon CloudWatch can read ECS task state changes and maybe trigger a Lambda function that reads this data and logs it into Amazon CloudWatch.

> **Important Note**
> A service in Amazon ECS is a network abstraction that makes it possible for a container application to be accessible.

The two examples given previously are just a few of the scenarios that CloudWatch can be used for to read an event and respond accordingly with another event. We will also be looking at practical setup configurations as we go further into the chapter, but let's first talk about an interesting service that is an improvement on Amazon CloudWatch Events. It is called Amazon EventBridge.

Amazon EventBridge

This is a newer version of Amazon CloudWatch Events. Amazon EventBridge is a serverless event bus service that is designed to respond to events by triggering other events. Very similar to Amazon CloudWatch, EventBridge receives events from other services and reacts accordingly. But one major feature makes EventBridge different from CloudWatch Events, which is the fact that it takes input from sources other than AWS services. Events from **Software as a Service** (**SaaS**) services and custom applications can be tied into Amazon EventBridge to respond accordingly. This makes EventBridge have wider applications than CloudWatch Events. It means you can configure an automated event trigger for your applications. It is serverless, meaning that it scales infinitely, and you do not have to worry about managing servers for your application that uses an event bus for its operation.

> **Important Note**
>
> An event bus is a technique or method that allows multiple components or services that do not have any direct method of communication to be able to interact with each other. Send events from one system to another system, and the second system responds based on the details of the event trigger it receives.

We have been able to understand the basic concepts of Amazon CloudWatch Events and EventBridge. We also compared CloudWatch Events and EventBridge, showing the similarities and differences. EventBridge is the new CloudWatch Events and according to Amazon, CloudWatch Events will be deprecated and EventBridge will replace it. We also talked about some of the applications of CloudWatch Events in Amazon ECS. This understanding of the use of CloudWatch Events and EventBridge will help us see the value in the practical sessions later in this chapter.

Now that we understand what CloudWatch Events is, let's look at the various components that make up a CloudWatch event, what they are, and how they are important in setting up a CloudWatch event.

Understanding the components of a CloudWatch event

For an Amazon CloudWatch event to function, it is made up of different moving parts to achieve a goal successfully. Each of these components is inter-connected and forms the life cycle of a CloudWatch Events operation. If any of these components is missing for any reason, then the CloudWatch Events life cycle will not be complete. Due to the similarities that exist between CloudWatch Events and Amazon EventBridge, we will be interpolating both services by describing the different components of CloudWatch Events. In scenarios where the features are unique to Amazon EventBridge, they will be uniquely spelled out. For an event to work completely, these are the three major components, which we will explore in the next sections.

Input trigger

This is the input data, service, or event that triggers the event to start. It can also be called the input signal of the CloudWatch Events life cycle. This is what starts the process or the CloudWatch event. The input trigger also contains information that is useful for the behavior of the resulting trigger and how the event pattern behaves. The input trigger or event source can range from different AWS services, some of which we mentioned during the examples for illustrating some scenarios where CloudWatch events can be used. Some of the input triggers for CloudWatch Events are as follows:

- **Elastic Container Service (ECS)**
- Elastic Load Balancing
- Elastic MapReduce
- Elastic Transcoder
- Elasticsearch
- Elemental MediaPackage
- EventBridge
- EventBridge Schema Registry
- GameLift
- Glacier
- Glue
- Greengrass
- Ground Station
- GuardDuty
- Inspector
- Kinesis
- Lambda
- Polly
- Redshift
- Step Functions

These are some of the input triggers that are used by Amazon CloudWatch Events. They trigger CloudWatch events based on a specific state or event they emit.

Since EventBridge can take input for SaaS applications, this means EventBridge not only supports AWS services but also other third-party services, such as the following:

- PagerDuty
- Opsgenie
- SugarCRM
- Shopify
- Datadog
- Zendesk
- Auth0
- Site24x7

There are other input triggers but this is a list of some of the SaaS services supported by EventBridge. Both the AWS services and SaaS form an event pattern, which is what defines the behavior of the event triggered by that service.

Rules/event pattern

When the input trigger is sent, there are rules that govern that trigger and it comes with an event pattern that is used by Amazon CloudWatch Events to recognize the trigger. This event pattern gives CloudWatch Events all the information it needs to react to it. The information in the event pattern is the determinant of how the event will react. In a case where the input trigger is a service that changes state, the event pattern will hold the information of this state. For instance, an EC2 instance has different state changes, such as *stopping*, *stopped*, *terminated*, *pending*, *running*, and *shutting-down*. These states are generated by the event pattern and this is how it is able to read the event when it is triggered by the service. This data is then sent over to the target that is responding to the event triggers. The following screenshot shows an example of an event pattern:

```json
{
  "source": [
    "aws.ec2"
  ],
  "detail-type": [
    "EC2 Instance State-change Notification"
  ],
  "detail": {
    "state": [
      "stopped"
    ]
  }
}
```

Figure 2.1 – Sample event pattern

The preceding event pattern is in JSON format with different keys and values. Let's explain what each of the keys and the associated values mean:

- source: This specifies the AWS service that the input trigger is coming from. All events from AWS services usually start with aws. to represent that it is coming from an AWS service.

- detail-type: This is an explanation in detail of the type of event that that particular service can emit or trigger.

- detail: A placeholder for the different states of a particular service.

- state: An array key for the specific state that is to be triggered by the AWS service. It could be a single value or multiple values.

> **Important Note**
> **JSON** is an acronym for **JavaScript Object Notation**. It is a method of transmitting data across disparate systems. It is an open-standard file format composed of human-readable text representing data in key/value pairs, and in some cases uses an array to represent groups of related data.

In the following example, the state has multiple values:

```
{
  "source": [
    "aws.glue"
  ],
  "detail-type": [
    "Glue Job Run Status"
  ],
  "detail": {
    "state": [
      "RUNNING",
      "STARTING",
      "STOPPING"
    ]
  }
}
```

Figure 2.2 – State with multiple values

The event pattern represented in the preceding figure is an abridged version. The pattern used within AWS and for cross-account configuration is a little bit more detailed and looks like this:

```
{
  "version": "0",
  "id": "651d5f8b-947c-4c0f-acb7-5ac4e41a1b8a",
  "detail-type": "EC2 Instance State-change Notification",
  "source": "aws.ec2",
  "account": "123456789012",
  "time": "2015-11-11T21:33:19Z",
  "region": "us-east-1",
  "resources": [
    "arn:aws:ec2:us-east-1:123456789012:instance/i-abcd3333"
  ],
  "detail": {
    "instance-id": "i-abcd3333",
    "state": "stopped"
  }
}
```

Figure 2.3 – Detailed event pattern

> **Important Note**
>
> Cross-account configuration is a setup in CloudWatch Events and Amazon EventBridge where events can be sent and received across different AWS accounts.

This event pattern contains more detailed information, such as the AWS account ID, the time the event was generated, the region, and the resource ARN in which the event is coming from. AWS usually generates the shortened version when using CloudWatch Events or Amazon EventBridge within the same account. In any case where events need to be transitioned from one account to the other, then this detailed event pattern will be needed to make that work.

Apart from the ability of CloudWatch Events to receive events from AWS services, a scheduled expression pattern can also be used to trigger an event. Personally, I use this to replace the popular Linux crontab. This scheduled expression is more or less a serverless crontab. It can be used to configure operations that need to happen at a scheduled later date or repeatedly. The scheduled pattern triggers itself when the condition for the particular time it was configured for is met. One major advantage of the scheduled expression is that it takes the crontab pattern, the Unix-like style, which makes it easy to configure mostly for those who are used to crontabs in Unix and Linux operating systems. The crontab expression is illustrated as follows:

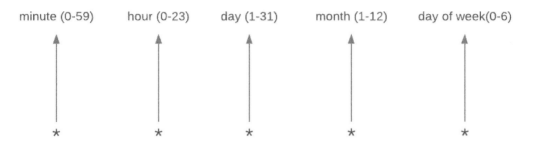

Figure 2.4 – Crontab expression syntax

Let's say we want to run a process every day at 12 a.m. to shut down a particular EC2 instance. The crontab expression that can be used for that configuration looks as follows:

```
*  0  *  *  *
```

The next section discusses the last part of the components of a CloudWatch event, known as the **target**.

Target

The target is the destination service that reacts to the input trigger. The target is usually another AWS service that responds based on the information that is sent to it from the event pattern. Any target can be chosen based on the service you need to respond to the event pattern. The target of a CloudWatch event does not depend on the event pattern, but it is totally independent of it. This means that the input trigger can be the change in state of an EC2 instance, while the target can be a batch job. This makes the possibilities quite dynamic and broad. Amazon EventBridge also supports targets the way it is supported in CloudWatch Events. The following is a list of a number of targets supported by CloudWatch Events that Amazon EventBridge also supports:

- Lambda function
- API Gateway
- Batch job queue
- Kinesis stream
- SNS topic
- SQS queue
- SSM automation
- Step Functions state machine
- CloudWatch log group
- CodeBuild Project
- CodePipeline
- ECS task
- Event bus in another AWS account
- Kinesis Firehose delivery stream

This list is of the services that are supported as targets for CloudWatch Events and Amazon EventBridge. The target services are tailored toward a particular resource in that service that has been created. For example, after selecting Lambda function as a target, the specific Lambda function that is responding to the event trigger needs to be selected from the list of Lambda functions in that specific AWS region. Because CloudWatch is region-specific, CloudWatch Events and Amazon EventBridge are also regional. This means that whatever configuration or setup that is done on CloudWatch Events and EventBridge is specific to a particular AWS region.

> **Important Note**
>
> An AWS region is a physical geographical location in the world, where there are clusters of data centers called availability zones. A region can contain from two to five availability zones. An example of a region is Milan in Italy or Cape Town in South Africa.

To be able to use any particular target, ensure that a resource exists in that target within the same region as CloudWatch Events or EventBridge. Targets also come with input parameters of the data to be sent over to the service selected as the specific target. This makes the target service behave according to the input data that is sent to it by the target configuration. The target configuration is of five types:

- **Matched events**: This sends all the information on the event pattern to the target service. This means if an event pattern has an EC2 instance state of STOPPED, that state and other information will be sent to the target event directly without any changes to the event pattern that was configured.

- **Part of the matched event**: This is used to extract part of the data sent in by the event pattern. This takes only part of the matched event specified and sends it to the target service. It uses the $ notation to filter through the event pattern. If only the *source* of the event pattern is needed, $.source is used to extract only the source of the event pattern. In the same way, if only the *region* is needed to be sent to the target service, $.region can be used to extract the region from the event pattern.

- **Constant**: This means a constant value will be sent to the target service resource. This constant value by default is usually JSON-formatted data. The onus is on the target service to read the constant data sent to it via the input parameter. No partial or full data of the event pattern is sent to the target, only constant JSON data that is sent. If an input trigger comes from an EC2 instance that contains the instance state, it does not send it to the target service; instead, it sends the JSON data at all times.

- **Input transformer**: This makes it possible to change or edit the values of one or more of the items in the event pattern. It makes it possible to manipulate the original value that is in the matched event and put in another value that is eventually sent to the target event.

- **Version/alias**: This keeps track of configurations for the purpose of rollback, or forward changes that have been made to the target configuration.

We have talked about the target section of a CloudWatch event and Amazon EventBridge. The next step is to create a simple CloudWatch event and an Amazon EventBridge for two different scenarios. We can see the similarities and maybe the differences in the method of configuration and setup.

Configuring a basic CloudWatch event

Let's take a real-life scenario of how CloudWatch Events can be quite important to use for a very simple solution. Let's assume that an organization, MCS Consulting, owns a bunch of staging servers used as EC2 instances. These servers are not used for 24 hours and are only used when the developers need to run application tests. This means that running the server just within the working hours, that is, between 9 a.m. to 5 p.m. or 6 p.m., is how much is needed for useful purposes. This means that between 6.01 p.m. and 8.59 a.m., the EC2 instance(s) can be shut down, which will result in some huge cost savings for running those instances. This configuration can be done using CloudWatch Events. For this to work, we need the instance ID(s) of the EC2 instance we wish to place on this schedule. Let's assume the instance ID is `i-1234567890abcdef0`.

For this setup, we will not be using the event pattern; instead, we will be going through the route of using a scheduled expression that is used for events that need to be triggered at a particular time. From the scenario given here, one schedule is to stop the EC2 instance at 6 p.m. and then to start it up at 9 a.m. the next day. This automatically makes it two schedules:

1. So, we will create two schedules for this setup, one to stop the instance and the other to start the instance. Let's go into the console and get this done. First, we log in to our AWS console (this is assuming we already have an AWS account).

2. Click on the **Services** top-menu item, and from the drop-down menu, click on the **CloudWatch** link, which should look like this:

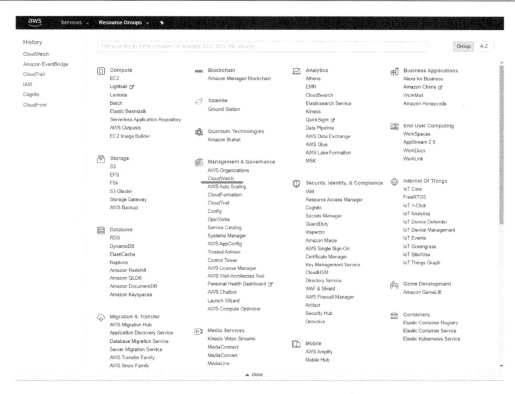

Figure 2.5 – AWS management console

3. After clicking the **CloudWatch** link, this will take us to the CloudWatch console, as shown in the following figure:

Figure 2.6 – AWS CloudWatch console

4. From the console, navigate to the left-side menu and click on the **Rules** item just directly below **Events**, as shown in the following screenshot:

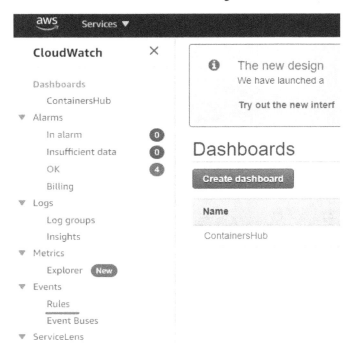

Figure 2.7 – Navigation to the CloudWatch event page

This will take us to the CloudWatch Events console, as shown in the following screenshot:

Figure 2.8 – CloudWatch Events console

5. Click on the **Create rule** button to create a new CloudWatch Events rule, as shown in the following screenshot:

Figure 2.9 – Creating a rule in CloudWatch Events

6. Click on the **Schedule** radio button to reveal the options to configure the scheduled time:

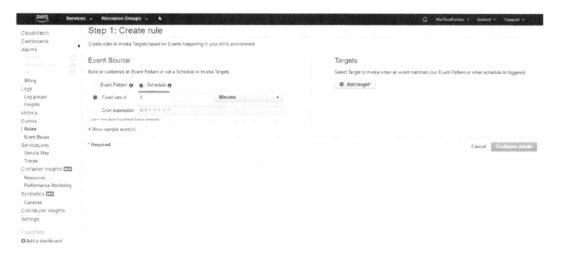

Figure 2.10 – Configuring a scheduled expression

7. At this point, we will need the right cron expression for the stop operation. The instruction says the EC2 instance will stop at 6pm. The cron expression that signifies 6 p.m. every day is 0 18 * * ? *.

8. Click on the **Cron expression** option and paste the preceding cron expression into the box beside it. It will automatically show the time of the events for the next 10 days. This is also another way to validate that the cron expression is correct:

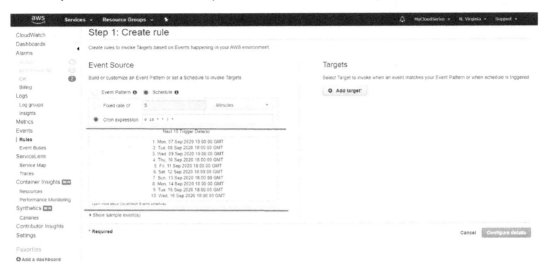

Figure 2.11 – Cron expression validation

9. The next step is to add the target we want this scheduled expression to trigger. To do this, click on the **Add target** button on the right-hand side under the **Targets** title:

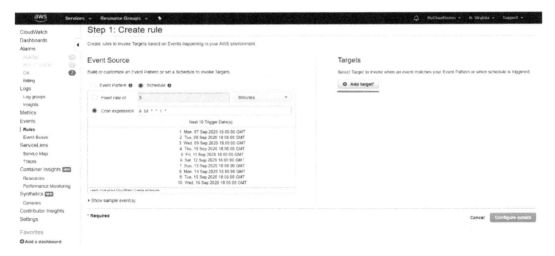

Figure 2.12 – Adding a target

10. Clicking on this will show the different target options that exist. Our setup requires that we stop an EC2 instance. So, from the list, we shall select **EC2 StopInstances API call**:

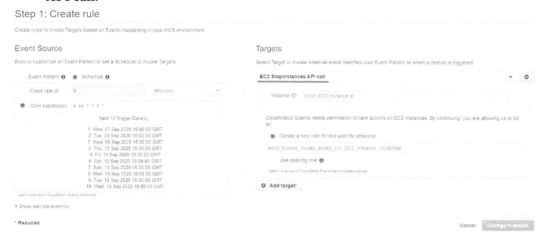

Figure 2.13 – Configuring a target

11. When the **EC2 StopInstances API call** option is selected, it gives the option to enter an instance ID. In this box, we are going to fill in the instance ID we were given: i-1234567890abcdef0.

12. The next step is to configure authorization. For this action to take place, an **Identity and Access Management** (**IAM**) role is required to be able to make an API call to the EC2 instance from CloudWatch.

> **Important Note**
>
> An IAM role is a feature in the AWS IAM service, which is responsible for managing inter-service communication within AWS. The role is assigned to a service to give it access to communicate with another service. A role is made up of a policy, which a JSON document that defines the rules that guide how service A communicates with service B. An IAM role is the authorization layer for all inter-service interactions in AWS.

13. There is the option to either create a new role or use an existing role. For our setup, we will be creating a new role. A value is already generated in the box, which is AWS_Events_Invoke_Action_On_EC2_Instance_22287866. This value might be different for your own setup.

14. The final configuration screen will look as in the following screenshot:

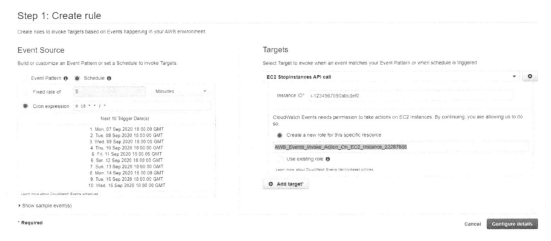

Figure 2.14 – Final configuration screen

15. When this configuration is confirmed, the next step is to click the **Configure details** button at the bottom-right corner of the screen to move to the next step.

16. The next step is to write the name and description of this event rule:

Figure 2.15 – Entering an event rule name

17. The last option there, labeled **State**, is to configure whether the event should be active or not. By default, it is configured to be enabled. This configuration can be useful in scenarios where you want to disable an event. The state can easily be changed and the checkbox clicked to make disable it.

18. The next step is to create the rule. To do this, click on the **Create rule** button in blue at the bottom-right of the screen.

This will create the rule and return to the event rule dashboard, like this:

Figure 2.16 – Dashboard showing the rule created

These steps have been to stop an EC2 instance. We can go through the same process for starting a start but this time, two parameters will change. The first is the scheduled expression while the second will be the target. The scheduled expression will become 0 9 * * ? *, which represents 9 a.m., and the target will be **EC2 RebootInstances API call**. The same instance ID will be used and the name has to be unique for this rule.

We now understand what Amazon CloudWatch Events is and how CloudWatch Events is gradually being transitioned into Amazon EventBridge. We also looked at the different components of CloudWatch Events and EventBridge. To help drive home all of these, we went on to create a basic example of a scheduled expression. The next step is to talk about alarms and the role of CloudWatch alarms in the monitoring process.

Introducing CloudWatch alarms

CloudWatch alarms are a managed alert and notification service used to send notifications when an anomaly is detected in an infrastructure setup. Alarms are configured in relation to specific metrics. What an alarm does is it checks changes in the metric it is attached to based on specific conditions that have been given to it. When those conditions have been met, the alarm is triggered. An alarm can be configured to consistently check and ensure that the CPU usage of an EC2 instance does not exceed 80%. If it does for any reason, the alarm will be triggered and will push those state changes to Amazon SNS.

CloudWatch alarms in conjunction with Amazon SNS make alarms and notifications much easier to manage by reducing the operational expression of managing different alert and notification systems for your monitoring infrastructure, thereby aggregating metrics, alarms, and notifications as a complete set of solutions for alerting when the state of a particular metric changes.

Importance of a CloudWatch alarm

When there is a change in state or an anomaly activity, the best way to know if something has gone wrong is through a notification that an alarm provides. Anomalies in a system vary from environment to environment, so it is essential to know the exact metric anomaly that occurs. Some of the things that CloudWatch alarms specifically help with are as follows:

- Visibility
- Infrastructure performance
- Infrastructure health

We now understand the meaning of CloudWatch alarms and also the importance of different aspects of an application, such as the visibility of metrics or logs that are anomalies or different from what they should be. Alerts on infrastructure performance, such as network speed alerts when it passes a certain threshold or an alert when a server CPU is peaking at 80–95%. The next step is for us to set up a very basic CloudWatch alarm.

Configuring a basic alarm

An alarm is usually configured based on a metric from any of the AWS services or from logs. This is the major aspect we will be covering in the rest of this chapter, how alarms can be configured on a service based on a specific metric.

For starters, we shall create a simple alarm that triggers when the AWS bill gets to a certain threshold that we are also going to configure. This can be very helpful in cutting down costs and ensuring that we do not spend more than a specific amount within a month. For this setup, we will be checking the estimated charges for a month and ensure that they are not greater than $15. If for any reason the estimated charge is greater than $15, we will get an email notification via SNS notifying us of the increase. Now, let's get to work and configure this alarm. The AWS account that was used in the previous practical guide is sufficient to carry out the next practical guide:

1. The **Receive Billing Alerts** setting needs to be enabled from the AWS billing console. Navigate to the AWS main menu. Click on the **Services** bar. In the search bar, type `Billing` and click on the **Billing** menu item.

2. The next page is the billing dashboard, which shows different information about the AWS bill, such as the bill-till date, the bill for the last month, and the forecast for the month. On the side menu, click on the **Billing preferences** link to load the billing preferences page:

Figure 2.17 – Billing preferences link

3. The next page we are going to see is the page showing the billing preferences. The following screenshot shows the billing preferences page:

Figure 2.18 – Billing preferences dashboard

4. On the screen, navigate to the bottom and look for the item called **Receive Billing Alerts**. Click on the checkbox beside it and click the **Save preferences** button. This will activate the billing metrics to be sent to CloudWatch.

5. The next step is to navigate to the Amazon CloudWatch dashboard. Click on the **Services** menu item and navigate to the **Management & Governance** list and locate **CloudWatch**, which is the second item in the list just after **AWS Organizations**.

6. Landing on the CloudWatch dashboard, click on the **Alarms** menu item on the list of items on the left-hand side of the screen:

Figure 2.19 – CloudWatch Alarms dashboard

7. The next step is to create the actual alarm. To do that, click on the **Create alarm** button on the top-right corner of the screen, which will lead you to the following screen:

Figure 2.20 – Creating a CloudWatch alarm

8. Click the **Select metric** button. This will open different metrics that you can choose from, as follows:

Figure 2.21 – The Select metric dashboard

9. Click on **Billing**, and then click on **Total Estimated Charge**. Then, click the checkbox beside the currency (for example, USD), and then click on the **Select metric** button on the bottom-left corner of the screen:

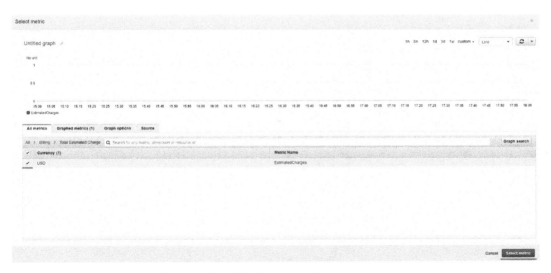

Figure 2.22 – Selecting a specific metric value

10. The next screen, titled **Specify metric and conditions**, allows us to configure the value for this metric that will trigger an alarm. We shall configure the value to be a **Static** value that should be **Greater** than 15. The following screenshot shows the configuration after we have set it up:

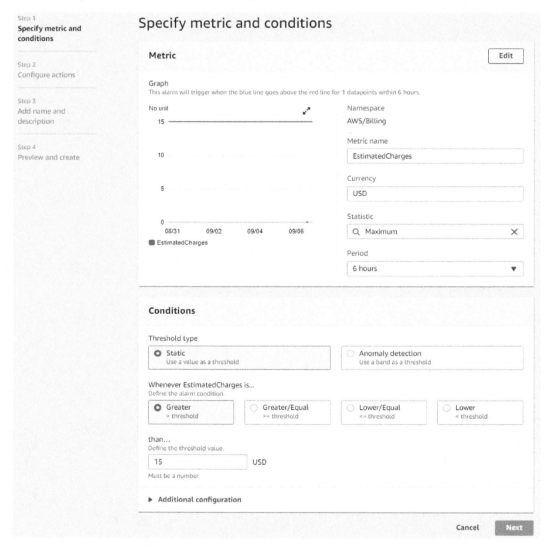

Figure 2.23 – Configuring the metric and conditions

11. When the configuration is confirmed, click the **Next** button on the bottom-right corner of the screen.

12. The next step is to **Configure actions**. First, select the **Alarm state trigger** option, in this case, **In alarm**, which is selected by default.

13. The next option is **Select an SNS topic**. This option has various selections, such as **Select an existing topic**, **Create new topic**, and **Use topic ARN**. For this setup, we will be creating a new SNS topic. Click on the **Create new topic** option. Enter the name of the topic and the email endpoints, as shown in the following screenshot:

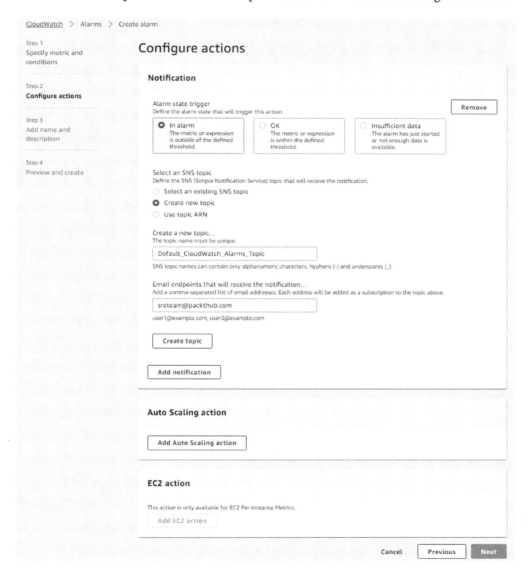

Figure 2.24 – Configure actions

14. Click on the **Create topic** button to create the topic. When the topic has been successfully created, review the other configurations and click the **Next** button to confirm.

15. Enter the name of the alarm and a description for the alarm. For this, we will call the alarm `BillingThresholdAlarm`. The description is optional, so we shall leave it blank:

Figure 2.25 – Entering a name and description

16. Click the **Next** button to continue.

17. The next stage is **Preview and create**. This gives us the choice to review all the configurations that have been made from the start. At this stage, we are allowed to edit or make changes to each section as we please. At this point, we really do not need to make any changes:

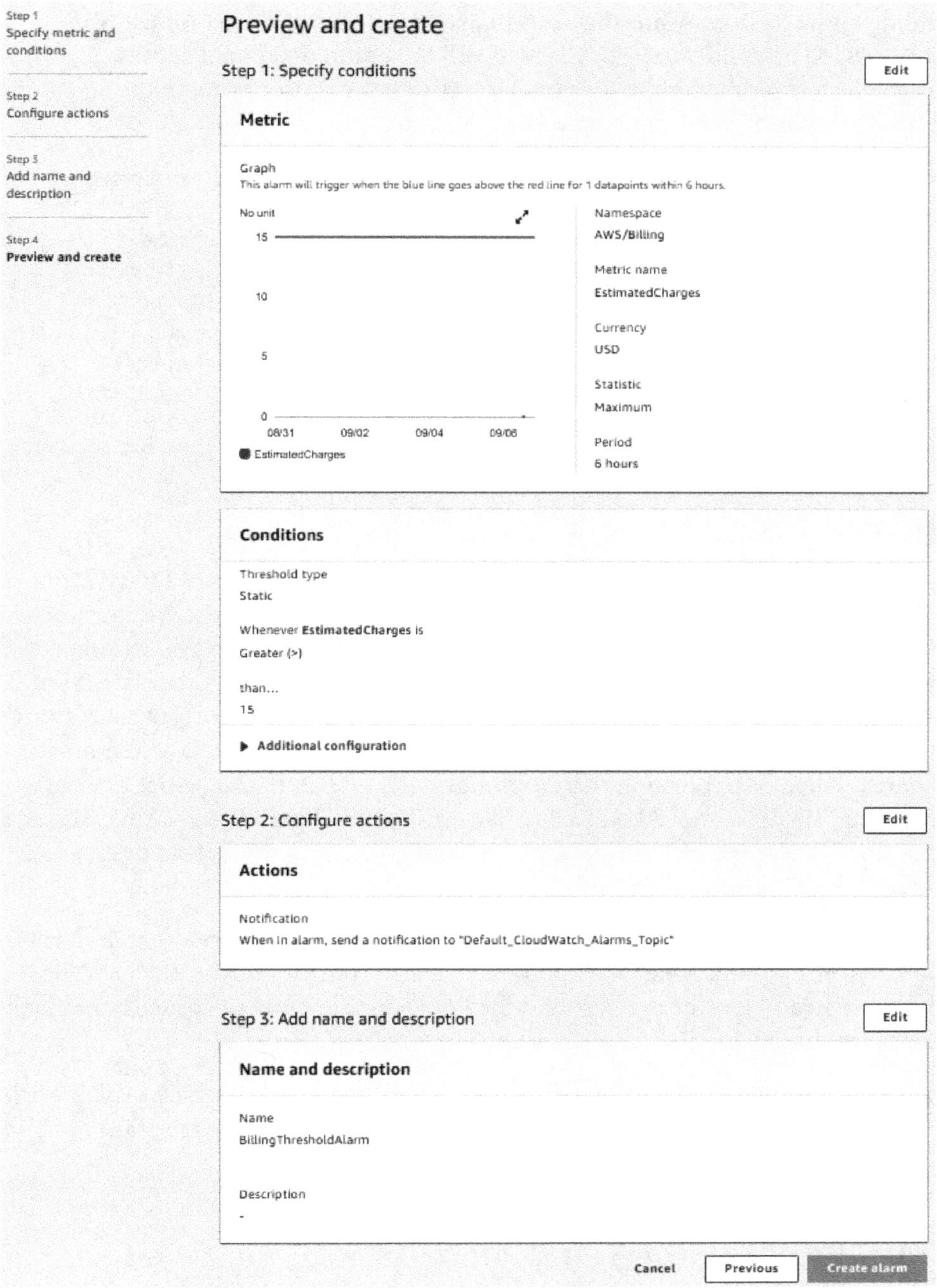

Step 1
Specify metric and
conditions

Step 2
Configure actions

Step 3
Add name and
description

Step 4
Preview and create

Preview and create

Step 1: Specify conditions   Edit

Metric

Graph
This alarm will trigger when the blue line goes above the red line for 1 datapoints within 6 hours.

No unit   ⤢   Namespace
    15 ──────────────────   AWS/Billing

                                               Metric name
    10   EstimatedCharges

                                               Currency
    5   USD

                                               Statistic
    0 ──────────────────   Maximum
      08/31   09/02   09/04   09/06
    ● EstimatedCharges   Period
                                               6 hours

Conditions

Threshold type
Static

Whenever **EstimatedCharges** is
Greater (>)

than...
15

▶ Additional configuration

Step 2: Configure actions   Edit

Actions

Notification
When in alarm, send a notification to "Default_CloudWatch_Alarms_Topic"

Step 3: Add name and description   Edit

Name and description

Name
BillingThresholdAlarm

Description
-

Cancel   Previous   Create alarm

Figure 2.26 – The Preview and create page

18. Click the **Create alarm** button to create the alarm.

The pending confirmation means that the email address that was used for the SNS endpoint needs to be confirmed. So, an email will be sent to that email address for confirmation. Click on the link in the email to activate the subscription to the SNS topic to start receiving alerts when the alarms trigger.

> **Important Note**
> Composite alarms are a feature in CloudWatch alarms that help to aggregate different alarms to decide whether an alarm should trigger. When there are multiple metrics and alarms configured, there are situations where they could be too much to track and become irrelevant in the end because too many emails or SMSes are being sent by Amazon SNS. Composite alarms can be used to aggregate and compute multiple alarms to decide whether a final alarm should trigger based on the data from different alarms combined.

Summary

This chapter started with an understanding of the meaning of Amazon CloudWatch Events and the different components that make up CloudWatch Events. We also learned that it is being deprecated and will be replaced with Amazon EventBridge. We learned that EventBridge is a serverless service for receiving events and triggering other corresponding services just the way CloudWatch Events does, but EventBridge supports triggers from SaaS applications, making it more extensive than CloudWatch Events. We then moved on to configure a schedule expression that stops and starts and an EC2 instance at a particular time of the day. Then, we moved on to introduce Amazon CloudWatch alarms, discussed the importance of alarms, and moved ahead to configure an alarm that sends an email when our AWS estimated bill reaches $15.

We have been able to not only learn the guiding principles behind CloudWatch Events, Amazon EventBridge, and Amazon CloudWatch alarms but also formulate a real-life practical scenario and use the services and the knowledge learned to create solutions to our scenario for both CloudWatch Events and CloudWatch alarms.

The next chapter is going to focus on CloudWatch logs and metrics, which explains how to understand data collecting from infrastructure and how to make sense of it.

Questions

1. An alarm is a feature of Amazon CloudWatch. But for the notification of an alarm to be sent, a particular AWS service is needed to perform that delivery. What is that service called?

2. What part of the Amazon CloudWatch Events components is responsible for defining the input trigger into CloudWatch Events?

3. Alarms and alerts are usually used for what type of monitoring?

Further reading

For more information on monitoring and alerting, refer to *Understanding Monitoring and Alerting Services in AWS*: `https://www.packtpub.com/product/aws-masterclass-monitoring-and-devops-with-aws-cloudwatch-video/9781788999533`

3
CloudWatch Logs, Metrics, and Dashboards

In the previous chapter, we talked about **Amazon CloudWatch Events, Amazon EventBridge**, and **CloudWatch alarms.** We defined the meaning of CloudWatch Events and talked about the components that make up a CloudWatch event. We further explained the importance of CloudWatch Events and gave real-life scenarios. We created an example of an automated start and stop of an EC2 instance based on a specific time of day. This was done using the **scheduled expression** feature in **Amazon CloudWatch Events**. We explained CloudWatch alarms and why it is important to integrate an alarm system into your monitoring infrastructure. Then, we implemented a basic alarm solution that sends an email when the **estimated AWS bill** gets to a specific amount for that particular month.

These scenarios used for CloudWatch Events and CloudWatch alarms are the criteria for understanding the basics. In subsequent chapters, the alarms will be tied to more specific and important metrics to trigger alarms for more critical systems and scenarios.

In this chapter, we will continue to talk about the components of **Amazon CloudWatch.** Our focus in this chapter will be on **CloudWatch Logs**, **metrics**, and **dashboards**.

This chapter explains how to understand data collected from infrastructure and how to make sense of it. To get a better understanding of applications and infrastructure, data needs to be collected about the infrastructure services. This data is the metric for measuring behavior over time. Combining this data will help to get more historic data and eventually help to get insights from the metric that has been collected. A pictorial representation in the form of graphs and charts can help give good analytics of the behavior of a system.

We will cover the following topics in this chapter:

- Introducing CloudWatch Logs
- Understanding metrics and CloudWatch metrics
- Introducing Amazon CloudWatch dashboards
- Creating a dashboard from metrics
- Working with dashboards

Technical requirements

To be able to accomplish the technical tasks in the chapter, you will need to have the following technical prerequisites:

- A working **AWS account** (you can opt for the free tier, which will cost $0/month for one year)
- A **Linux EC2** instance set up in the AWS account
- Basic knowledge of **Linux**
- An understanding of **AWS IAM**

Check out the following link to see the Code in Action video:

https://bit.ly/3l7RXk4

Introducing CloudWatch Logs

We previously defined logs in *Chapter 1, Introduction to Monitoring*, and this time we are going to streamline our understanding of logs in the context of **CloudWatch**. But for the purpose of reminding us, let's go back to what logs are. Logs are a series of events captured in a text format. The text format could be **unstructured** or **semi-structured** data formats.

> **Important Note**
>
> Unstructured data is a kind of data that does not have a specific defined model with which the data is stored. It does not conform to a specific consistent pattern. Unstructured data usually comes with a few data types, such as string, number, or date and time. Most web server logs are unstructured data.
>
> Semi-structured data is a form of storing data that is not fully structured data; it does not conform to the relational (table) method of storing data in rows and columns. Instead, it uses its own unique pairs and grouping of data in a unique way to help the data look a little more structured. A popular example of semi-structured data is **JavaScript Object Notation (JSON)**.

For most application logs, web server logs, and system logs, they are usually stored as unstructured data that takes note of specific information and important metrics, and most times the application or web server outputs the data in a particular format.

Life cycle of a log

To look further into logs, we need to understand the **life cycle** of logs. We already defined a **log** as the documentation of an event. This documentation needs to be stored in a particular location. In most cases, a log is stored in the location where it is generated. For example, **Apache Web Server** generates different types of logs, such as access log, and error logs. These logs are stored in a particular directory specified by the Apache configuration file. This same concept applies to other applications and application servers.

To be able to monitor and draw insights from the data, the insights need to be collected, aggregated, and in some cases properly re-formatted or cleaned to allow easy analytics operations. There are a few principles that cover the life cycle of a log. They are as follows:

1. **Collection/extraction**: This involves the extraction of the logs from their original source. Due to the fact that the logs are generated from the specific location where the application or service is running, it is necessary to move and aggregate them into a central location. This central location will be responsible for housing the data. This collection or extraction of logs is done using a log agent. A log agent is a daemon process or application that helps to extract this data from a specific location. The log agent is usually configured to read the location where the log is written and intermittently pick the data and send it to the location where it will be stored.

   Amazon CloudWatch has an agent. This agent can be installed in multiple operating systems (Windows or Linux) and can be used to extract both operating system logs and applications logs and send them over to CloudWatch for storage. Without the collection point for the logs, there is no data to work with for monitoring, metrics, dashboards, and alarms. When the data has been collected, it needs to be stored somewhere, which is the storage location. Let's talk about how CloudWatch stores logs.

2. **Storage**: When the data has been collected, it needs to be stored in a particular location. This location could be a database, a filesystem, or a storage service. The data that is collected is going to be large, so the storage needs to be resilient, scalable, and highly available. CloudWatch Logs is a solution that meets all the requirements for storing log data and more. When you use CloudWatch to store your infrastructure and application logs, you do not have to worry about the capacity of the storage or the availability of the storage service. The CloudWatch Logs service is built with extra features, such as a log retention policy, which helps with managing how long the logs will be visible and accessible.

   Logs usually stay forever in Amazon CloudWatch Logs, but that could make the log interface quite cumbersome. With log retention configuration, logs can be configured to expire or rotate when a specific condition is met. Another feature that CloudWatch Logs has is the query feature. This feature makes it easy to sift through the large number of logs that have been stored in CloudWatch Logs. Archiving is another unique feature of CloudWatch Logs. It gives you the ability to store old logs in an archiving solution such as Amazon S3 or Amazon S3 Glacier. This data can be retrieved anytime it is needed. This can be quite helpful when performing compliance operations and data needs to be audited by external auditors.

3. **Analytics**: When logs have been extracted and stored, the next thing is to make sense of them. That is where analytics comes in. Analyzing data comes in different forms and different tools and techniques can be used to analyze data. The simplest way of analyzing data is by using metrics. We drill down through all the logs that have been collected and select a specific part of the data that is necessary to draw out more meaning from the data.

Important Note

A daemon process is a background application that sits inside of your operating system to perform tasks without any user interaction. Daemons have various uses and can be very useful in managing tasks and operations that require system autonomy. One of the best examples of a daemon process is the time on your computer. The clock ticks on its own without you needing to do anything and it continues to run in the background. In all operating systems, there are different background/daemon processes that keep the operating system running perfectly, hence their importance in system operations.

These three states, **collection**, **storage**, and **analytics**, are different states a log can be in at different times. In each state, there are different activities that occur. These states are common to any monitoring service. One state of a log that has not been mentioned is the archive state. This is a state where logs are archived in a location for future purposes. They are not actively available for day-to-day analysis but can be kept in cold storage and can always be retrieved when needed. CloudWatch logs can be exported to **Amazon S3** or **S3 Glacier**. Our focus here is on CloudWatch, so the next section is to understand how CloudWatch Logs interprets these different stages of a log, and the unique components of CloudWatch that are used to perform extraction, storage, and analytics.

Understanding the components of CloudWatch Logs

The first state of a log is the extraction or collection of the data from the location where it is stored. Most times, the logs are stored in a particular file location, and an application writes the log output to that path. It is the job of the collector to read the data from the location and send it to a specific destination. In CloudWatch, the application responsible for this is the **Amazon CloudWatch agent**. The Amazon CloudWatch agent is an application that is installed into your **Amazon EC2** instance. It is further configured to read the particular file where the logs are written to and send those logs to the destination where they need to be stored.

This application runs as a daemon or background application that is not visible but continues to run to pull data from the log file and send it to the storage destination. The source where data is pulled and the destination of where the data is sent are all configured in the Amazon CloudWatch agent configuration file. It also has the option of configuring the rate, in time, at which the log is extracted from the file. This will mean the frequency at which new data extracted is available in the storage service. Whether you are using a Linux operating system or Windows operating system for your Amazon EC2 instance, the Amazon CloudWatch agent is designed to work across both operating systems. There might be differences in terms of the path of conventions but in the end, the same goal will be achieved.

The configuration snippet that follows is a sample of the CloudWatch agent configuration file:

```
[general]
state_file = /var/lib/awslogs/agent-state
[applications_logs]
region = eu-west-1
datetime_format = %b %d %H:%M:%S
file = /var/log/secure
buffer_duration = 5000
log_stream_name = {instance_id}
initial_position = start_of_file
log_group_name = server_logs
```

Let's break down each part of the configuration file:

- `state_file`: This is the file that the CloudWatch agent application will use to track the file when pulling logs from it. From time to time, it needs to know where it stopped when pulling logs from the file to avoid repetition. If for any reason the CloudWatch agent stops or the server was shut down, which also stops the CloudWatch agent from running, the state file will help to keep track of where the agent stopped reading the log file from.

- `region`: Amazon CloudWatch is region-specific; this configuration is specifying the AWS region of Amazon CloudWatch that the agent will be sending the logs to. For the sample configuration file, the region selected is `eu-west-1`. Any region can be used from the 20 AWS public regions. The short name for the region must be used for the selection. This is a list of regions and their short names:

Region Name	Short Name
N. Virginia	us-east-1
Ohio	us-east-2
N. California	us-west-1
Oregon	us-west-2
Cape Town	af-south-1
Hong Kong	ap-southeast-2
Mumbai	ap-south-1
Seoul	ap-northeast-2
Singapore	ap-southeast-1
Sydney	ap-southeast-2
Tokyo	ap-northeast-1
Canada (Central)	ca-central-1
Frankfurt	eu-central-1
Ireland	eu-west-1
London	eu-west-2
Milan	eu-south-1
Paris	eu-west-3
Stockholm	eu-north-1
Bahrain	me-south-1
São Paulo	sa-east-1

Table 3.1 – AWS regions and short names

- `datetime_format`: This is used to specify the date and time format in which the log data will be stored. Every entry of the logs collected needs to be stored with a date and time. This specifies the date and time format to be used. Based on our configuration, the date and time format will look like so: `2020-09-24T16:31:44.097+01:00`.

- `file`: This parameter is used to specify the file path where the log should pull data from. The path specified must point to a specific file within the operating system where the log data is being populated for the agent to be able to pull the data written to it.

- `buffer_duration`: This specifies the time duration for batching up log events. The unit of measurement is milliseconds. The larger the time, the longer it takes for the log to be visible on CloudWatch Logs. For our configuration, the value used is `5000`. This means the agent will delay for 5 seconds before it pushes new log data to CloudWatch Logs.

- `log_stream_name`: The log stream name is the name given to the category of log that is sent to CloudWatch Logs. The log stream is the label used to identify the type of log that is being sent to CloudWatch Logs. In the configuration we have, the name of the log stream is `serverauditlogs`. A log stream name could be `nginxlogs` or `apachestream`, to signify NGINX logs and Apache logs, respectively. It is a good practice to give the log stream a good name for the purpose of easy identification when it gets to the CloudWatch Logs console. A log stream is a sequence of log events that share the same source.

- `initial_position`: This means the position where the agent starts reading the file from. The possible options for this are either `start_of_file`, which means it will go to the first line and start reading the logs from the top or beginning of the file, or `end_of_file`, which means that it will start reading from the last line in the file.

- `log_group_name`: Just like `log_stream_name`, `log_group_name` is used to label the log group that the log stream will be grouped under. The log group is used to group streams of logs that share the same retention, monitoring, and access control settings. The screenshot that follows shows an example of a log group with its configuration details and log streams just below the log group:

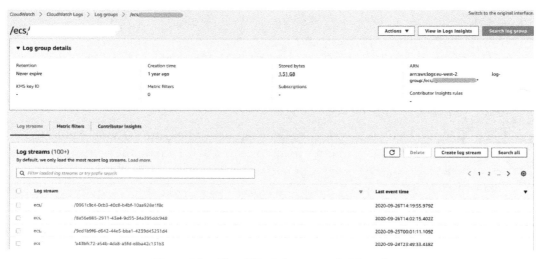

Figure 3.1 – CloudWatch log group dashboard

Now we have explained what CloudWatch logs are and the different components that make up Amazon CloudWatch. Let's go into the steps involved in configuring an Amazon CloudWatch agent and push logs to Amazon CloudWatch.

Configuring a basic CloudWatch agent

These are the steps involved in configuring a basic CloudWatch agent to push CloudWatch logs from a server to the CloudWatch Logs dashboard. As stated earlier, CloudWatch Logs works with Linux and Windows operating systems. For this scenario, we will be using a Linux operating system to demonstrate these steps. The steps are as follows:

1. Create an Amazon EC2 instance with any version of Linux (Amazon Linux, Ubuntu, Red Hat, or any that suits you). You can also use an existing Linux instance that runs in your AWS environment.

2. Log in to the EC2 instance created previously with the login credentials provided by AWS after instance creation. If you already have an EC2 instance login, use the credentials you already have.

3. Install the Amazon CloudWatch agent for Linux using the following command:

    ```
    yum install awslogs -y
    ```

    It is recommended to run this on Amazon Linux and not Amazon Linux 2 to get the best experience.

4. When the installation is complete, the next step is to configure the CloudWatch agent to be able to send logs from a specific file location to CloudWatch. To do that, we will locate the file that needs to be configured. The file is located at `/etc/awslogs/awslogs.conf`.

5. Open the file with your favorite Linux text editor (such as Vim, nano, or vi). Delete all the contents of the file and update the file with the contents in *Figure 3.1*.

6. Next is to configure **IAM** access to allow the instance to write logs to Amazon CloudWatch. To do this, we will need to create an AWS IAM role.

> **Important Note**
>
> An AWS IAM role is a set of permissions defined by an AWS IAM policy that determines the privileges and rights a service has to communicate with another AWS service. When one AWS service needs to communicate with another AWS service, permissions need to be given to one to be able to communicate with the other, and this can be done using either `AccessKey` and `SecretKey` or an IAM role.

7. To create an IAM role, log in to your AWS management console and navigate to the **Services** menu item on the top bar.

8. Click on the **Services** menu item. In the dropdown, type `IAM` and click on the pop-up search result. This will lead to the IAM management console. The following screenshot shows part of the IAM console:

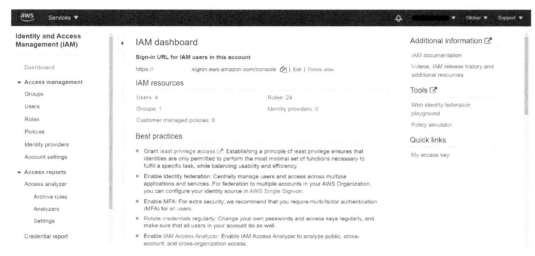

Figure 3.2 – AWS IAM management console

9. Click on the **Roles** option on the left-side menu bar to show the existing roles and display where we can create a new role.

10. On the **Roles** page, click on the **Create Role** button to create a new role. This will give us the form to fill in to create a new role.

11. The next action to take is to choose a trusted entity. For this scenario, our use case is EC2, so we shall select **EC2**:

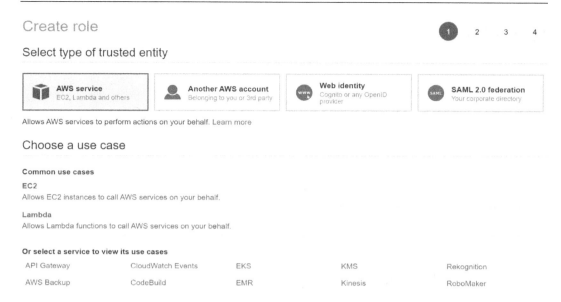

Figure 3.3 – Creating an IAM role

12. Click the **Next: Permissions** button on the bottom-right corner of the screen.

13. The next step is to create a policy. We do not have a policy that fits directly into our use case, from the list of AWS **managed policies**. For that reason, we will create our own policy. Then, use a policy statement that will give EC2 access to CloudWatch. In this case, give EC2 instances access to write logs to CloudWatch Logs. To create a policy, click on the **Create Policy** button.

> **Important Note**
>
> A policy is a JSON document that defines the level of access one service has over another. The policy defines the service(s) that requires permission and users who can have access to that service and allows configuration of conditions that need to be met before access can be allowed for a particular service or set of services. AWS managed policies are policies created by AWS by default. This does not stop you from creating your own custom policies.

14. A new tab will be created to create a new policy. On the page, click the **JSON** tab. This tab allows the imputation of the JSON policy document:

Figure 3.4 – Creating a policy

15. Enter the following policy into the page and click on the **Review policy** button:

```
{
    "Version": "2012-10-17",
    "Statement": [
        {
            "Effect": "Allow",
            "Action": [
                "logs:CreateLogGroup",
                "logs:CreateLogStream",
                "logs:PutLogEvents",
                "logs:DescribeLogStreams"
            ],
            "Resource": [
                "arn:aws:logs:*:*:*"
            ]
        }
    ]
}
```

16. The policy statement is reviewed and validated for errors, both for JSON syntax errors and an IAM policy grammar check.

17. If everything checks out fine, the next step is to write the name of the policy and a brief description of what the policy does. Enter a name for the policy and a short description, for example, `ec2cloudwatchpolicy`. Then, click on the **Create policy** button.

18. Navigate back to the **Create IAM Role** tab, and click on the refresh icon to reload the list of policies.

19. Then, type the name of the new policy we just created, `ec2cloudwatchpolicy`. It will show up on the list. Click on the checkbox beside it and click the **Next: Tags** button.

20. Tags are not compulsory here, so we shall leave them blank and click the **Next: Review** button.

21. Enter the name for the role and a brief description of the role. We can call this `ec2cloudwatchrole`. Then, click the **Create role** button to create the role.

    This will lead to the IAM role dashboard with a message at the top saying that the role has been created.

22. The next step is to attach the created role to the EC2 instance. Navigate to the EC2 instance console and select the instance to attach the IAM role. Click on the **Actions** button to list out different actions on the EC2 instance.

23. On the drop-down list, navigate to **Instance Settings | Attach/Replace**.

24. On the next screen that displays, select the role from the list of roles, and then click the **Apply** button to apply the role to the EC2 instance.

    This will apply the role to the EC2 instance.

25. The final step is to start the CloudWatch agent, which has already been installed. For the Linux version, we use the `service awslogs start` command. This will start sending the logs from the file that was configured in the CloudWatch agent to the AWS CloudWatch Logs console. The following screenshot shows the logs being written to the Amazon CloudWatch Logs console:

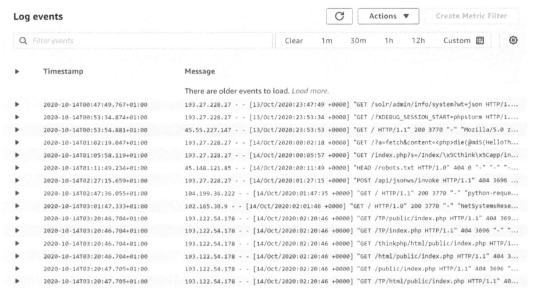

Figure 3.5 – Sample view of the CloudWatch stream

That was quite a long process but going through it step by step is advised so that no stage is missed to ensure everything works perfectly. With that working, we finally have logs being sent to CloudWatch, and the next question is, how do we draw meaning and sense out of these logs that are being collected by CloudWatch Logs? CloudWatch provides three ways to draw insights from the logs that are sent from an EC2 instance. They are as follows:

- CloudWatch Logs Insights

- CloudWatch metrics

- The CloudWatch dashboard

In the next section, we will be talking about metrics and how CloudWatch metrics help to give meaning to logs, as well as the different types of metrics that exist in Amazon CloudWatch.

Understanding metrics and CloudWatch metrics

A metric is a specific data point that is singled out and further computed to derive meaning from a huge set of data or logs that has been collected. In some cases, there are standard metrics for systems such as operating systems, application servers, or web servers. It is also possible to set up and configure a specific data point that you believe is important to the status and behavior of a system that gives specific insight into all the data that has been collected. The goal behind a metric is to be able to draw insights from data. As mentioned earlier, a metric can be pulled from logs, or it can exist as an entity of its own. Whichever form a metric takes, it is the focal point and is paramount to decision making for monitoring systems. A metric directly feeds into how an alarm is triggered and the conditions surrounding a metric are what determine the state of an alarm in Amazon CloudWatch. There are various terms associated with CloudWatch metrics. Let's talk about a few of them.

Terms associated with CloudWatch metrics

The following are terms you will commonly find associated with CloudWatch metrics. They are major components that make up CloudWatch metrics and are necessary for understanding how CloudWatch metrics work. They are as follows:

- **Metric namespaces**: These are used to group and categorize metrics to prevent them from being ungrouped. Grouping metrics makes it easier to work with them. Namespaces do not exist for metrics by default, but they can be created when a metric is being created or when a metric filter is being created from a log.

- **Custom namespaces**: Custom namespaces are namespaces created by a user from a particular log that has been generated. AWS namespaces are namespaces generated by AWS that are used to group metrics from different AWS services.

- **AWS namespaces**: An AWS namespace is automatically generated for services that have metrics created by default in CloudWatch without any manual configurations. For example, when an EC2 instance is launched, CloudWatch by default starts monitoring metrics such as CPU utilization, disk reads, network packets in, and network out. These metrics are stored in the AWS namespace for EC2 instances.

- **Metric dimensions**: A metric dimension is a key/value pair that defines how data is stored within a metric. A single metric can have up to 10 dimensions. For example, a billing metric can be grouped by different dimensions, such as **By Linked Account and Service**, **By Linked Account**, **By Service**, and **Total Estimated Charge**.

- **Metric filter**: This is a feature that originates with CloudWatch Logs but works fully within CloudWatch metrics. This feature makes it possible to clamp down on specific touchpoints or data points you intend to monitor within the stream of logs that are received in CloudWatch Logs. The metric filter is able to filter through the logs as the logs come and the metric can be fed into graphs and used to configure a CloudWatch alarm. A metric filter can search for a specific word within the logs, or a pattern match can be used to create a metric filter. An example of a metric filter is creating a filter that is able to identify all the errors that exist within a stream of logs that have been sent to the CloudWatch log stream. Let's look at a basic example of a CloudWatch metrics filter to help drive home this point.

Creating a metric filter from CloudWatch Logs

Let's see how we can create a log stream based on the logs that we created in the previous section. In the previous section of this chapter, we talked about logs and also saw a demonstration of sending logs from a particular path, /var/log/secure, to **CloudWatch Logs**. What we are going to do this time is to create a metric filter based on a CloudWatch log that has been sent to Amazon CloudWatch. But to do that, we need to first take a look at a unit log event and try to see what kind of metric we would like to get out of the log and possibly configure a CloudWatch alarm based on the metric that we have been able to filter out and identify in the logs. Let's assume we want to find out the invalid user ssh attempts on our EC2 instance, which means we want to see the number of times or occurrences when a login to the EC2 instance failed and has an invalid user. This could be a malicious user trying to use a fake username to log in to the EC2 instance, which can be picked up by the log. Then, we will use the filter to get that activity and tie an alarm to that occurrence. The alarm triggers whenever it finds an invalid user trying to log in. The following screenshot is a sample of the ssh log that shows an invalid user called avanthi:

```
Sep 30 07:14:12 ip-172-31-71-23 sshd[25088]: Connection reset by 222.186.31.166 port 34979 [preauth]
Sep 30 07:21:54 ip-172-31-71-23 sshd[25361]: Received disconnect from 222.186.42.155 port 47824:11: [preauth]
Sep 30 07:21:54 ip-172-31-71-23 sshd[25361]: Disconnected from 222.186.42.155 port 47824 [preauth]
Sep 30 07:26:28 ip-172-31-71-23 sshd[25507]: Did not receive identification string from 182.23.84.218 port 64044
Sep 30 07:26:37 ip-172-31-71-23 sshd[25508]: Invalid user avanthi from 182.23.84.218 port 64054
Sep 30 07:26:37 ip-172-31-71-23 sshd[25508]: input_userauth_request: invalid user avanthi [preauth]
```

Figure 3.6 – Sample of logs to be filtered

So, our metric filter will be focused on looking for the word Invalid in the pool of logs. Let's set up a metric filter based on this data. These are the steps to set up a metric filter:

1. Log in to your AWS console and navigate to the Amazon CloudWatch console.

2. Click on the **Logs | Log groups** link on the side menu of the Amazon CloudWatch console. This will lead us to the log group that we already created. Click on the log group called `server_logs` to open up the log stream.

3. On the log stream dashboard, there is a search bar at the top. Type the word `Invalid` to get all occurrences of `Invalid` in the log streams.

4. When the results load, the **Create Metric Filter** button will be active on the top-right corner of the screen.

5. Click on the button to create the metric filter.

6. On the popup that displays, fill in the form with all the required parameters, as shown in the following screenshot:

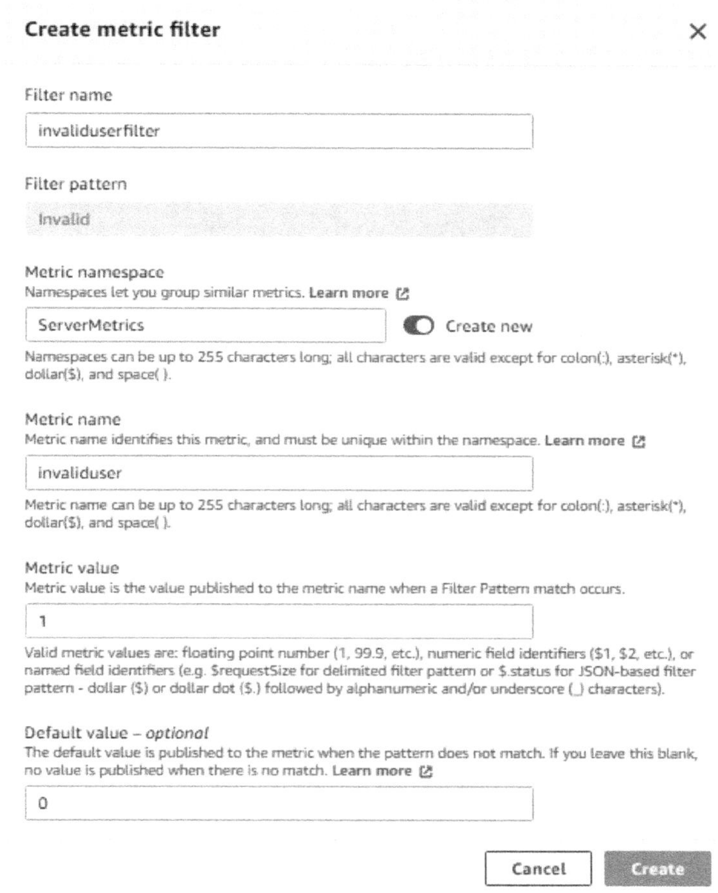

Figure 3.7 – Form filled with all the required parameters

Creating the dashboard

To create a dashboard in Amazon CloudWatch, we click on the **Dashboards** link on the left-hand side of the Amazon CloudWatch console. Click on the **Create dashboard** button and enter the name of the dashboard from the popup, and then click on the **Create dashboard** button to create the dashboard. The dashboard will become visible in the list of dashboards.

The next step will be to add a widget to the dashboard. As mentioned earlier, widgets are actually what contain the pictorial representation of data. Widgets are created using either metrics or logs.

For this scenario, we will create a widget for our dashboard based on the metric that was created before, which is the `invaliduser` metric under the `ServerMetrics` custom namespace.

To create this widget, we take the following steps:

1. On the Amazon CloudWatch console, click on the **Dashboards** link on the left-hand side of the screen.

2. On the list of dashboards, we should find the dashboard that was just created, `sampleboard`. Click on the link to open the dashboard page.

3. Click on the **Add widget** button to add a new widget. From the list of options, click on the **Line** option:

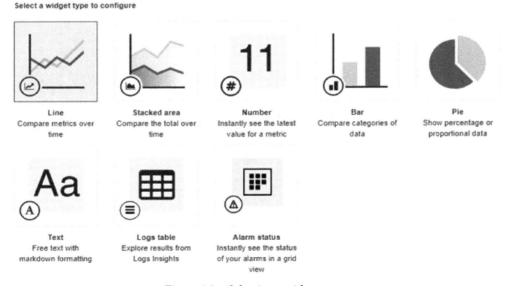

Figure 3.8 – Selecting a widget type

4. Click on the **Next** button. You will find that there are two options used to create a dashboard. The two options are metrics or logs. For our scenario, we will pick **Metrics**.

5. Click the **Metrics** option, and click the **Configure** button.

6. Click on **ServerMetrics | Metric** with no dimensions and then click the checkbox beside **invaliduser**. The graph will automatically get populated with the data on the metric and show the points and lines.

7. Finally, click the **Create widget** button to create the widget.

8. The widget will become available on the dashboard. It will have the default name of the metric, which can be edited to a specific name that will be easily recognized.

With this, we have been able to successfully create a custom dashboard based on a specific metric that was created previously. We can now see that it is possible to create different kinds of custom dashboards based on a custom metric that has been created. The next step is to understand how to work with some of the features of the dashboard.

Working with dashboards

Sometimes, a graph might look empty as maybe the data is not available at that time. Using the time configuration in the top-right corner of a dashboard can work like a time machine to go back in time to view historic data on the dashboard. It has the option of going back in time by minutes, hours, days, weeks, or months:

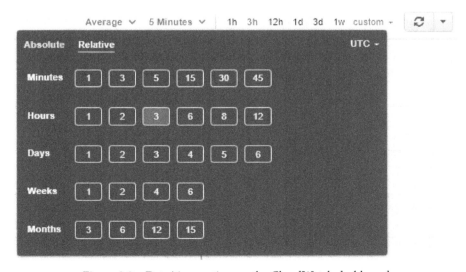

Figure 3.9 – Date/time option on the CloudWatch dashboard

The dashboard can also lead you to the raw logs that are generating the dashboard, making it possible to view the raw data that is collected directly from the source, which could be an EC2 instance, a Lambda function, or any other AWS service where the raw logs are coming from:

Figure 3.10 – Viewing logs

The red underlined icon gives access to view the logs for this particular dashboard. The other icons after that are to refresh, expand, and get more options on the dashboard, which include editing, deleting, or even changing the widget type. These options can allow you to manipulate the widget and the dashboard too.

The essence of this section was to show a few of the features of the widgets in the CloudWatch dashboard. Most of these features will be more valuable when applied to real-life scenarios to drill down to get deeper insights and other manipulations that can be done with the feature capabilities of the CloudWatch dashboard and widget.

Summary

We have spent time in this chapter talking a lot about logs and how to work with logs. We started by defining what a log is and the life cycle of the log, which goes from collection, to storage, to analytics. We also talked about the different ways that CloudWatch Logs groups and categorizes logs. There are log groups and log streams. We went on to do a practical demonstration of how to collect logs from an Amazon EC2 instance and send them over to CloudWatch Logs. After that, we moved on to define CloudWatch metrics and talked about how metrics are represented in metric namespaces and metric dimensions. We then explained that metrics are what make logs become more meaningful by drawing out specific insights from the logs that have been collected. Then, we went further to create a simple metric based on the logs that have been collected.

The last part of this chapter was focused on CloudWatch. We defined CloudWatch and the value of using CloudWatch, in that it helps to give a pictorial summary of logs and metric data and a proper bird's-eye view of application and infrastructure behavior. We also created a widget based on the metric that was created previously and attached it to the dashboard. We went further to interpret the dashboard to understand what is being represented in it.

Now that we have a basic understanding of all of these components of Amazon CloudWatch, the next chapter is going to help us in deepening our understanding and look at more real-life scenarios based on the Amazon EC2 compute service. We will talk about the core components of Amazon EC2 and how CloudWatch can help ensure uptime for your EC2 instances.

Questions

1. A combination of events in a system is called what?

2. How do you get a visual of the logs that have been collected by the CloudWatch agent?

3. What tool is used to sift through logs and create a specific metric based on different parameters in the logs?

4. How do you bring together a couple of log streams in the Amazon CloudWatch console?

5. What authorization feature do you need to configure to allow logs to leave the EC2 instance and go to the Amazon CloudWatch console?

Further reading

For more information on topics covered in this chapter, refer to the following links:

*   AWS CloudWatch dashboards: `https://www.packtpub.com/product/aws-masterclass-monitoring-and-devops-with-aws-cloudwatch-video/9781788999533`

*   The need for log analysis: `https://www.packtpub.com/product/learning-elk-stack/9781785887154`

*   Centralized logging: `https://www.packtpub.com/virtualization-and-cloud/docker-swarm-advanced-centralized-logging-and-monitoring-video`

Section 2: AWS Services and Amazon CloudWatch

After whetting your appetite in the first part with the meaning of monitoring and the various pillars that make up monitoring, we shift gears and move faster to see real-life applications of monitoring using CloudWatch as our monitoring tool. Every AWS service can be monitored and tracked and understanding can be drawn from the behavior of the infrastructure. Every service is unique in its own way. A better understanding of its metrics will help improve the availability of the system, improve system performance, and cut down unnecessary costs in other applications.

The following chapters are included in this section:

- *Chapter 4, Monitoring AWS Compute Services*
- *Chapter 5, Setting Up Container Insights on Amazon CloudWatch*
- *Chapter 6, Performance Insights for Database Services*
- *Chapter 7, Monitoring Serverless Applications*
- *Chapter 8, Using CloudWatch for Maintaining Highly Available Big Data Services*

4
Monitoring AWS Compute Services

The previous chapter focused on CloudWatch Logs, the life cycle of a log, and how to capture, store, and perform analytics on a log. All these were practicalized using a basic example of Linux server logs and we used the concept of metrics to draw out meaningful insights from the logs that have been collected from the EC2 instance. After that, we introduced CloudWatch dashboards, and created a dashboard based on the metric that had been created previously. Armed with an understanding of the life cycle of logs, we are able to understand the character of our system. By collecting logs, we understand over time every activity of the system, and with metrics we are able to draw insights from the logs collected. The more logs and metrics we can obtain, the more insights we can derive and the better we can understand the behavior of our system(s). This chapter is going to expose how we can collect more logs and generate more meaningful insights.

In this section, starting from this chapter onward, we will be taking key AWS services and understanding how monitoring and CloudWatch work within those specific systems. The first part is the compute services in AWS. The compute service is usually the first service that practitioners and experts use extensively in AWS. We could not start this section of this book without opening with compute services. But before we go on, I want to set out some expectations in relation to compute services here, usually, services such as Amazon **Elastic Kubernetes Services (EKS)**, **Elastic Container Services (ECS)**, and AWS Lambda.

For this chapter, we will be focused on Amazon EC2, Elastic Beanstalk, and AWS Batch as our compute services. We will begin this chapter by talking about the major metrics that need to be understood and monitored when running an **Infrastructure as a Service (IaaS)** model in the AWS environment. We will be covering the fundamentals of IaaS, as it aids in the proper understanding of IaaS as a method of cloud delivery, and the service we will be monitoring is a major component of IaaS. We will then shift our focus to Amazon EC2, exploring some of the basics around monitoring Amazon EC2 instances and applications deployed within an EC2 instance. We will then look at the various metrics that make up EC2 instance monitoring, talking about the importance of each component and how it ties back to the type of EC2 instance, CloudWatch dashboards for EC2 instances, AWS Batch, and monitoring with Elastic Beanstalk.

By the end of this chapter, you will understand what IaaS is as a method for delivering cloud computing resources. You will also understand how the major components of an EC2 instance are monitored to get information regarding system performance. We will also learn how to configure a CloudWatch unified agent to collect custom metrics and logs from an EC2 instance. Finally, we will look at the dashboard generated when the metrics and logs have been collected.

We will cover the following topics in this chapter:

- Understanding the fundamentals of IaaS monitoring
- Collecting custom metrics on EC2
- Creating an Amazon EventBridge instance for Amazon EC2
- Monitoring Elastic Beanstalk workloads
- Monitoring AWS Batch
- Case study on CloudWatch custom metrics

Technical requirements

To be able to accomplish the technical tasks in the chapter, you will need to have the following technical prerequisites:

- A working AWS account (you can opt for the free tier, which will cost $0/month for 1 year)
- A Linux EC2 instance set up in the AWS account

- A basic knowledge of Linux

- A basic understanding of Amazon SNS

- An understanding of AWS IAM

The code files for this chapter can be downloaded from `https://github.com/ PacktPublishing/Infrastructure-Monitoring-with-Amazon- CloudWatch/tree/main/Chapter04`.

Check out the following link to see the Code in Action video:

`https://bit.ly/2PW3nM7`

Understanding the fundamentals of IaaS monitoring

Compute services are the first entry services for anyone studying cloud computing for the first time. Even power users and professionals in cloud computing use compute services. That is where applications built by developers are deployed. Cloud computing can be delivered in three models:

- **Infrastructure as a Service (IaaS)**

- **Platform as a Service (PaaS)**

- **Software as a Service (SaaS)**

In the IaaS model of cloud computing delivery, the user is given remote access to on-demand virtual machines, or some dedicated hardware, to host applications. In this chapter, our focus will be on IaaS, as the IaaS model of cloud computing is the building block of cloud computing and where starters and applications migrated to the cloud begin to get a grip of the cloud. So, most users of cloud computing services use the IaaS service. In AWS, the paramount IaaS service is Amazon EC2. Amazon **EC2** is an acronym for Amazon **Elastic Compute Cloud**, which is a service that allows users to rent compute power via a virtual machine or a dedicated physical hardware device. This forms the IaaS part of the AWS infrastructure.

A virtual machine is an emulation of a physical computer. It has the same characteristics as a physical computer, the only difference being that it is virtual. Virtual machines are created on top of physical machines. A single physical machine can house multiple virtual machines. A virtual machine has the ability to run an operating system just like physical hardware does. It also has the physical components of a hardware virtualized and shared across all other virtual machines running on the same physical hardware. These virtual components are essential to running any kind of software on the physical hardware and the virtual machine. These components are as follows:

- **Central Processing Unit (CPU)**
- Memory
- Hard disk

These three components get virtualized in a virtual machine and are partitioned based on what exists on the physical hardware. An AWS data center is made up of thousands of pieces of physical hardware. From this physical hardware, the AWS console gives you the ability to rent a part of the physical hardware in the form of a virtual machine, which is called an EC2 instance. This EC2 instance gives you the ability to choose from the vast array of operating system options available in EC2. You can also build a customized operating system if you do not find what you want. EC2 instances have both Windows and Linux operating system variations. With these operating systems installed, applications can be deployed and configured inside the virtual machines.

Now that we understand what an EC2 instance is, and how AWS rents it out via physical hardware, let's look at monitoring associated with EC2 instances and how CloudWatch works with an EC2 instance to ensure proper monitoring of EC2 instances.

When an EC2 instance is created. AWS automatically creates a monitoring dashboard and metrics, some of which we mentioned earlier – the CPU, memory, and hard disk utilization. However, AWS measures other metrics that are associated with running an EC2 instance effectively. Two important metrics that determine the state of an EC2 instance are **system status check** and **instance status check**. There are other metrics that are used to track and monitor the status of an EC2 instance. Here is a list of these:

- Network in (bytes)
- Network out (bytes)
- Network packets in (count)
- Network packets out (count)
- Disk reads (bytes)

- Disk read operations (operations)
- Disk writes (bytes)
- Disk write operations
- CPU credit usage
- CPU credit balance

These metrics/graphs can be easily located just below the EC2 instance that is created. These graphs and metrics are automatically generated by AWS when an EC2 instance is launched. They also give you the option to create a dashboard from these graphs and widgets to put everything together in a single place.

The screenshot that follows shows the default widgets generated by AWS when an EC2 instance is created:

Figure 4.1 – CloudWatch default dashboard for an EC2 instance

These seem like a lot of metrics and can be a lot to monitor all the time. But understand that they are all important in terms of ensuring that the EC2 instance runs perfectly well. Any anomaly in any of the graphs or metrics means something is not right with the EC2 instance. Looking at the graphs, they are all of different types, ranging from the CPU utilization in the EC2 instance to the status check to the disk reads/writes and the network packets in/out. Thankfully, this book will cover the networking part in *Chapter 10, Monitoring Network Services*.

In all these graphs and metrics that have been mentioned, we will be singling out about five major metrics that require close attention by a system administrator, DevOps engineer, or a **Site Reliability Engineer** (**SRE**). These metrics directly affect the infrastructure itself and, in turn, affect the applications running in it. But before pointing out these metrics, we need to understand that, in application monitoring, mostly when we are talking about IaaS monitoring, it can be shared into two broad categories:

- Infrastructure monitoring
- Application monitoring

Infrastructure monitoring deals with monitoring the virtual machine and the components that keep it running. A virtual machine, just like a physical machine, is made up of some major hardware components – CPU, memory, and disk. Infrastructure monitoring is focused more on the utilization and health of these three major components. The networking part of the virtual machine or EC2 instance is also essential because when the EC2 instance is in a network, that is how it can share resources such as internet connection and **Virtual Private Cloud** (**VPC**) resources, which is the bedrock of networking and connectivity in the cloud. In infrastructure monitoring, we look at the CPU, memory, and disk utilization from time to time and create alarms, dashboards, and metrics based on this (we will talk more about network monitoring in *Chapter 10, Monitoring Network Services*). If any of these components get fully utilized at any point, it will have a direct impact on all the applications running within the EC2 instance. Each of these components has a major role to play in keeping the applications running. Let's briefly look at each component in terms of functionality.

Understanding CPU in IaaS

The CPU is more or less the brain of the computer. It is the component of a computer that thinks and makes decisions in terms of what to do based on the commands and instructions issued to it, ensuring that every application installed runs as it was designed to. It works in tandem with other hardware components to keep the EC2 instance running. There are applications that are usually high in CPU processes. Mathematical calculations, searching for information, and the sorting of information through a huge chunk of data are all CPU-intensive operations. A complex mathematical operation could need about 60% of the CPU power and another might need 30% running in the same EC2 instance. This will automatically consume 90% of the CPU available, leaving only 10% of CPU left. Any other application that requires the CPU to run will not work optimally because it is already deficient in CPU availability. CPU power is measured in what is called clock-cycles or **gigahertz** (**GHz**). The number of GHz used by an application is the measure of how much CPU that particular application consumes.

Understanding memory in IaaS

This component serves as a buffer and temporary storage for the data being processed by the CPU. Instead of sending every instruction at the same time to the CPU, the memory stands in between to take these instructions and intermittently sends them to the CPU for processing. **RAM**, as it is also called, is an acronym for **Random Access Memory**. It stores information sent to it temporarily and discards it when a particular operation is done, thereby helping to offload stress from the CPU. In programming languages, the variables and arrays and other data types that are declared to perform any kind of compute operation are actually stored in the memory. So, it is usually good practice to empty a variable after it has been completely used.

In some programming languages, it is a good practice to ensure that all variables declared are used or else they should be deleted. Lastly, ensure that you use the appropriate data type for a specific variable declared. For example, in the Java programming language, it has primitive data types, which are `int`, `float`, `long`, `char`, `boolean`, and `string`. The `int` and `long` data types are both designed for numerals, one is for an integer holding 4 bytes of information, and the other is for a higher size of 8 bytes of information. Ensuring the right data type is used ensures that an unused block is not created. This can increase the amount of memory allocated for an operation to be over-provisioned and not used.

In the same way that there are CPU-intensive applications, there are also memory-intensive applications and operations. This could affect the efficient running of other applications that also require that same memory from the same EC2 instance in order to run. The memory is measured in **gigabytes** (**GBs**) or, in some cases, **terabytes** (**TBs**). The more memory-intensive the application is, the more in GBs it is consuming from the memory, leaving fewer GBs for other applications and services in the operating system to work with.

Understanding the disk in IaaS

The disk, or hard disk as it is called, is the computer's permanent storage. It is where files, applications, and even the operating system are stored. This is also where the operating system boots from. Unlike the RAM, information stored in the hard disk is not volatile. Hard disks have evolved over time from spinning disks in a spindle to more of static memory storage, called **solid-state drives** (**SSDs**). SSDs are usually more efficient and have better IOPS. The major metric for measuring a hard disk is in its capacity in terms of how much information it can store. This is usually measured in GBs and TBs. The higher the GBs and TBs, the more information the hard disk can store. So, the more information stored in a hard disk, the more it gets filled up.

In AWS, a hard disk is called an **EBS** volume, which is an acronym for **Elastic Block Storage**. It is an abstraction that allows you to provision different types of disks, from magnetic to HDD to SSD disk. In all the different configurations of an EBS volume, GB and TB are still the metrics used to measure the amount of data the hard disk can hold.

> **Important note**
> **IOPS** is an acronym for **Input/Output Per Second**. It is used to measure the speed at which data is written to a hard disk and the speed at which data can be read from a hard disk. This metric is crucial for applications that require a quick response in terms of reading data and also need data to be written quickly to the hard disk. The higher the IOPS, the faster the read/write operation. An EBS volume (hard disk in AWS) could have from 300 IOPS to 5,000 IOPS.

The three aforementioned metrics are the three major devices that make an operating system function. We have also explained the basic metrics that make up each of these three components (memory measurement in GB, CPU speed in GHz, and disk size in GB or TB), and how to optimize the metrics used to measure the capacity for the different components. There are two other metrics that are peculiar to the running of EC2 instances, and these are as follows:

- **Instance status**: This metric is used to check the status of an instance. It is a check that is performed by AWS in the background to verify that the EC2 instance that is created is in good working condition. When everything about an instance looks fine and is running perfectly well, this is one of the metrics that can be checked to verify whether it is working fine. It is AWS' way of making sure that every virtual machine/EC2 instance that is running is working in an optimal state.

- **System status check**: Similar to the instance status, the system status checks the physical hardware device that is provisioning the EC2 instance. It checks to ensure that the physical hardware is working optimally. If there is any issue, this is immediately reported on the EC2 console of the EC2 instance.

These two metrics, added to the three talked about initially, make five very key basic metrics to look at when looking at monitoring EC2 instances. Any anomaly in any of these metrics can lead to an EC2 instance being unavailable or inaccessible. So, my advice is that when there is any issue with an EC2 instance, these five metrics can serve as the first five places to check and ensure that the instance is working optimally. The questions to answer in monitoring these five metrics are as follows:

- Is the disk space filled up, or do we have enough GB or TB to store more information?

- Is there a sufficient CPU percentage available?

- What application is taking up all the memory (RAM)? Can we free up memory or optimize the app to reduce memory consumption?

- What is the information from the instance status check and system status check?

The act of troubleshooting in this scope is what we call **infrastructure monitoring**. This is the concept of checking metrics that make up the IaaS part of our application. The focus here is less on the application and more on what houses the application. Hence, we have been looking at the different operating system components all along. This is the perspective the system administrator looks at when monitoring.

There is another perspective to this, which is **application monitoring**. This is more from the SRE and software engineering perspective and focuses more on the application that is running in the server. In most cases, issues found on the infrastructure layer emanate from the applications. But there are also instances of infrastructure malfunction, hence, infrastructure monitoring is also important. The techniques and cadence of application monitoring are pretty different from infrastructure monitoring, and will be talked about in *Chapter 6*, *Performance Insights for Database Services*, where we will talk about containers, and also in *Chapter 8*, *Using CloudWatch for Maintaining Highly Available Big Data Services*, where we will be talking about serverless.

We now understand what IaaS is all about and the components that make up the IaaS services, that is, the virtual machines, or EC2 instances as they are called in the AWS ecosystem. The virtual machines are made up of the CPU, memory, and disk as major components needed to run an IaaS service.

To be able to answer the questions listed previously, we need to be able to collect this data/metrics from the EC2 instance. Fortunately, the Amazon EC2 console helps us to collect some of this information. From *Figure 4.1*, we can see that CPU consumption, from the list of metrics mentioned previously, is the only visible metric. The next step is to see how we can get other metrics that are not provided by AWS by default.

Collecting custom metrics on EC2

In *Chapter 3, CloudWatch Logs, Metrics, and Dashboard* (under the *Life cycle of a log* section), we talked about how to collect logs from an EC2 instance and send those logs to the CloudWatch Logs console. But the tool we used in that example is the former log collection tool from CloudWatch – the **CloudWatch agent**. CloudWatch has a new agent called the **unified CloudWatch agent**. This new agent is designed to be able to collect both logs and metrics from an EC2 instance, unlike the old setup that had two different agents to collect logs and metrics, respectively. It has the ability to collect system-level EC2 metrics (CPU, disk, memory, network), system-level metrics for on-premises servers, and it is also supported on a wide range of Linux distributions (such as Amazon Linux, Red Hat Enterprise Linux, Ubuntu, CentOS, and Kali Linux) and on Windows servers. It is also able to collect logs from a particular file, and can be configured to point to a specific file within the operating system and send the events or data recorded in the file just like the old agent does. This makes the new agent the go-to agent for any type of EC2 monitoring and log collection.

The agent is important in the collection of metrics because it is able to collect a lot of system-specific metrics that are not collected by the EC2 dashboard by default. One very important metric that it collects are the memory metrics. The CloudWatch agent is able to collect different metrics relating to the memory of an EC2 instance. This makes the CloudWatch agent a very important tool in the CloudWatch monitoring ecosystem. The following table is an abridged version of the number of metrics the unified CloudWatch agent can collect:

Metric	Description
cpu_time_active	The amount of time the CPU is active Unit: None
cpu_time_idle	The amount of time the CPU is inactive Unit: None
cpu_usage_system	Percentage of the time of the CPU in system mode Unit: Percent
disk_free	Displays the amount of space left in the disk Unit: Bytes
disk_total	Displays the used and free space on all disks Unit: Bytes
disk_used	Displays the space used in the disk Unit: Bytes

Metric	Description
disk_used_percent	Displays the total disk space that is used Unit: Percent
mem_active	Amount of memory used during the last period Unit: Bytes
mem_available	Total amount of memory available to be released to a process Unit: Bytes
mem_available_percent	Total percentage of available memory Unit: Percent
mem_free	Total amount of memory that is free Unit: Bytes
mem_total	Total amount of memory Unit: Bytes
mem_used	Amount of memory in use Unit: Bytes
mem_used_percent	Percentage of memory that is currently in use as a percentage Unit: Percent
net_bytes_recv	Total number of bytes received by the network interface Unit: Bytes (use the sum statistic)
net_bytes_sent	Total number of bytes sent by the network interface Unit: Bytes
netstat_tcp_close	Total TCP connections without a state Unit: Count
netstat_tcp_established	Total number of established TCP connections Unit: Count
netstat_tcp_listen	Total number of TCP ports that are currently listening for a connection request Unit: Count
netstat_udp_socket	Total number of UDP connections Unit: Count

Table 4.1 – Some CloudWatch agent metrics that can be collected

From the table, we can see a lot of metrics that this agent can collect. The column of the table labeled **Description** also describes what the metric means and the unit of measuring the metric. When creating a metric in *Chapter 3, CloudWatch Logs, Metrics, and Dashboard* (under the *Metrics and CloudMetrics* section), we saw the importance of the unit of measurement. It is what determines the value of the information that has been collected, it acts as an aggregator of that particular data, and the unit of measurement can vary from metric to metric. Looking at some metrics, their unit of measurement is count, some are in bytes, or percent, and, in a number of interesting cases, none. This is how you can determine the status of the system based on the unit of measure and pipe the value of this metric to an alarm that can be triggered based on the condition tied to a specific threshold. Without the unit of measurement of a metric, the metric status cannot be properly evaluated, making the metric useless in the first place. So, the unit of measure of a metric is a key factor.

We have been introduced to the new agent and have seen just a glimpse of the number of detailed metrics it can collect. There are more, but I have summarized it to highlight some of the metrics that it can collect. Enough with the theory; it is time to get to work. Let's actually see how this metric can be collected from the EC2 instance, sent over to CloudWatch metrics, and dashboard(s) created from this information that has been collected. Hence, from time to time, the dashboard will be a true measure of the status of the infrastructure.

Using a unified CloudWatch agent

As mentioned earlier, a unified CloudWatch agent can be used to collect metrics from an EC2 instance. The next step in this chapter is to go through a step-by-step process on how to set up a unified CloudWatch agent. The steps are similar to what was done in *Chapter 3, CloudWatch Logs, Metrics, and Dashboard* (in the section entitled *Configuring a basic CloudWatch agent*), using a CloudWatch agent, but there are some changes, because the unified CloudWatch agent does both log collection and metric collection.

There are various forms of metrics that can be collected by the unified agent, and these metrics vary from category to category and also from Windows to the Linux operating system. The category of metric and the operating system you choose determine the metric that can be collected from that particular operating system. The following table sheds more light on this:

	Linux OS	Windows OS
Basic	Memory and swap	Memory and paging
Standard	Memory, swap, CPU, and disk	Memory, paging, processor, PhysicalDisk, LogicalDisk
Advanced	Memory, swap, CPU, disk, disk I/O, and netstat	Memory, paging, processor, PhysicalDisk, LogicalDisk, and TCP

Table 4.2 – Metric categories matched with operating systems

The unified CloudWatch agent can be installed in both Linux and Windows environments. For this setup, we will be installing and configuring the unified CloudWatch agent in a Linux environment. The unified CloudWatch agent can be installed in two different ways. The first method involves using the AWS SSM service.

> **Important note**
> AWS **SSM** is an acronym for AWS **Systems Manager** and is a service that has the ability to connect to Amazon EC2 instances and on-premises virtual machines and perform different system management operations, such as installing, updating, and managing resources and applications within the server. It requires the SSM agent to be installed in the EC2 instance or on an on-premises virtual machine in order for the SSM service to connect and perform any system management operations. In scenarios where there is a need to install an application in a fleet of virtual machines or EC2 instances, AWS SSM is the go-to tool to do that seamlessly.

This service makes it easier and faster to install the unified CloudWatch agent across various EC2 instances. The second method of installing the unified CloudWatch agent is to do it manually by connecting to the EC2 instance and downloading and installing the agent. The following steps are used to set up and configure the unified CloudWatch agent manually. There is an automated method using SSM, but we will cover this in *Chapter 11, Best Practices and Conclusion*:

1. Set up an EC2 instance. If you have an existing EC2 instance, this will suffice. To set up an EC2 instance, observe the following instructions: `https://docs.aws.amazon.com/AWSEC2/latest/UserGuide/EC2_GetStarted.html`.

2. Create an IAM role called `CWUnifiedAgentRole` and attach it to the EC2 instance (follow the steps as demonstrated in *Chapter 3, CloudWatch Logs, Metrics, and Dashboard*). Instead of creating a fresh policy, select `CloudWatchAgentAdminPolicy`, which is an AWS managed policy, and attach it to the created role.

3. The next step is to download and install the agent using the command line. In the Linux terminal, type the following command to download the agent:

    ```
    wget https://s3.amazonaws.com/amazoncloudwatch-agent/
    linux/amd64/latest/AmazonCloudWatchAgent.zip
    ```

4. When the file is successfully downloaded, unzip the file called `AmazonCloudWatchAgent.zip` using the `unzip` command in the Linux terminal.

5. After unzipping the file, the following files in the screenshot are the files that were unzipped:

Figure 4.2 – View of files from the AmazonCloudWatchAgent.zip file

6. The next step is to install the agent by running the `install.sh` script. The following screenshot shows how to run the `install.sh` file:

```
[root@ip-172-31-71-23 ec2-user]# ./install.sh
```

Figure 4.3 – Installing the CloudWatch agent

7. Next, we create a configuration file that the CloudWatch agent will use. This file will be created using the CloudWatch agent wizard. A couple of questions will be asked by the wizard, and the answers will form the configuration file that will be created. The file to trigger the wizard is located at `/opt/aws/amazon-cloudwatch-agent/bin`. Change the directory to the location using the `cd` command. Then, run the wizard file, which is the `amazon-cloudwatch-agent-config-wizard` file, using the same command as for the `install.sh` file:

```
[root@ip-172-31-71-23 bin]# ./amazon-cloudwatch-agent-config-wizard
```

Figure 4.4 – Starting the CloudWatch agent wizard

This will start the CloudWatch agent wizard

8. The first question involves choosing the type of operating system you want to install and run the agent on:

```
=================================================================
= Welcome to the AWS CloudWatch Agent Configuration Manager =
=================================================================
On which OS are you planning to use the agent?
1. linux
2. windows
default choice: [1]:
```

Figure 4.5 – Select the operating system option from the wizard

For this, we select the default choice of [1], which means we are using the Linux option. The next step is to press the *Enter* key to accept. The second option can be selected if the operating system is Windows. Press the *Enter* key to continue.

9. The next question involves establishing whether the current machine is an EC2 instance or an on-premises server and it goes thus:

```
Trying to fetch the default region based on ec2 metadata...
Are you using EC2 or On-Premises hosts?
1. EC2
2. On-Premises
default choice: [1]:
```

Figure 4.6 – Choosing the type of virtual machine

Two things are happening here. The agent is trying to get the region from the EC2 metadata and it is also asking to confirm whether it is an EC2 instance or an on-premises server.

For this option, we will select option [1] because our system is an EC2 instance. Press the *Enter* key to continue.

10. The next question concerns the user who will be running the agent. The agent is a daemon process in the operating system. The agent is trying to understand which operating system user will be responsible for running the daemon process. For this, the default option is [1], meaning the root user. To select and continue, press the *Enter* key:

```
Which user are you planning to run the agent?
1. root
2. cwagent
3. others
default choice: [1]:
```

Figure 4.7 – Selecting the user to run the agent

11. The next question from the wizard involves asking whether you are going to turn on the `StatsD` daemon. The `StatsD` daemon is designed to collect application metrics, which is not in the scope of this chapter. So, we will not turn it on at this moment. The option chosen here will be `[2]`, which means no. Press the *Enter* key to accept and continue:

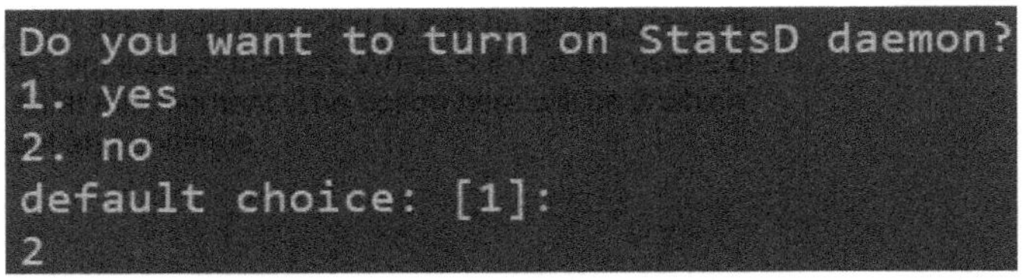

```
Do you want to turn on StatsD daemon?
1. yes
2. no
default choice: [1]:
2
```

Figure 4.8 – Deactivating StatsD

12. The next step involves turning on `CollectD`. `CollectD` is a process used to collect system metrics from a Unix/Linux operating system. Our monitoring is focused on infrastructure monitoring, so we are going to enable `CollectD` to enable the collection of operating system metrics. We will leave the default option of `[1]`, which is `yes`, and press *Enter* to continue:

```
Do you want to monitor metrics from CollectD?
1. yes
2. no
default choice: [1]:
```

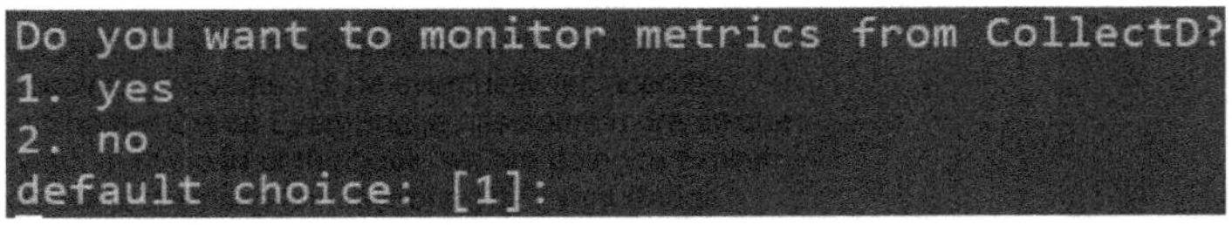

Figure 4.9 – Activating CollectD

13. The wizard will next ask whether we are interested in monitoring host metrics, such as CPU and memory. This is also part of the infrastructure we want to monitor, so the answer will be `yes` again for this. Press *Enter* to continue:

```
Do you want to monitor any host metrics? e.g. CPU, memory, etc.
1. yes
2. no
default choice: [1]:
```

Figure 4.10 – Activating host metrics collection

14. The next option involves asking in more detail about getting deeper metrics on the CPU; if we want to collect CPU metrics per core. This also comes with a condition of additional CloudWatch charges. We are not interested in such detailed metrics at the moment, so the option will be `[2]`, which means no. Then, press *Enter* to continue:

```
Do you want to monitor cpu metrics per core? Additional CloudWatch charges
may apply.
1. yes
2. no
default choice: [1]:
2
```

Figure 4.11 – Disabling CPU metrics per core monitoring

15. The next question in the wizard relates to the dimensions of the metrics. Dimensions, as talked about in *Chapter 3, CloudWatch Logs, Metrics, and Dashboard*, assist with grouping metrics of the same namespace into proper categories for easier navigation and filtering. For this we will select option [1], which is yes. Then, press the *Enter* key to continue:

```
Do you want to add ec2 dimensions (ImageId, InstanceId, InstanceType, AutoS
calingGroupName) into all of your metrics if the info is available?
1. yes
2. no
default choice: [1]:
```

Figure 4.12 – Adding dimensions to metrics

16. The frequency of metric collection determines how up to date the metrics are based on what is going on within the EC2 instance. For this option, we will be taking the default of 60 seconds, which is option [4]. Other options exist, but we will stick with the default for this one. The other option of a reduced timeframe is available if you need to get the metrics quicker. Press *Enter* to continue:

```
Would you like to collect your metrics at high resolution (sub-minute resol
ution)? This enables sub-minute resolution for all metrics, but you can cus
tomize for specific metrics in the output json file.
1. 1s
2. 10s
3. 30s
4. 60s
default choice: [4]:
```

Figure 4.13 – Metric collection frequency configuration

17. There are three types of metrics used for EC2 instances: *Basic*, *Standard*, and *Advanced*. The Basic metric configuration only collects the memory and disk space used, whereas the Standard metric configuration collects all the metrics from the basic configuration along with other metrics such as disk I/O time, CPU usage idle, CPU usage I/O wait, CPU usage user, and CPU usage system. The Advanced configuration of metrics is able to collect the same metrics as the *Standard* configuration and more besides. We talked about the specific metrics each of these categories collect. This next option is to select which of the categories we will want to use. One of the major reasons for this setup is to collect custom metrics that Amazon EC2 metrics on CloudWatch do not have by default. One of those metrics is memory utilization. From *Table 4.2*, we can see that all categories capture memory metrics. For our example, let's use `Standard` and collect a little more information than just memory. So, the option we choose will be 2, which tallies with `Standard`:

```
Which default metrics config do you want?
1. Basic
2. Standard
3. Advanced
4. None
default choice: [1]:
2
```

Figure 4.14 – Choosing monitoring category metrics

18. The wizard will now generate the configuration file based on all the input values that have been given and prompt to accept or reject the configuration. This is the configuration based on the wizard answers given so far: `https://github.com/PacktPublishing/Infrastructure-Monitoring-with-Amazon-CloudWatch/blob/main/Chapter04/config.json`.

The following screen will ask whether we are satisfied with this configuration, so choose `yes` or `no`. You can always change the configuration manually if there are updates that need to be made in the future. The default option is [1]. Press *Enter* to continue:

```
Are you satisfied with the above config? Note: it can be manually customized after the
wizard completes to add additional items.
1. yes
2. no
default choice: [1]:
```

Figure 4.15 – Finalizing to confirm the configuration file

19. The next question is to establish whether we have any existing CloudWatch Logs agent configuration files to import for migration. If we do, we choose option 1, which is `yes`, or otherwise 2, which is `no`. Press *Enter* to continue.

20. Since this is a unified agent, the wizard will ask whether we have a log file to monitor, meaning whether we have a path that we would like to configure. For the moment, we will select option 2, which is no. Then, press *Enter* to continue.

21. The wizard will ask for confirmation a second time. This time, it will specify the path where the configuration file is. For our setup, it is in the `/opt/aws/amazon-cloudwatch-agent/bin/config.json` path. It will also ask whether we want to store the `config` file in the SSM parameter store. Storing it in the SSM parameter store means that we will have a backup in the AWS SSM parameter store in case this configuration is missing. This is also good when working with an EC2 fleet or virtual machine fleet, so that they all have a single source of truth in the AWS SSM parameter store for their CloudWatch agent configuration file. This makes it easier to apply across the instance from a single centralized location. For our setup, we will say no, which is option 2. Then, press the *Enter* key.

22. Since the configuration is now complete, the next step is to start CloudWatch and start sending metrics to CloudWatch metrics. Use the following command to start the agent:

```
./amazon-cloudwatch-agent-ctl -a fetch-config -c
file:config.json -s
```

This will start the CloudWatch agent as a daemon process, using the `config.json` file, which is the file that has the configuration that we have created. It also has the option of using the SSM option, that is, if the config file is stored in the AWS SSM parameter store.

23. The CloudWatch agent will immediately start pushing the metrics that have been configured to the CloudWatch metric. The following screenshot shows the new metric in the custom metric namespace:

Figure 4.16 – New custom metric from the unified CloudWatch agent

The custom namespace, **CWAgent**, shows that there are 10 metrics, which are the number of metrics that have been collected based on the configuration. To view the actual metrics, click on the **CWAgent** custom metric namespace. This will lead us to the different metric dimensions.

On the metric dimension, you can select the particular EC2 metric you would like to see from the custom metrics that have been collected. Let's view the percentage of disk space consumed and the percentage of memory that has been consumed.

24. To be able to view disk and memory metrics, click on the third metric dimension with a value, `ImageId`, `InstanceId`, and `InstanceType`. After clicking the metric dimension it further shows that there are two metrics.

These two metrics are part of the metrics that we configured to collect with the unified CloudWatch agent. The first is `mem_used_percent`, while the second is `swap_used_percent`. The following screenshot shows both metrics:

Figure 4.17 – Memory metrics and graph

The preceding screenshot shows that the memory used on the EC2 instance is about **31.2** percent. The swap used is **0** percent. Both metrics are custom metrics and are not usually available by default on EC2 instance metrics and dashboards. Hence, the unified CloudWatch agent was able to collect these metrics and post them to the CloudWatch metric, thereby making it visible on a CloudWatch dashboard.

> **Important note**
>
> You may notice that when you try to start the agent, it fails. This might be because some of the components we decided to run are not installed. So, run the following command to install some dependencies:
>
> ```
> yum update && yum install epel-release && yum
> install collectd
> ```

We were able to configure the unified CloudWatch agent to send metrics to CloudWatch and view the metrics on a CloudWatch dashboard. This agent can collect other metrics and also collect logs and send these to CloudWatch Logs.

Our takeaway from this section is that we now know how to configure a unified CloudWatch agent to send logs and metrics over to Amazon CloudWatch. We have also gone further and viewed the metrics present on the Amazon CloudWatch console.

The next section of this chapter involves looking at a practical example of creating an event, using Amazon EventBridge, which can detect a spot instance interruption and react based on that.

Creating an Amazon EventBridge for Amazon EC2

We have already introduced Amazon EventBridge previously, and juxtaposed it with Amazon CloudWatch Events. We previously talked about CloudWatch Events, and we also explained that **Amazon EventBridge** is going to be taking the place of CloudWatch Events in the near future. The following screenshot is taken directly from the CloudWatch Events dashboard:

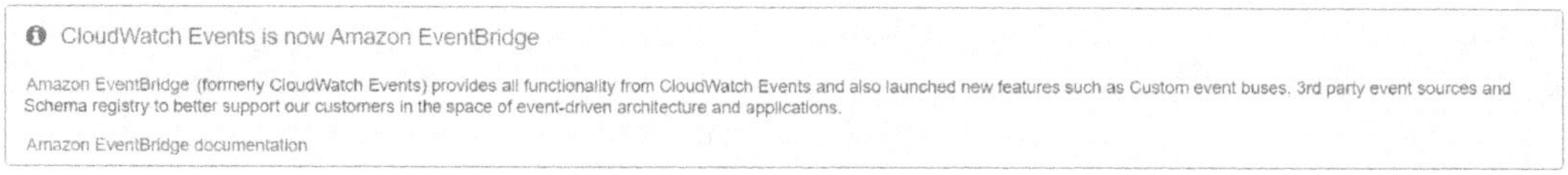

> ❶ CloudWatch Events is now Amazon EventBridge
>
> Amazon EventBridge (formerly CloudWatch Events) provides all functionality from CloudWatch Events and also launched new features such as Custom event buses, 3rd party event sources and Schema registry to better support our customers in the space of event-driven architecture and applications.
>
> Amazon EventBridge documentation

Figure 4.18 – CloudWatch Events deprecation

We also explained in *Chapter 2, CloudWatch Events and Alarms* (in the section entitled *Amazon EventBridge*), that EventBridge has some more unique features that do not exist in CloudWatch Events. In this section, we are going to explore what we can do to EC2 instances, based on event checking and responses by EventBridge. Amazon EC2 instances have various events that can be monitored, and an event triggered to respond to that particular event. The following list includes some of the events that can be triggered automatically:

- Calling an AWS Lambda function
- Triggering an Amazon EC2 run command
- Transferring the trigger to an Amazon Kinesis data stream
- Turning on an AWS setup function alert, an Amazon **Simple Notification Service (SNS)** topic, or an Amazon **Simple Queue Service (SQS)** queue

We are going to demonstrate an Amazon EventBridge event that is an example of an **EC2 Spot Instance interruption**. This event reads the spot instance from time to time to ensure that you are notified just before a spot instance is terminated.

> **Important note**
>
> An Amazon EC2 spot instance is a type of instance that allows you to take advantage of unused Amazon EC2 capacity, reduce your compute costs, and improve application throughput. These instances are available at up to a 90% discount compared to on-demand prices. With this pricing model, you can scale your existing workload throughput by up to 10 times and still stay within budget.

Spot instances are an important part of the EC2 instance pricing model and are very valuable when designing volatile workload systems. Spot instance storage is ephemeral, even if it uses EBS volumes for storing data, meaning that data can be instantly lost when the spot instance is terminated. The best way to architect spot instances is to ensure that whatever data is processed by the spot instance is permanently stored in non-volatile storage, such as **Simple Storage Service (S3)** or **Elastic File System (EFS)** storage, to keep the data persistent. Another major advantage of a spot instance is that they are among the cheapest in terms of pricing in all EC2 instance pricing models.

Our focus in this section is to create an Amazon EventBridge event that will notify us before a spot instance get terminated so as to give enough time to perform a cleanup before the instance is lost. You can also configure a Lambda function that could request another spot instance as one is being lost. Without further ado, let's get our hands dirty with Amazon EventBridge:

1. Log in to the AWS management console, click on the **Services** menu item, and then search for EventBridge on the search bar.

2. When it is visible on the pop-up menu, click the **Amazon EventBridge** menu item. This will take you to the **Amazon EventBridge** console page.

3. On the landing page, click the **Create rule** button to start the process of creating a new rule. The following screenshot shows the button to be clicked:

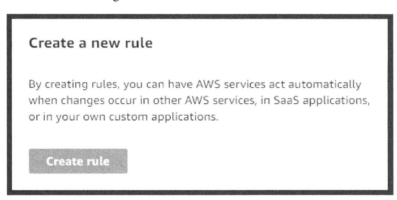

Figure 4.19 – Creating a rule on Amazon EventBridge

4. A form will be displayed with a bunch of information to be filled in. The first item is the name of the event rule. This is a unique name; we want to use it to identify the rule. Enter a name in the box. For this setup, we will use the name spot-terminate-rule.

5. The next box is the description, which is optional. We will leave this and move on to the next item to be configured.

6. The next option is **Define pattern**. For this we will select the **Event pattern** option, which gives us the ability to configure the specific **event pattern** and **event trigger** required for spot instance interruption. Click on the radio button to select **Event pattern**, as shown in the following screenshot:

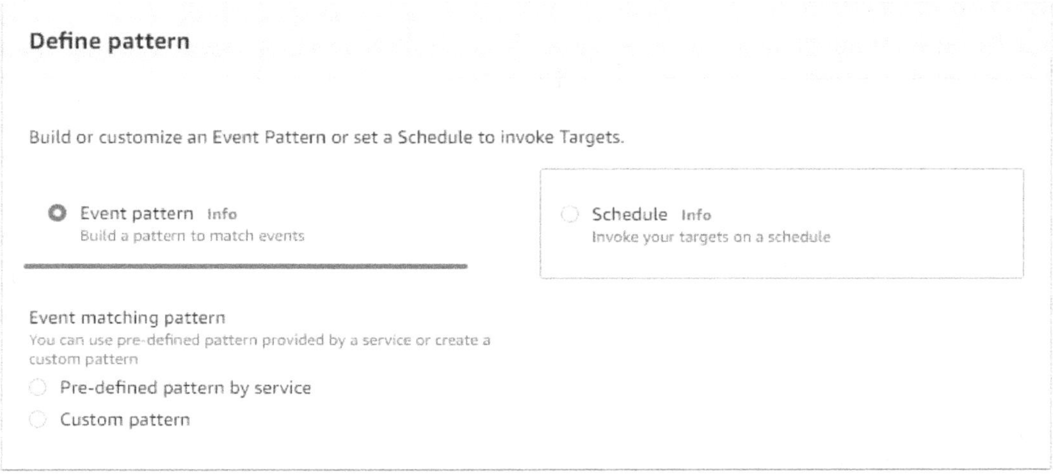

Define pattern

Build or customize an Event Pattern or set a Schedule to invoke Targets.

○ Event pattern   Info
   Build a pattern to match events

○ Schedule   Info
   Invoke your targets on a schedule

Event matching pattern
You can use pre-defined pattern provided by a service or create a custom pattern
○ Pre-defined pattern by service
○ Custom pattern

Figure 4.20 – Selecting Event pattern as the defined pattern

7. Click on the **Pre-defined pattern by service** option. This will reveal other options. Click on the dropdown on the item labeled **Service provider** and **AWS**, which is part of the options in the list. The next option is to select **Service name**. On the drop-down list, search for EC2. The last option is **Event type**. Click the dropdown and select **EC2 Spot Instance Interruption Warning**.

8. The next option is **Select Event bus**. We will ignore this option and leave the default as is – **Enable the rule on the selected event bus**.

9. The next option is to select a target. We actually want to get a notification when the spot instance is going to be interrupted, so the target for this will be Amazon SNS. Click on the dropdown under **Target** and select **SNS topic**. Then, select a topic that this notification will be sent to. Ensure that you have an SNS topic already created and subscribed to. Click on the SNS topic that has been created. Follow this link for guidelines on how to create an SNS topic: https://docs.aws.amazon.com/sns/latest/dg/sns-create-topic.html.

10. The final option is the tags, which is pretty optional. Then, click on the **Create** button to create the rule.

The steps we just went through will trigger an email notification or any type of notification that was configured on that SNS topic whenever a spot instance is going to be interrupted. This is a very good use case of Amazon EventBridge, serving as a monitoring tool that can track events within AWS and third-party services and respond based on that event. The preceding practical exercise shows how this can be achieved.

The next thing we will be looking at is how to monitor another compute service in AWS called Elastic Beanstalk. We will look at monitoring through the eyes of Elastic Beanstalk and understand how CloudWatch comes into the picture in monitoring applications deployed in the Elastic Beanstalk environment.

Monitoring Elastic Beanstalk workloads

Elastic Beanstalk is a PaaS that gives developers, cloud engineers, and cloud administrators a turnkey solution for deploying, managing, and scaling applications on AWS. Elastic Beanstalk eliminates the hassle and stress involved in setting up a fresh server, installing all dependencies required for the application to run. This makes it faster to orchestrate the environment for the application and deploy the application immediately once the environment is ready. Elastic Beanstalk supports a couple of programming languages, including Node.js, Python, .NET Core, Java, Golang, Ruby, and PHP.

> **Important note**
> PaaS is a method of cloud delivery just like its counterpart, IaaS. In PaaS, the underlying infrastructure is no longer managed by you; the service provider creates an abstraction layer that makes it easy to deploy, manage, monitor, and scale your application without bothering about the underlying infrastructure. PaaS makes it easy for developers to deploy applications without the need for a system administrator or infrastructure engineer. Examples include Heroku, Azure App Service, and Google App Engine.

Since we now understand what Elastic Beanstalk is all about, let's look at how monitoring works in Elastic Beanstalk. Under the hood of an Elastic Beanstalk setup, there is an EC2 instance running there. So, the same requirements as an EC2 instance come to pass here. But, with a little bit of help from the Elastic Beanstalk engine, the job of managing an EC2 instance is totally abstracted from the user. Elastic Beanstalk presents an interface that makes it easier to monitor, manage, and scale your application.

When an application is deployed in Elastic Beanstalk, a couple of monitoring facilities are automatically set up to monitor both the application and the underlying infrastructure. In this case, the underlying infrastructure is an EC2 instance hosting the application. Elastic Beanstalk creates logs of the application and monitors the health of the application. These three features are used to monitor both the application and the underlying infrastructure. These are the functionalities of each of them:

- **Logs**: This feature is used to view/download the application and server logs of the application running within the EC2 instance. The following screenshot shows logs that have been requested from the Elastic Beanstalk environment. To get the logs, click on the **Request Logs** button, and then click on **Last 100 Lines** or **Full Logs** as required. The first option will retrieve the last 100 lines of the logs, while the second will retrieve all the logs from inception. Click on the **Download** link to download the logs and view them:

Figure 4.21 – Elastic Beanstalk Logs console

- **Health**: This feature is in charge of reporting the status of the underlying EC2 instance hosting the application. It also lists the number of EC2 instances that are running in the current Elastic Beanstalk environment. You can also manage the instance by either rebooting or terminating the instance if need be. This option can be found in the top-right corner button, **Instance actions**. It also holds some other vital information, including the number of requests per second the application has received, and the number of 2xx, 3xx, 4xx, and 5xx response counts, which is key in knowing how the application is performing at any point in time. The following screenshot shows the **Health** dashboard in Elastic Beanstalk:

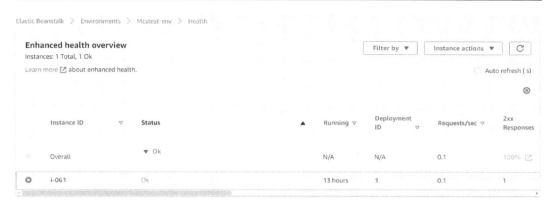

Figure 4.22 – Elastic Beanstalk Health console

- **Monitoring**: Elastic Beanstalk will not be complete without the monitoring feature. This feature is a summarized dashboard of application monitoring and infrastructure monitoring metrics. It contains specific dashboards that capture some important metrics for the EC2 instance(s) running within the Elastic Beanstalk environment. Some of the metrics it collects include **CPU Utilization**, **Environment Health**, **Target Response Time**, and **Sum Requests**. These can be seen in the monitoring console screenshot that follows:

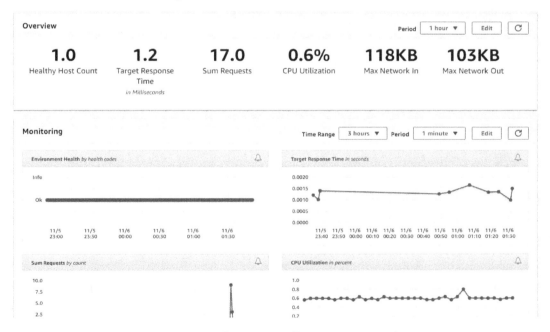

Figure 4.23 – Elastic Beanstalk monitoring console

Those are the various monitoring features that exist in Elastic Beanstalk. The major advantage here is that you do not have to install any agent or configure any dashboards or metrics. Elastic Beanstalk handles all that for you in your stead, thereby making monitoring much easier, faster, and much more fun. From the monitoring console, alarms can be created to trigger based on the specific thresholds that you configure. The alarms will still be plugged to an SNS topic to be able to send notifications based on the topic configuration.

Monitoring AWS Batch

AWS Batch is a managed service that is used for running huge batch jobs. It is designed to help eliminate the cost that goes with configuring and setting up your own batch processing infrastructure. With AWS Batch, you configure the job, and the compute required the run the job, and the rest is history. AWS Batch can be used to run hundreds to thousands of parallel jobs.

The underlying infrastructure of AWS Batch is AWS compute resources (EC2 and containers). The compute resources used to process batch jobs range from EC2 instances to AWS Fargate (serverless containers). So, the monitoring for the EC2 instances that we already explained previously in this chapter will also apply to EC2 instances used for batch processing. As regards AWS Fargate, we will explain this more in *Chapter 5, Setting Up Container Insights on Amazon CloudWatch*, when we talk about the monitoring of containers.

In AWS Batch, there are different components that make up a batch processing job. These are as follows:

- Jobs
- Job definitions
- Job queues
- Compute environments

The reason for monitoring AWS Batch jobs is to understand the state of a job at any given point in time and also to get logs of what happened to a job in situations where the job must have failed. Logs are always the source of truth for the history of what happened with an operation or an application. Logs are generated for a job that is submitted to AWS Batch. For every job submission and run, logs are sent to a CloudWatch Log group called /aws/batch/job and the log stream will have a value that contains the name of the job that was submitted. The AWS Batch dashboard gives instant metrics of the status of a job, including whether the job that was submitted failed or is successful. This is usually the first point of call in understanding what happened instantly. The logs help to provide more details. To view the logs of a batch job, perform the following steps:

1. Log in to the AWS management console.

2. Navigate to the AWS CloudWatch console.

3. Click on the **Logs | Log groups** link on the left-hand side.

4. You should locate the /aws/batch/job log group. This log group holds all the log streams for AWS Batch:

Figure 4.24 – AWS log groups showing AWS Batch

5. Click on the log group to view the log streams:

Figure 4.25 – Log streams from AWS Batch

6.   The log streams in *Figure 4.25* are the streams for the jobs that have been submitted with the logs of the activity of the job. Click on any of the streams to get the logs:

Figure 4.26 – Log events from the log stream of AWS Batch

With this we now understand how to view logs and understand the status of any job submitted to AWS Batch. CloudWatch can automatically aggregate all the log streams into a log group, making it a one-stop shop for anything to do with logs in AWS Batch. It is also possible to create metrics and dashboards from the logs that have been collected to get faster feedback and insights from the logs sent to CloudWatch Logs by AWS Batch.

With this knowledge, we can now monitor and understand how logging and monitoring work in AWS Batch, which is also a compute service from AWS, with the underlying EC2 instance and AWS Fargate being the compute engines to power batch job processing. We can also see how logs are sent to CloudWatch and how we can view the logs from the CloudWatch log groups and, eventually, in the log streams.

Case study on CloudWatch custom metrics

The applications in your organization have something in common. They have all been built in the Java programming language running on the JVM runtime. The marketing team in your organization did a campaign that led to a huge spike of traffic in the application. This led to the application becoming very unstable and having frequent downtimes. You have gone through the Amazon CloudWatch automated dashboard for EC2 instances. The automated CloudWatch dashboard collects a lot of relevant information about the EC2 instances but still does not provide any insight into behavior due to the absence of a certain important EC2 metric. What is this metric? How do we go about collecting this metric to help us figure out what exactly is wrong with the application?

Solution

What is peculiar about Java applications and JVM is memory consumption. This can be figured out by installing the unified CloudWatch agent. This agent can help to collect memory-related metrics to see what is going on in terms of the memory metric of the application.

Summary

In this chapter, we deliberately created two practical operations to allow for the practical application of the concepts that have been spoken about. We introduced the idea of compute and the different AWS compute services and categories. We then went further and talked about the categories of monitoring – infrastructure monitoring and application monitoring.

Our focus in this chapter was more on infrastructure monitoring. We defined it and brought in the concept of IaaS, which is a model of cloud delivery. IaaS is focused more on virtual machines, which in AWS are called EC2 instances. We also talked about the key metrics in monitoring EC2 instances, such as the instance status check, CPU, memory, and disk metrics. After that, we looked at how CloudWatch monitors EC2 instances by default, and the loopholes that exist in default CloudWatch monitoring. We moved on and rectified this deficiency by using the new unified CloudWatch agent to collect more metrics, including memory and swap utilization.

Next, we looked at Amazon EventBridge, which is the service that will replace CloudWatch events. We then created a rule in EventBridge to monitor a spot instance interruption and trigger an alarm that sends a notification when a spot instance is interrupted.

To top everything off, we looked at monitoring through the eyes of Elastic Beanstalk, and how it creates basic metrics needed to monitor and understand the state of the application and infrastructure at any point in time.

In the next chapter, we will be talking about another method of compute – tagged containers. We will also look at container services in AWS and see how to monitor container applications.

Questions

1. What are the major components of IaaS monitoring for understanding the status of the infrastructure?

2. What is the difference between a CloudWatch agent and a unified CloudWatch agent?

3. What service is used to notify a user when an event is triggered on Amazon EventBridge?

4. What is the difference between a metric and a dashboard?

Further reading

- Getting started with EC2: `https://www.packtpub.com/product/aws-certified-developer-associate-guide-second-edition/9781789617313`

- CPU management: `https://www.packtpub.com/product/linux-5-performance-monitoring-and-tuning-video/9781838559250`

- Introducing cloud service models – IaaS, PaaS, and SaaS: `https://www.packtpub.com/product/learning-aws-second-edition/9781787281066`

- Managing servers on AWS with EC2: `https://www.packtpub.com/virtualization-and-cloud/aws-certified-sysops-administrator-associate-guide`

- Amazon EC2 basics: `https://www.packtpub.com/networking-and-servers/amazon-ec2-master-class-auto-scaling-and-load-balancer-video`

- Selecting and configuring EC2 instances: `https://www.packtpub.com/product/amazon-ec2-cookbook/9781785280047`

5
Setting Up Container Insights on Amazon CloudWatch

The previous chapter focused on monitoring some AWS compute resources such as **Elastic Compute Cloud (EC2)** and Elastic Beanstalk. We also spent some time setting up the **unified CloudWatch Agent** in an EC2 instance to send logs to Amazon CloudWatch Logs. We now understand **Infrastructure as a Service (IaaS)** and **Platform as a Service (PaaS)**, which are different methods of cloud delivery. We also looked at the metrics that make up the IaaS cloud setup, and then for PaaS, we set up Elastic Beanstalk and described how monitoring works in Elastic Beanstalk applications.

Let's understand what objectives we will cover by the end of this chapter. Since containers are pretty different from **virtual machines (VMs)**, it means that a lot of things are going to be different: deploying, scaling, configuration, and most importantly, monitoring. We will talk about the AWS services used for container orchestration and management, then we will talk about how monitoring works on these different services.

We will then connect this knowledge to how CloudWatch exclusively manages container applications with its unique feature called CloudWatch Container Insights. This makes it easier to monitor, manage, and work with container monitoring, because this feature is specifically tailored to containers both within the AWS ecosystem and any other kind of system that runs containers for their applications. We will corroborate all this understanding by doing a practical setup of metrics, monitors, and dashboards based on the different AWS container services.

We will cover the following topics in this chapter:

- Introducing the concept of containers
- Orchestrating container services in AWS
- Triggering ECS events on Amazon EventBridge
- Configuring CloudWatch Container Insights
- Monitoring of EKS applications and services
- Setting up custom dashboards and metrics for containers
- Case study of Amazon EKS logging and monitoring

Technical requirements

To be able to accomplish the technical tasks in the chapter, you will need to have the following technical pre-requisites:

- A working AWS account (you can opt for the free tier, which will cost $0/month for 1 year)
- Basic knowledge of Linux
- Basic understanding of Docker and Linux containers
- Understanding of Kubernetes and Amazon ECS

The code files for this chapter can be downloaded from `https://github.com/ PacktPublishing/Infrastructure-Monitoring-with-Amazon- CloudWatch/tree/main/Chapter05`.

Check out the following link to see the Code in Action video:

`https://bit.ly/3chkpMa`

Introducing the concept of containers

Moving on to more advanced and new technologies is what this chapter is focused on. In this chapter, our focus is on containers. Containers are not very new. The story of containers starts as early as 1979. Fast forward some years down the line to 2006, when Google launched the idea of **process containers**, which made it possible to isolate and limit hardware resources such as the CPU, memory, and disk to specific resources in the Linux operating system. In 2013, Docker was born, and this took containers to a whole new level and the adoption grew extremely fast. Now, small-, medium-, and large-scale organizations are finding ways to re-architect their systems to take advantage of the power and value of containers. There are different types of container runtimes, but Docker has stood out to be the most used.

Containers are designed to make application deployment, release, versioning, and scaling much easier and faster. This is possible due to the unique features containers have. We mentioned one of them previously, which is resource limitation, and others are resource isolation, application isolation, and sharing the same kernel with the host operating system. Containers can be similar to VMs due to the similarities in the features that have been mentioned previously. But one major difference containers have over VMs is that containers share the host operating system kernel, while every VM has its own kernel that is different from that of the host operating system. Containers tend to start up faster too compared to VMs, which need to go through the normal operating system boot process. This has made containers a great option for DevOps engineers and top tech executives to quickly deliver applications and makes it faster for applications to recover in the eventuality of failure of any kind. This is because containers do not boot-up; they just start up and run the application and configurations that are embedded within them.

Orchestrating container services in AWS

The introduction was more about understanding the basics of containers and the advantages of containers over VMs. Moving forward, let's look at the concept of **container orchestration**. When an application is packaged as a Docker image, for the purposes of running it as a container, it is quite easy to manage, deploy, and monitor when it is just a single container or a few containers running in a single VM. But as these containers increase, say from 1 to 10 to 15, it becomes more difficult and complicated to manage, deploy, scale, and even monitor that number of containers. Moreover, containers require high availability when the application is in production (customer-facing), hence there should be a more automated way to manage these operations that is more flexible and easier to manage. This is where container orchestration comes in. Without a container orchestration tool, it is quite difficult to perform all the necessary operational tasks to keep the applications/containers up and running optimally.

Container services in AWS are all container orchestration services. Container orchestration applications/services are made up of various components. The monitoring of container applications is made up of two parts. One is the underlying infrastructure that manages the containers themselves, then we also have to monitor the applications running within the container. In AWS, there are cases where we might not focus on monitoring the components of the container orchestration tool/service.

There are two major container orchestration services within AWS. They are as follows:

- Amazon ECS
- Amazon EKS

Let's overview them both in the following sections.

Overviewing Amazon ECS

Amazon **ECS** is AWS proprietary service for container orchestration. It is an acronym for **Elastic Container Service**. This was AWS's response to customer requests for a service that will help in managing tens to hundreds of applications that have been containerized. It is a managed service, meaning that the orchestration part of the service is managed and monitored by AWS themselves, just the way it is done for other managed services. What this means is that you do not have to worry about managing the core of the orchestration service itself but just other components and the container itself that have been deployed into ECS. Over time, Amazon ECS has evolved to having various features. When Amazon ECS was released, it came with one launch type: the EC2 launch type. This means that when the containers are deployed, they are orchestrated by the ECS service to run within EC2 instances. The EC2 instance in the **ECS cluster** will need to have the engine needed for the container to run (Docker is the most popular container runtime, so we will be referring to Docker as our default container runtime environment).

> **Important Note**
> An ECS cluster is a combination of all the services and resources running within the cluster. An ECS cluster contains components such as tasks, services, EC2 instances, and containers. All these work together to help with effective container orchestration and application management.

Therefore, monitoring in this space is focused on two things: firstly, the EC2 instance running the containers, and secondly, the monitoring of the containers to ensure the availability of the container applications. The previous chapter on compute monitoring already covered how we can monitor an EC2 instance, so installing and configuring the Amazon unified CloudWatch agent for the EC2 instance should cover monitoring the EC2 instance itself. Hence, there is still the need to monitor core metrics of the EC2 instance, because anything affecting the instance will affect the applications running within the EC2 instance, which includes the container runtime and the containerized applications themselves. Next is the containers themselves. ECS has a nice dashboard that helps us to understand the behavior of containers running within the ECS cluster. Every container in ECS is configured using a JSON payload called a **task definition**. The task definition tells you everything you need to know about the container, from the image that the container will be running from to the application configurations and the network configurations that the container will be running on top of. This task definition file is given to the ECS service task to create a container out of. The first level of monitoring is ECS giving updates on the status of the container, telling us if the container is running or not. This is easily identified by the state of the task. The different states of a task in ECS are as follows:

- **PROVISIONING**: Tasks performed when the container is starting up, such as network setup.

- **PENDING**: This state is when the task is waiting for the ECS agent to take further action.

- **ACTIVATING**: These are tasks or activities performed when the task has been launched, which leads to the **RUNNING** state of the container.

- **RUNNING**: This is the state showing that the tasks/containers are running.

- **DEACTIVATING**: This shows that the task is being deactivated and performing initial operations before the task gets permanently deactivated.

- **STOPPING**: This is the state where the task triggers the stopping of the container and waits for the Amazon ECS agent to stop the container.

- **DEPROVISIONING**: Just like the provisioning operation, this operation deallocates all the resources and tasks that were done during the provisioning operation as part of the **STOPPING** process.

- **STOPPED**: This signifies that the task/container has stopped successfully.

Each of these statuses is reported by the Amazon ECS task manager, to report intermittently the status of the task running the container so that the cloud engineer can know what is going on at any particular point in time and whether there needs to be some form of action taken. Interestingly, each of these states is also an event that can be forwarded to Amazon EventBridge and further actions can be taken based on any of the events that have been triggered. We shall configure a scenario on this in the *Triggering ECS on Amazon EventBridge* section:

Desired task status: Running Stopped

Filter in this page | Launch type ALL | < 1-7 > Page size 50

Task	Task definiti...	Container in...	Last status ...	Desired stat...	Started at	Started By	Group	Launch type...	Platform ver...
1ade34b245b...		--	RUNNING	RUNNING	2020-11-05 0...	ecs-svc/6489...	service:	FARGATE	1.3.0
1ba3e3a5a56...		--	RUNNING	RUNNING	2020-11-11 1...	ecs-svc/0794...	service:	FARGATE	1.3.0
1bccd19b755...		--	PENDING	RUNNING		ecs-svc/0794...	service:	FARGATE	1.3.0
303c70b3542...		--	RUNNING	RUNNING	2020-11-05 0...	ecs-svc/6489...	service:	FARGATE	1.3.0
8bdd4280368...		--	RUNNING	RUNNING	2020-11-10 0...	ecs-svc/6171...	service:	FARGATE	1.3.0
92f39ca1090...		--	RUNNING	RUNNING	2020-11-11 1...	ecs-svc/0778...	service:	FARGATE	1.3.0
a6e874caa74...		--	RUNNING	RUNNING	2020-11-09 2...	ecs-svc/6171...	service:	FARGATE	1.3.0

Figure 5.1 – EC2 tasks and current running states

The preceding screenshot shows a list of various tasks, and in the screenshot, they are all in the **RUNNING** state. This is all for the EC2 launch type for the Amazon ECS orchestration service. Next, we will look at another launch type for ECS.

ECS is also made up of another launch type, called **Fargate**. Fargate is a serverless option for launching containers in Amazon ECS. What this means is that you do not need servers to run containers anymore. You just need to specify the CPU and memory needed to run the container and the container starts running. Fargate saves the operational cost involved in running EC2 instances, operations such as management, scaling, and securing. Just like the EC2 launch type, Fargate also has task transition events for orchestrating containers and the states are the same as that of the EC2 instance launch type. It also creates an internal container network for the application to be able to send and receive traffic. The screenshot in *Figure 5.1* shows a list of containers and the tasks are launched using the Fargate launch type.

Overviewing Amazon EKS

EKS is an acronym for **Elastic Kubernetes Service**. It is AWS's version of the open source Kubernetes service. Kubernetes is made up of two parts: the master node and the worker nodes. In Kubernetes, the master node is what controls and manages the operations and activities of the worker nodes. The master node itself is made up of four major components:

- Control plane
- Scheduler
- API server
- etcd

Each of these components has different functionalities that maintain the Kubernetes cluster. Together they ensure that containers orchestrated in the Kubernetes cluster are running based on the configurations that have been made for them. In the open source setup for Kubernetes, the master node is a VM that houses all the components that have been listed previously. In AWS, the master node is a service that is managed and scaled by AWS, taking away that responsibility from the user.

The worker nodes are the second major component of the Kubernetes cluster. The worker nodes are made up of the following components too:

- kubelet
- kubeproxy
- Container runtime (Docker)

These components ensure that containers deployed in the cluster run as they were designed to. They maintain constant communication with the master node to send and receive updates based on the behavior of applications and services within the cluster. A Kubernetes cluster is usually made up of one master node and multiple worker nodes.

In most cases, worker nodes are VMs and in the case of AWS, they are EC2 instances. The worker nodes are the components that house the containers that are deployed to the Kubernetes cluster. In Kubernetes, a container is given a different name. It is called a **pod**. A pod is an abstraction of a container, which means that a container runs within a pod, and various containers can run within a pod. The logs generated by the containers are collected by the pod. There are unique features that make Kubernetes abstract the container into a pod. One of them is a **deployment** object in Kubernetes. The deployment object makes it possible to set up **ReplicaSets**, which are a feature that make it possible to create multiple pods for the high availability of your containers.

This feature also allows the self-healing of your application. This means that if for any reason a pod fails due to a bug in the application running in the container, Kubernetes has the ability to re-create the pod that hosts the container and your application without any manual intervention.

With all these moving components of a Kubernetes cluster, it is essential to have monitoring to be able to know what is going on across the Kubernetes cluster from time to time. This monitoring ranges from core Kubernetes component monitoring to the monitoring of the pods, which translates to the application running within the pod. We shall continue this in the *Monitoring of EKS applications and services* section.

We now understand the basics of ECS and EKS and the different moving parts that make them container orchestration services to ensure high availability for applications deployed within their environment. EventBridge is a part of event monitoring that can trigger feedback based on a system's behavior. In the next section, we shall configure Amazon EventBridge to respond to an ECS event.

Triggering ECS events on Amazon EventBridge

We have understood that ECS is made up of events via tasks. This section will focus on how we can turn these events into meaningful triggers and responses in the form of a feedback system.

The events sent by ECS help us to understand more about the status of the tasks and containers. Each of these states can be captured as events and sent to Amazon EventBridge, and also be used to trigger another type of event. This can help make our tasks within Amazon ECS responsive to events when an Amazon EventBridge target is attached to the specific event. It is essential to know the status of the tasks from time to time, as the system administrator or DevOps engineer in charge of the ECS cluster. You are not going to log in to the console and continue to check for states, but the state events can be forwarded to another AWS service for action to be taken when that event triggers. ECS is made up of different moving parts, and it is essential to keep track of the important parts of your container orchestration to be able to maintain high availability for the applications running in the container.

For this EventBridge example, using ECS, we shall configure Amazon EventBridge to respond to a state change in ECS. This can be helpful to know when something happens in an ECS cluster. We already explained the different states a task can be in. But it isn't just tasks that change in ECS. There are other components of an ECS cluster that also change. Some other components of an ECS cluster that have state changes include the following:

- **Services**: Some state changes include `SERVICE_STEADY_STATE`, `TASKSET_STEADY_STATE`, `CAPACITY_PROVIDER_STEADY_STATE`, and `SERVICE_DESIRED_COUNT_UPDATED`.

- **Deployment**: Some state changes include `SERVICE_DEPLOYMENT_IN_PROGRESS`, `SERVICE_DEPLOYMENT_COMPLETED`, and `SERVICE_DEPLOYMENT_FAILED`.

For this EventBridge scenario, we will be using a custom **event pattern**, which is not in EventBridge by default. This pattern is designed to read a deployment state change event from Amazon ECS. It is going to check whether a service deployment fails, is in progress, or is completed, and will trigger an SNS topic to send an email of the status of the deployment. This event will be targeted to a particular ECS Fargate cluster we have already created. The name of the cluster is `samplefargate`. To link up the event to the ECS cluster, we will be using the **ARN** of the ECS Fargate cluster.

> **Important Note**
>
> **ARN** is an acronym for **Amazon Resource Name**. It is the unique identifier for every service or resource created within the AWS environment. It is a string that comprises your AWS account number, AWS region, and a short name of the AWS service. An example ARN could be `arn:aws:lambda:us-east-1:123456789024:function:token_verifier`. This ARN means that it is a Lambda function with the name `token_verifier`, in the AWS `us-east-1` region, and the account number of the AWS account is `123456789024`.

These are the steps to create EventBridge for the ECS deployment status:

1. Log in to your AWS console and navigate to **Amazon EventBridge**.

2. Click on the **Create rule** button to create a new rule.

3. Enter the name of the rule and the description, then click on **Event pattern**. Then, click on the **Custom pattern** radio button.

4.   In the **Event pattern** box, enter the following event pattern (code can be obtained from the following URL: `https://github.com/PacktPublishing/ Infrastructure-Monitoring-with-Amazon-CloudWatch/blob/ main/Chapter05/event-pattern.json`), as shown in the following screenshot:

Figure 5.2 – Custom event pattern in Amazon EventBridge

5.   Scroll to the bottom and select a target. For this example, we shall use **SNS topic** (use the following link to create an SNS topic: `https://docs.aws.amazon. com/sns/latest/dg/sns-create-topic.html`). Select a topic that has been created previously, or a new topic can be created for this use:

Select targets

Select target(s) to invoke when an event matches your event pattern or when schedule is triggered (limit of 5 targets per rule)

Target   Remove

Select target(s) to invoke when an event matches your event pattern or when schedule is triggered (limit of 5 targets per rule)

SNS topic ▼

Topic

spotalert ▼

▶ Configure input

▶ Retry policy and dead-letter queue

Add target

Figure 5.3 – Choosing a target for the ECS custom event pattern

6. When that has been configured, click on the **Save** button to save the rule configuration.

With this, we have an Amazon EventBridge rule that is able to track state changes of any deployment in ECS and send alerts when the state of the deployment changes. This can be very helpful in monitoring a deployment made to ECS to know when it fails, when it is successful, or when it is in progress.

Visit this link for more information on service deployment events and other ECS events: `https://docs.aws.amazon.com/AmazonECS/latest/developerguide/ ecs_cwe_events.html`.

The next thing is to see how we can configure Container Insights for an ECS cluster to obtain container- and ECS-level metrics, for whatever launch type is used for the ECS cluster.

Configuring CloudWatch Container Insights

CloudWatch has an intelligent way of collecting container metrics using a feature called **Container Insights**. To be able to use Container Insights, it needs to be enabled from CloudWatch. But first, let's understand why we need to activate Container Insights.

Why activate Container Insights?

There are a lot of metrics that can be collected in any application or infrastructure setup. But you do not want to flood your CloudWatch with both necessary and unnecessary metrics. So, using Container Insights will narrow down the metrics collected from ECS to more specific and useful metrics for your ECS deployments. It also serves as a turn-key solution for metrics aggregation. Instead of looking for which monitoring tool will be used to collect logs from the running container and sifting through the logs to find the most important metrics needed for your container running in ECS, activating Container Insights on ECS will help in collecting these important metrics without any need for manual configuration. The following page shows the list of metrics collected by Container Insights:

`https://docs.aws.amazon.com/AmazonCloudWatch/latest/ monitoring/Container-Insights-metrics-ECS.html`

Now that we understand why we need to activate Container Insights, let's go through the activation process.

Activating Container Insights for ECS

We shall go through the process of enabling Container Insights for CloudWatch, and then move further to see the insights it is able to pull into CloudWatch.

We will perform the following steps to enable Container Insights:

1. Log in to the AWS management console.

2. Navigate to **Services | CloudWatch**.

3. On the CloudWatch dashboard, click on **Container Insights** on the left-side menu:

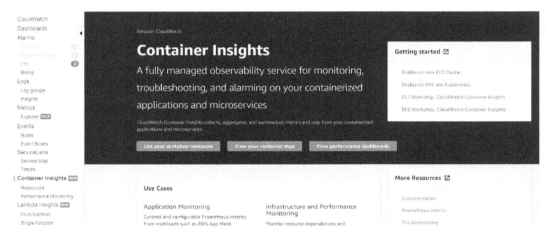

Figure 5.4 – Container Insights home page

4. Click on the **Enable on new ECS Cluster** link to enable Container Insights on ECS.

5. This will open up a new window, which is the ECS settings. Scroll to the bottom of the screen and locate the **CloudWatch Container Insights** section:

Figure 5.5 – Enabling Container Insights for ECS

6. Click the checkbox beside **Container Insights** and click the **Save** button to activate CloudWatch Container Insights.

7. Confirm the update to your AWS account. Click the **Confirm** button to confirm it:

Figure 5.6 – Confirm Container Insights activation

This will automatically activate Container Insights for all your ECS deployments.

> **Important Note**
> Please note that Container Insights is usually activated by region. If you activate
> it for a specific AWS region, it does not mean it is activated for all regions. So,
> if you need it in another region where you have your AWS resources, you will
> need to activate it separately for that specific region.

Now, we have activated Container Insights on ECS and understand why it is important
and the metrics it helps us to collect without any manual setups or configurations. Let's
view the insights and metrics that have been collected by Container Insights.

To view these insights, we shall use the following steps:

1. Navigate to the Amazon CloudWatch console using the **Services** menu item on
   your AWS console: click the drop-down menu, locate CloudWatch in the menu item
   list, then click it.

2. On the CloudWatch console, click on the **Container Insights** link menu item on the
   left-hand side of the console.

3. On the Container Insights page, click on **View performance dashboards**. This will
   lead us straight to the performance dashboard for Container Insights.

4.   By default, it selects EKS clusters. We just activated this for ECS, so we shall click on the drop-down menu and click on **ECS Clusters**. From the drop-down list, you can see a couple of other options that Container Insights can monitor and give metrics based on them. But for this example, we are focused on ECS clusters:

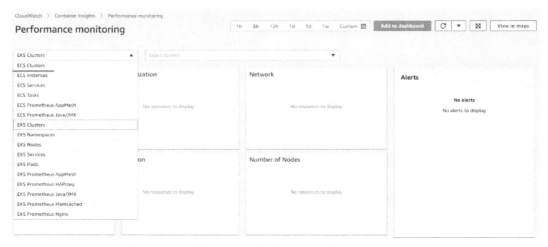

Figure 5.7 – Selecting ECS Clusters for Container Insights

5.   This will give us an option to select the appropriate cluster we want to get performance monitoring information on. For our example, we have an ECS cluster with Fargate running a container. The cluster is called `samplefargate`. That is selected by default, and the metrics for that cluster will be shown on the **Performance monitoring** dashboard, as shown in the following screenshot:

Figure 5.8 – Performance monitoring metrics from Container Insights

The dashboard in *Figure 5.8*, shows the performance metrics of the cluster called `samplefargate`. From the dashboard, we can see **CPU Utilization**, **Memory Utilization**, **Network**, **Container Instance Count**, **Task Count**, and **Service Count**. These are the metrics and automated dashboards that have been automatically generated by CloudWatch Container Insights based on our cluster. Due to the fact that the cluster was set up using Fargate, which is serverless, **Container Instance Count** will remain at **0**. This is because there is no EC2 instance used to orchestrate the currently running container. If the ECS launch type was EC2, then the instance count would be a count of the number of EC2 instances running in the cluster.

We have seen how Container Insights is able to collect essential metrics for monitoring the ECS cluster. Let's see how to collect logs for the containers in the ECS cluster.

Collecting logs for ECS applications

The metrics we have seen from Container Insights are mostly infrastructure metrics and not application logs, that is, metrics from the system(s) that hosts the container. The applications in the containers themselves also have logs that they generate. We need to be able to collect these logs from the containers. There are a couple of methods that can be adopted for this. We shall be making use of the `awslogs` driver. This is a configuration that can be activated during the creation of the **task definition** (see how to create a task definition here: `https://docs.aws.amazon.com/AmazonECS/latest/developerguide/create-task-definition.html`). It is activated when adding a container to the task definition. This is the point when we configure the Docker image and other configurations needed for the container to run efficiently.

The following screenshot shows the area of configuration to activate logging for your ECS containers:

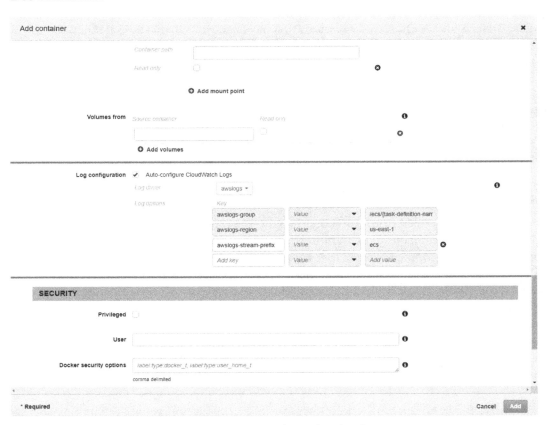

Figure 5.9 – Activating the awslogs log driver

The area shown in the screenshot of *Figure 5.9* is the section that allows us to activate logging for our container. It uses the `awslogs` driver by default. Within the configuration, we are also able to see where to configure the log group, AWS logs region, and the log stream. This helps to properly categorize the container logs as they are sent to CloudWatch Logs. When the container is created, this will send the logs to CloudWatch.

Let's navigate to where the logs have been created for our container. We do that with the following steps:

1. Navigate to the Amazon CloudWatch console using the **Services** menu item on your AWS console, click the drop-down menu, and locate **CloudWatch** in the menu item list, then click it.

2. Click on the **Log groups** link just below the **Logs** link, on the left-hand side of the screen.

3. A list of log groups will appear. Navigate to the one for ECS. It usually has a format based on what we had created. It has the format /ecs/{taskdefinition} where {taskdefinition} represents the name of our task definition we defined in ECS. For this scenario, our log group is /ecs/first-run-task-definition. So, we will click on that:

Log group	Retention	Metric filters	Contributor Insights
/aws/batch/job	Never expire	-	-
/aws/codebuild/mcshello	Never expire	-	-
/aws/ecs/containerinsights/ecs-ec2/performance	1 days	-	-
/aws/ecs/containerinsights/samplefargate/performance	1 days	-	-
/aws/lambda/billingms-dev-billinit	Never expire	-	-
/aws/lambda/billingms-dev-billresp	Never expire	-	-
/aws/lambda/billingms-dev-health	Never expire	-	-
/aws/lambda/billingms-dev-hello	Never expire	-	-
/aws/lambda/book-render-prod	Never expire	-	-
/aws/lambda/mcsbillingms-dev	Never expire	-	-
/aws/lambda/token_verifier	Never expire	-	-
/ecs/first-run-task-definition	Never expire	-	-

Figure 5.10 – Select the log group for ECS logs

4. This will take us to the different log streams in the log group. For this scenario, we have two log streams that have been configured, because we are running two containers: one in ECS for the EC2 launch type, and another for the ECS Fargate launch type.

Missing out activating the log configuration during the task definition configuration could mean no logs will be sent from the containers running in that ECS cluster. We have also learned that the logs will be sent to a specific log group and log stream. There, we can find the logs of the application running in the container. This will help us to understand the status and behavior of our containers, without necessarily having to log in to the container. EKS is our next stop; since we have looked at ECS, let's see how these monitoring configurations are done on EKS. EKS has both a master node and worker nodes. In the next section, we shall configure monitoring for both the master node and applications running in the worker nodes.

Monitoring of EKS applications and services

We already mentioned earlier the different aspects of an EKS cluster. This time, we will be talking about how we activate and configure monitoring for the master node (also called the control plane), and then we will talk about how to collect logs for the pods that are deployed in the worker node. But first, let's talk about how to configure monitoring for the EKS control plane.

Monitoring the control plane

First, let's see how to enable monitoring on Amazon EKS. When an EKS cluster is set up, the monitoring features are usually not activated by default. We shall activate them on the EKS console when we have a control plane running. To do this, we go to the EKS console of the cluster that has been created.

To activate the different components of the control plane, we take the following steps:

1. Log in to the AWS management console and navigate to **Amazon EKS** on the services menu.

2. Click on the **Clusters** link on the side menu to view the list of EKS clusters that have been created.

3. Click on the cluster that needs the logging features enabled. This will take us to the cluster configuration page:

Figure 5.11 – Configuring logs for the EKS control plane

4. Click on the **Logging** option to take us to the **Control Plane Logging** tab. This will show the different components of the control plane that can be monitored. In the screenshot in *Figure 5.11*, they are disabled by default.

5. Click on the **Manage logging** button to change the settings for the logging option:

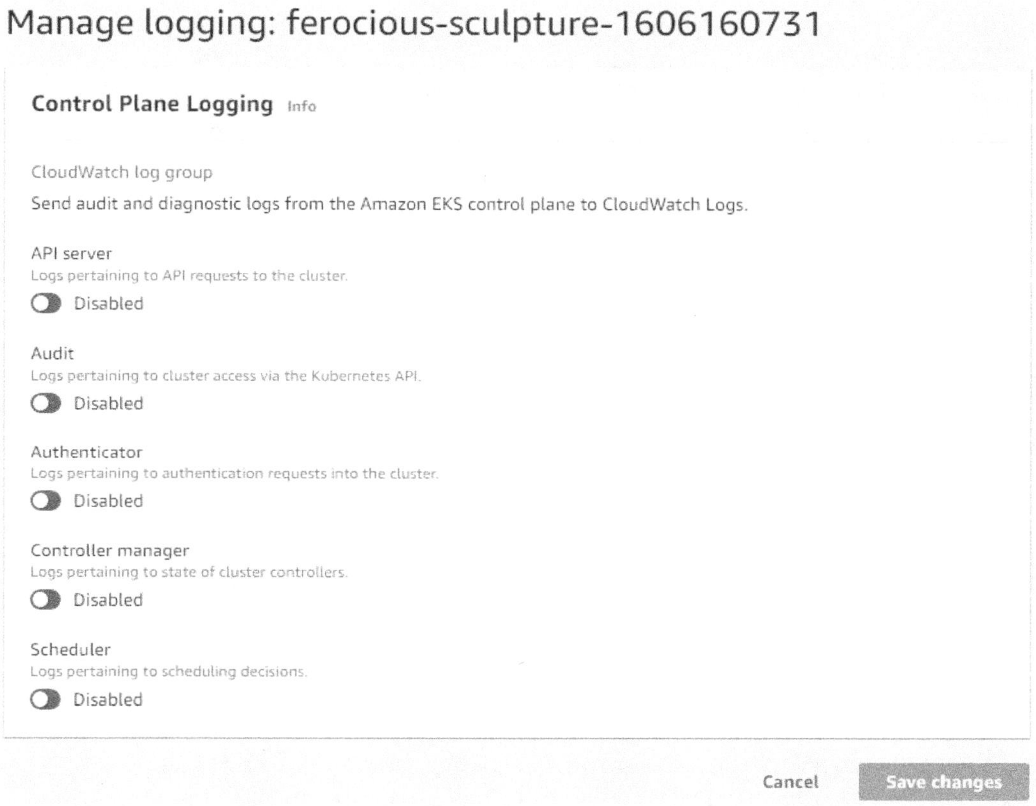

Manage logging: ferocious-sculpture-1606160731

Control Plane Logging   Info

CloudWatch log group
Send audit and diagnostic logs from the Amazon EKS control plane to CloudWatch Logs.

API server
Logs pertaining to API requests to the cluster.
⬤ Disabled

Audit
Logs pertaining to cluster access via the Kubernetes API.
⬤ Disabled

Authenticator
Logs pertaining to authentication requests into the cluster.
⬤ Disabled

Controller manager
Logs pertaining to state of cluster controllers.
⬤ Disabled

Scheduler
Logs pertaining to scheduling decisions.
⬤ Disabled

Cancel   Save changes

Figure 5.12 – Activating logging for different control plane components

6. To activate logging for any of the components, click on **Disabled** (or the switch beside **Disabled**) to make it **Enabled**, and then click on the **Save changes** button. For our example, we only activated **API server**.

The logs will get written to a CloudWatch log group in a specific format, as shown in the following screenshot:

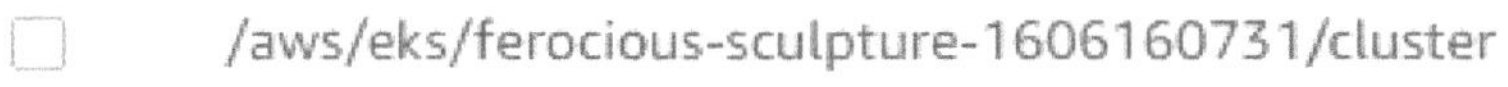

☐   /aws/eks/ferocious-sculpture-1606160731/cluster

Figure 5.13 – Log group for the EKS control plane

7. Click on the log groups to reveal the log stream for the EKS cluster. Then, click on
    the log stream to view the logs:

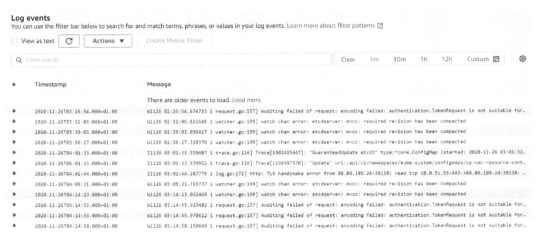

Figure 5.14 – CloudWatch log events for the KubeAPI server

This will finally enable logging for the specific components for which we need logging.
With this, we can start monitoring the control plane to get metrics and behaviors of the
different components of the control plane.

Important Note

An EKS cluster in AWS can be set up in different ways. You can use
CloudFormation, Terraform, or eksctl. It is quite easy to use eksctl as
it is a simple command that is used to set up the Kubernetes cluster. To learn
more about the tool, visit eksctl.io.

With this understanding of the activation of different components of the EKS control
plane, we can say that we can now collect information on the activity of the different
parts of the master node. The next focus will be on the worker nodes and the **pods**
running within the Kubernetes cluster. In the next section, we shall configure a log
collector for the pods in the Kubernetes cluster.

Collecting logs for EKS resources

Before starting the process of log collection in EKS, ensure that the worker nodes have
the appropriate IAM role so that the fluentd daemon can push logs to Amazon
CloudWatch. To do that, attach a CloudWatch policy to the IAM role attached to the
worker nodes of the Kubernetes cluster.

To attach the IAM role, use the following steps:

1. Log in to the AWS console and go to the EC2 console to get the IAM role attached to it.

2. Click on the attached IAM role to land in the AWS IAM console:

Figure 5.15 – IAM role for the EC2 instance

This will open up the particular role with the policies listed below the role.

3. Click on the **Attach policies** button to attach the policy for CloudWatch:

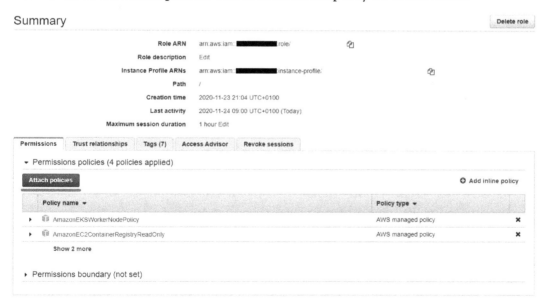

Figure 5.16 – CloudWatch role with IAM policies listed

4. Search for `CloudWatchFullAccess` from the list and click the checkbox beside it to select it.

5. Then, click the **Attach policy** button in the bottom-right corner of the screen. This will eventually attach the policy to the role.

With this, the Kubernetes worker nodes can now send logs to CloudWatch Logs.

The next step for us now is to activate/configure Container Insights for EKS, which will both give us automated dashboards and collect logs for all pods and services running within the Kubernetes cluster. This gives us a bird's-eye view of everything running in our Kubernetes cluster: **pods**, **services**, **namespaces**, worker nodes, memory, and CPU utilization. Let's walk through the steps of configuring Container Insights for EKS. This configuration works for both Amazon EKS and if you are running Kubernetes on EC2:

1. Log in to the machine used to manage your Kubernetes cluster. Ensure that the machine has the `kubeconfig` file, which has the ability to administer the Kubernetes cluster.

2. Ensure that you can communicate with the Kubernetes cluster via the `kubectl` command.

3. Enter the following command in the command line:

```
curl https://raw.githubusercontent.com/aws-samples/
amazon-cloudwatch-container-insights/latest/
k8s-deployment-manifest-templates/deployment-mode/
daemonset/container-insights-monitoring/quickstart/
cwagent-fluentd-quickstart.yaml | sed "s/{{cluster_
name}}/MyCluster/;s/{{region_name}}/us-west-2/" | kubectl
apply -f -
```

Replace `MyCluster` and `us-west-2` with the appropriate values where `MyCluster` should be the name of your EKS cluster/control plane and `us-west-2` is replaced with the specific AWS region that the EKS cluster is in, which is where the CloudWatch metrics will be sent to.

4. Press the *Enter* key to apply the changes to the cluster:

```
namespace/amazon-cloudwatch created
serviceaccount/cloudwatch-agent created
clusterrole.rbac.authorization.k8s.io/cloudwatch-agent-role created
clusterrolebinding.rbac.authorization.k8s.io/cloudwatch-agent-role-binding created
configmap/cwagentconfig created
daemonset.apps/cloudwatch-agent created
configmap/cluster-info created
serviceaccount/fluentd created
clusterrole.rbac.authorization.k8s.io/fluentd-role created
clusterrolebinding.rbac.authorization.k8s.io/fluentd-role-binding created
configmap/fluentd-config created
daemonset.apps/fluentd-cloudwatch created
```

Figure 5.17 – Apply configuration to the Kubernetes cluster

This will create the required Kubernetes resources for monitoring.

Allow a few minutes for some logs to be collect and then visit the CloudWatch dashboard and navigate to **Container Insights | Performance monitoring**. This will present the automated dashboard that comes with your Kubernetes cluster, showing a visual representation of essential metrics such as CPU, memory disk, and more. See the following screenshot for an example:

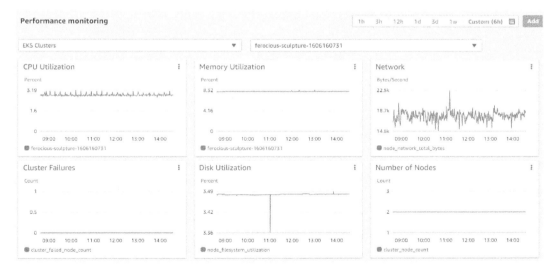

Figure 5.18 – EKS metrics on Container Insights

You can also view the logs from each of the metrics and logs from the pods in the cluster. Navigate to **Container Insights | Resources**. This option shows the list of all resources both in ECS and EKS. Navigate to a pod running in EKS. For our example, we already deployed nginx in the Kubernetes cluster:

Figure 5.19 – EKS pod in Container Insights

Clicking on the pod will give more information about the pod, such as the CPU, memory, and network information:

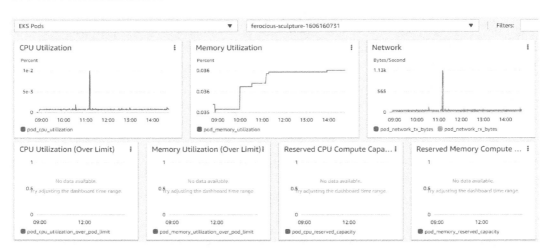

Figure 5.20 – Resource metrics in the EKS pod

To view the logs, scroll to the bottom of the page, where you have the container performance, and tick the pod on the list. Click on the **Actions** button, and then click on **View application logs**. This will take us to the **Logs Insights** page. Click on the **Run query** button to run the query to view the application logs:

Figure 5.21 – Pod logs in CloudWatch Logs Insights

> **Important Note**
> The kubeconfig file in Kubernetes is a configuration file that contains
> both authorization and authentication information used to communicate with
> the Kubernetes cluster. The kubeconfig file is made up of certificates and
> the Kubernetes API server URL. The certificates serve the password used to
> authenticate every request made to the Kubernetes API server to perform all
> types of Kubernetes administration operations.

We have successfully configured Container Insights for EKS. Let's help to streamline the automated dashboard(s) from EKS and create a more specific dashboard. The next section is about how to use the CloudWatch dashboard to configure a more specific dashboard.

Setting up custom dashboards and metrics for containers

Just like every other dashboard in CloudWatch, CloudWatch dashboards are usually generated automatically, when Container Insights has been activated. Be it Amazon ECS or Amazon EKS, CloudWatch dashboards are automatically generated that take note of the top relevant information of the cluster in which the Container Insights agent is actively running. It is also possible to create a custom dashboard from the logs that have been collected from the containers running within the cluster setup.

These dashboards can be generated and then added to a unified dashboard that contains information on not only the metrics from what Container Insights displays but also your custom metrics from your logs. An example could be creating a metric that counts the number of **exceptions** found in the applications logs, then creating a widget with a line graph based on that. The widget can then be attached to a unified dashboard that already has other widgets that contain the CPU and memory metrics.

This gives a 360 degrees view of the major metrics of the full system and helps to configure appropriate alarms that are needed to avoid and reduce **alert fatigue**.

Important Note

Alert fatigue is a scenario where you have too many alarms configured, and they keep sending messages from time to time. This makes it hard to know which alarms are important and the ones that are not important. It eventually makes it impossible to understand underlying issues and problems because there are too many alarms/alerts being sent.

We will be creating a custom dashboard that is a combination of the ECS dashboard and the EKS dashboard so that we can have a unified container dashboard for all our container workloads. We will also delete some widgets we really do not need from the dashboard and finally, generate a sharable link that can be used to project the dashboard on a larger screen so that it is visible to the DevOps and SysAdmin team so that they can easily get a glance of the status of our containers, whether they reside in ECS or EKS.

To configure this dashboard, we will use the following steps:

1. Navigate to the CloudWatch console from the **Services** menu in your AWS console.

2. Click on the **Dashboard** link on the left hand-side menu. This will lead us to the **Dashboards** home page:

Figure 5.22 – CloudWatch Dashboards page

3. Click on the **Create dashboard** button in the top-right corner to create a new dashboard.

4. Enter the name of the dashboard in the dialog box and click the **Create dashboard** button. We shall call our dashboard ContainersHub.

5. The next popup will ask you to select the particular widget you would like to add to the dashboard. Ignore this by clicking the **Cancel** link in the dialog box.

6. Click on the **Performance monitoring** link under the **Container Insights** link on the left-hand side. This will open the **Performance monitoring** page with the default selection of **EKS Clusters**, and the cluster that we configured previously will be selected by default. The metrics will also be shown in the automated dashboard below that.

7. Click on the **Add to dashboard** button.

8. A pop-up dialog will display showing the dashboard we just created, named ContainersHub. If there are other dashboards, the list gives us an option to pick from any other dashboard we choose to add the widgets to. For this scenario, we shall pick the dashboard we already have.

9. Click on the **Add to dashboard** button to add the widgets to the dashboard.

    This will take us to the dashboard, showing that the widgets have been added successfully:

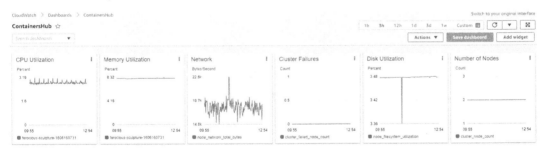

Figure 5.23 – EKS widgets added to a dashboard

10. The next step is to add the ECS dashboard. We shall follow the same procedure, but this time, instead of EKS clusters, we shall click on the dropdown and select **ECS Clusters**:

Figure 5.24 – Selecting ECS Clusters

11. Click on **Add to dashboard** again to add the ECS widgets to the same dashboard, which is the ContainersHub dashboard.

    This will give us an aggregated dashboard that contains both ECS and EKS metrics.

12. Click on the **Save dashboard** button to save the widgets that have been added to the dashboard.

We can modify the dashboard by removing some widgets that are not very crucial for us to monitor at all times. For this scenario, I will be removing a couple of widgets, such as **Task Count**, **Container Instance Count**, **Cluster Failures**, **Service Count**, and **Number of Nodes**, as I just want the CPU, memory, disk, and network widgets. We can delete a widget by clicking on the menu button on the widget and clicking on the **Delete** option, as shown in the following screenshot. When done, click the **Save dashboard** button to save all the changes that have been made to the dashboard:

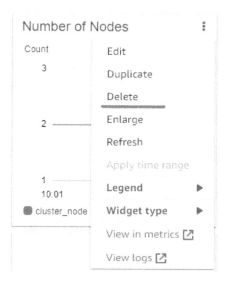

Figure 5.25 – Deleting a widget

We shall delete all the other widgets and then we'll have a final dashboard that is more concise and looks like this:

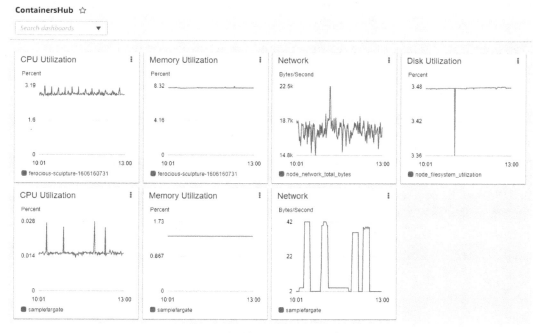

Figure 5.26 – Concise dashboard with specific widgets/metrics

Now that we have configured a proper dashboard to monitor our ECS and EKS clusters, let's look at a case study that will cover all that we have learned so far.

Case study of Amazon EKS logging and monitoring

You are a DevOps engineer who has just been employed to help migrate a couple of monolithic applications into microservices. The choice made for managing the microservices is to use a container-based system due to the advantages containers have. The company has gone further to say that they will be using Amazon EKS as the service for orchestration of the Docker images that have been built. Your company has just got the ISO 27001 certification for information security. So, things such as auditing applications and services are taken very seriously. Logs of applications are to be kept and audited from time to time to ensure that the company continues to remain compliant. Added to that, close monitoring of the applications and notification alarms needs to be configured to receive notifications when applications have any kind of behavior that is not normal.

Solution

From the preceding case study, a couple of things need to be taken into consideration to make this setup successful and meet the requirements that have been stated:

- An EKS cluster needs to be set up with monitoring enabled on the EKS cluster.

- Container Insights needs to be able to collect logs and be stored with a long retention period, or logs to be sent over to Amazon S3 for later auditing.

- Metrics and alarms will need to be configured for the logs collected to trigger an alarm when anything that has to do with ERROR is found in the logs.

This case study helps us to mimic a real-life scenario of the kind of task that will be expected of a DevOps engineer or a cloud engineer when we have acquired monitoring skills. We shall be covering more real-life scenario case studies of what will be required as an engineer with monitoring knowledge.

Summary

From the beginning of this chapter, our aim has been to be able to use Amazon CloudWatch Container Insights to perform monitoring and logging. We first started by talking about the different container orchestration services provided by AWS, which are Amazon ECS and Amazon EKS. We then went further to explore some of the features of ECS and the different launch types that exist within Amazon ECS, which are the EC2 instance launch type and Fargate. We looked at how the monitoring of containers/applications works in ECS. It involves activating the `awslogs` driver during the process of adding a container on ECS. This will make the log driver automatically pull logs from the container and send it over to CloudWatch Logs and CloudWatch Container Insights, which gives logs and metrics for both container applications and the components running the containers.

We then moved on to Amazon EKS, which is another container orchestration service in AWS. We explained what EKS means and talked about the different components that make up Kubernetes. We then moved on to talk about monitoring for the different components, including monitoring for the master node, which involves activating which particular component of the master node we want to monitor. For the worker nodes, we demonstrated how to install CloudWatch Container Insights in the Kubernetes cluster, to be able to collect logs from the containers that are deployed in the worker nodes, which are eventually sent to Amazon CloudWatch Container Insights and CloudWatch Logs.

In the next chapter, our focus will be on database monitoring and we will see how CloudWatch integrates with AWS database technologies.

Questions

1. What is the function of AWS worker nodes in a Kubernetes cluster?

2. What do you need to activate in ECS to allow logs to be sent to CloudWatch?

3. What do ECS and EKS have in common?

4. Is there a difference in the monitoring of the ECS EC2 launch type and the ECS Fargate launch type?

Further reading

Refer to the following links for more information on topics covered in this chapter:

- Understanding Kubernetes architecture: https://www.packtpub.com/ product/mastering-kubernetes-third-edition/9781839211256

- ECS basics using Fargate: https://www.packtpub.com/product/ aws-container-services-ecs-ecr-with-fargate-and-ec2-video/9781800567580

- Getting started with Amazon ECS and Amazon Fargate: https://www. packtpub.com/product/amazon-fargate-quick-start-guide/9781789345018

- What are containers and why should they be used? https://www.packtpub. com/product/learn-docker-fundamentals-of-docker-19-x-second-edition/9781838827472

- Kubernetes command center: https://www.packtpub.com/product/ the-kubernetes-workshop/9781838820756

6
Performance Insights for Database Services

The first facing system users come across in any service is the application they are interacting with. We spent the previous chapter talking about monitoring in containers. Since containers are a major part of compute and will continue to be in the future, we looked at the different types of container services in AWS.

Now that we have understood how to monitor applications that are being run in AWS compute services, we also need to understand database services and how to monitor and ensure better availability for them. An application is not complete without the database serving as the source of truth for all the information that has been collected by the application.

This chapter will focus on understanding what a database is and what database management is about. The different types of database technologies and database services that exist within the AWS ecosystem will also be covered. Then, we will look at the different scenarios where these different database technologies and services can be used, and then we will learn how monitoring works for them. Lastly, we will look at a more holistic case study that will cover both compute and database scenarios.

We will cover the following topics in this chapter:

- Introduction to database management
- Understanding the different types of AWS database technologies
- Configuring metric monitoring in RDS
- Logging operations in Amazon DynamoDB
- Monitoring events in ElastiCache
- Monitoring Redshift and Amazon DocumentDB cluster status
- Case study on monitoring an RDS database

Technical requirements

Check out the following link to see the Code in Action video:

`https://bit.ly/3cB419F`

Introduction to database management

As old as time, man has been storing data in different formats. From writing it on stones and tablets, to the invention of the quill, reed pen, and ballpoint pens. These instruments were designed as tools for recording and storing different types of data, for reference and historical purposes. Fast forward to the 20th century and computers were born, and they provided us with a new way of storing information. Data in computing is stored in different formats, and the format that we store this data in is dependent on what we intend to use that data for.

Database management is a group of activities that involves how data is created, updated, retrieved, and deleted. It also involves how the data that's been created is secured and designing proper policies around who has access to the data to do what and when. The primary activities that are performed in database management go by the acronym **CRUD**. Let's take a look:

- **Create**: This involves creating new data.
- **Retrieve**: This involves searching for or querying data that has been created for viewing purposes.
- **Update**: This involves making changes to existing data.
- **Delete**: This involves deleting or removing existing data.

Every type of database has these four operations as the bedrock for managing the data that is stored in them.

Data can be stored in various forms. We could be storing data for various reasons and for various purposes. For example, there are certain types of data that are stored and represented in a tabular form. This gives the user a way to understand and assimilate the data when it is stored in that format. Sometimes, data is stored in text form, which is not as structured as the tabular form of storing data. This categorizes data storage into three major categories, as follows:

- **Structured data**: This is data stored in more of a tabular form.
- **Semi-structured data**: This is data stored in a format that is not fully structured.
- **Unstructured data**: This is data that is neither stored in a tabular form or as semi-structured data.

These labels, which are given to the method and category of storing data, are used as an umbrella nomenclature. There are also more technical terms for categorizing data. These terms are generally recognized by software engineers, system administrators, and DevOps engineers. Let's match these more technical categories with the categories we mentioned earlier:

Technical	Non-Technical
Relational database system	Structured data
NoSQL database system	Semi-structured data
Documents and files	Unstructured data

Table 6.1 – Technical and non-technical database categories

As we described earlier, the relational database system stores data in a tabular form, just like structured data. The relational database system keeps data in rows and columns. To write data, you must create a new row of information containing a couple of fields with specific names and values to go with them. The following table is an example of how a relational database system stores data:

First name	Last name	Gender
John	Doe	Male
Jane	Doe	Female
Mary Chloe	Diagboya	Female
Cynthia	Diagboya	Female

Table 6.2 – Sample of a relational database

The preceding table is a logical design of how relational database technology works. It stores data in the form of rows and columns. Every column has a specific name that is used to identify the type of data the column collects.

The other database technology we mentioned is a NoSQL database, which falls under the semi-structured category. This category of data storage was designed to solve the challenges of following the structural form of data storage. There is certain information that needs to be collected that is not in a structured form, so there needs to be a storage format or technology that can accommodate that. This is how the NoSQL database model was born. It was given the name NoSQL because the programming language that's used by relational databases is called SQL.

> **Important note**
> **SQL** is an acronym for **Structured Query Language**. This is the default language used by most relational database management systems. It is used to perform the four most basic database operations (create, read/retrieve, update, and delete). It is also used to define the structure of the table that will be used to store the data in the database. SQL statements are categorized into **DDL** or **data description language** (for describing the structure of the data to be stored) and **DML** or **data manipulation language** (for performing database management operations on the data).

NoSQL is anti-SQL, which means it's different from the SQL method of storing data in a more structural format. To buttress this point, the following screenshot show a sample of how the NoSQL technology stores data:

```
{
  "firstname":"Chloe",
  "lastname":"Sullivan",
  "contact": [ "phone":+12344454542, "address":"44 Downing Street","homephone":"+4455224"]
  "gender": "female"
}
```

Figure 6.1 – NoSQL format of data storage

The format this data is in is used by most NoSQL database engines. This style of storing data is called **JSON**.

> **Important note**
> **JSON** is an acronym for **JavaScript Object Notation**. It is a method of representing, storing, and exchanging data across disparate systems.

The last format of data, known as unstructured data, falls under the category of files and documents, and is where other forms of representative data is stored. Word documents, PDF documents, images, and so on all fall under the unstructured data category. This type of data is hardly usable or readable by machines and for programmatic purposes, but machine learning is bringing many new techniques with it to make it possible to read unstructured data written in documents. This can be converted into a semi-structured or structured data format.

These database technologies are part of the **Relational Database Management System (RDMS)** and the NoSQL technology for specific brands that have built database systems based on these technologies. This is similar to how we have different types of televisions being produced by different types of manufacturers. There are plasma televisions, curved televisions, and cathode-ray tube televisions – they are all produced by different manufactures. So, the RDMS and NoSQL databases have companies that have produced databases that use those technologies. Some examples can be seen in the following table:

Database Brand Name	Database Technology
Amazon Aurora	RDMS
MySQL	RDMS
MongoDB	NoSQL
Cassandra Database	NoSQL
Oracle	RDMS
Microsoft SQL Server	RDMS
Amazon DynamoDB	NoSQL

Table 6.3 – Database brands and technologies

With that, we have gone through some of the fundamentals of databases. This will be relevant in helping us understand the next few sections of this chapter. In the next section, we will focus on the database technologies supported in the AWS environment.

Understanding the different types of AWS database technologies

AWS is an ecosystem of different cloud services for different purposes. The focus of this chapter is on the database services provided by AWS. The AWS database suite has a wide array of options for different database technologies, all of which were mentioned in the previous chapter. These database services cover both RBMS and NoSQL databases. The AWS services that we will discuss in this chapter are **relational database services (RDSes)**, DynamoDB, ElastiCache, and Amazon DocumentDB.

RDS

The RDS service is an umbrella service for all popular relational database services. AWS used this code name to group different relational database technologies.

The service makes it easy to set up, secure, scale, back up, and monitor relational databases. This would have been much more difficult if a user were to set up, secure, scale, back up, and monitor on their own. AWS abstracts all the operational complexities involved with that. Within the RDS service, you can create the following databases: Amazon Aurora MySQL, Amazon Aurora PostgreSQL, PostgreSQL, Oracle, MySQL, MariaDB, and Microsoft SQL Server.

There are various metrics and log information that are generated by an AWS RDS database. The performance of the RDS database is usually measured by a metric called DB load (database load). This DB load is an aggregate of various metrics. We will talk more about this in the *Configuring metric monitoring* in RDS section.

DynamoDB

This is an AWS propriety NoSQL database service. Like the RDS service, it is a managed service, which means that AWS handles the operations of the infrastructure concerning the DynamoDB database. Unlike other databases that have a database and a document structure, DynamoDB is made up of strictly tables. So, in DynamoDB, you create just the tables and write data to them. The performance of the database is measured by the provisioned read capacity and provisioned write capacity. There are other metrics for measuring the behavior of a DynamoDB table. We will explore all these in more detail in the *Logging operations in Amazon DynamoDB* section.

ElastiCache

ElastiCache is a category name for other types of NoSQL databases, and they are generally called **cache databases**. The sole reason for a cache database is to improve the performance of reading data from a database. Traditionally, databases write data into the hard disk of the computer. So, when an application connects to a database to retrieve information, that data is retrieved from the database, where this data was written to the database engine. Due to the nature of hard disks, this can be a little slower than using the memory of the system.

Hence, cache databases write and read data from the memory of the system instead of the hard disk. Memory originally serves as a buffer and communication link between the hard disk and the CPU. We discussed memory in more detail in *Chapter 2*, *CloudWatch Events and Alarms*, in the *Understanding memory in IaaS* section. However, cache databases are designed to be able to write and read data from memory, hence making I/O operations faster. Amazon ElastiCache has two services within it: ElastiCache for Redis and ElastiCache for Memcached.

Amazon DocumentDB

This is another umbrella name for document databases in AWS. DocumentDB is a sub-category of NoSQL databases. Amazon DocumentDB currently supports MongoDB. MongoDB is an open source NoSQL database that stores data in JSON format. This data is also called documents, hence the name document database.

Now that we understand the basic concepts behind the different AWS database and cache services, let's learn how monitoring and performance insights work in these different databases.

Configuring metric monitoring in RDS

RDS is the codename that AWS uses to group all the relational database technologies that it supports. In the previous section, we mentioned the database technologies that are powered by the AWS RDS technology. We won't be covering logging and monitoring for all the databases in this book, but we will take one of the databases and see how logging and monitoring works for it. The knowledge and concepts you will learn about here can be applied to other RDS database technologies; the differences might just be slight in regard to the terms that will be used to described certain metrics for the different database technologies.

The first thing we must do before we start monitoring is ensure that we have a database set up. Use the following URL to create a simple RDS database instance: `https://docs.aws.amazon.com/AmazonRDS/latest/UserGuide/CHAP_GettingStarted.CreatingConnecting.MySQL.html#CHAP_GettingStarted.Creating.MySQL`. It will take a couple of minutes for the instance to be created.

If you followed the instructions provided in the preceding link, a database will be created for you using the default RDS settings. These settings come automatically with the option to activate **Performance Insights**. This is a feature within RDS that makes it possible for us to perform monitoring on all RDS instances.

There are a lot of metrics to check for in a database, but RDS's Performance Insights has been well-designed by the AWS team to draw key insights that will give you the relevant information you need to understand the behavior of the database. The following screenshot shows where Performance Insights is activated, as well as other monitoring and logging configurations for our RDS instance:

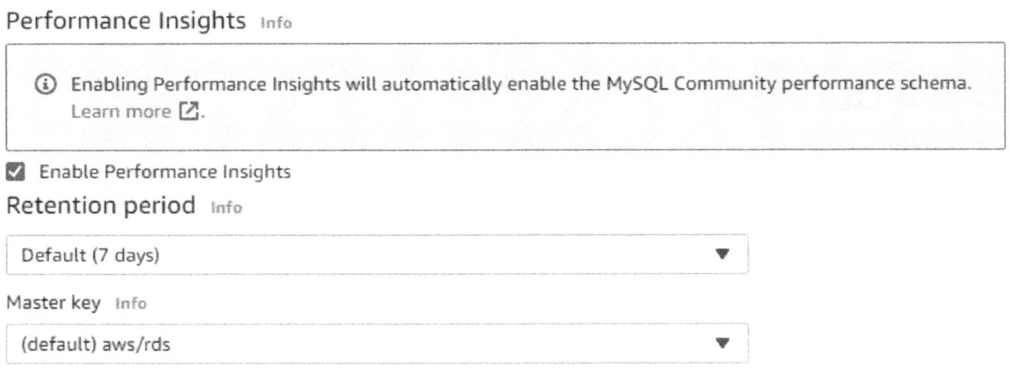

Performance Insights Info

> (i) Enabling Performance Insights will automatically enable the MySQL Community performance schema. Learn more 🗗.

☑ Enable Performance Insights

Retention period Info

Default (7 days)   ▼

Master key Info

(default) aws/rds   ▼

Figure 6.2 – Enabling Performance Insights

The preceding screenshot shows where Performance Insights can be enabled. Log collection is not activated by default. The next section, just after Performance Insights, provides a collection of general and error logs from the database option. The following screenshot shows where enhanced monitoring and logging can be activated:

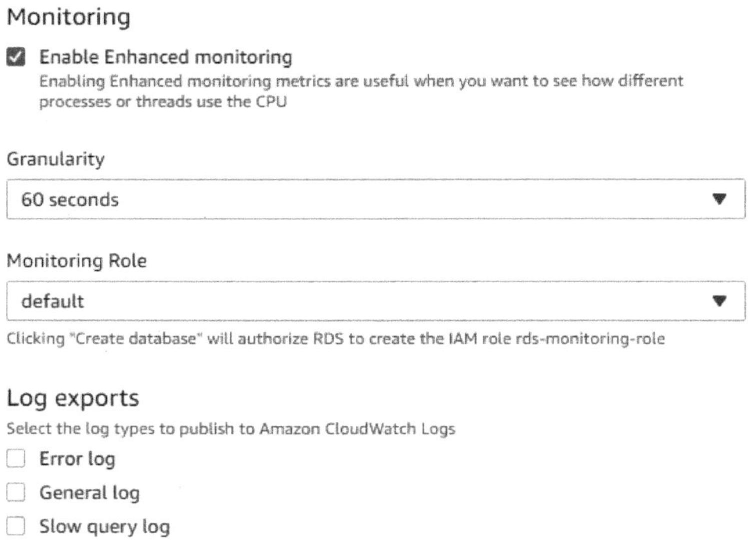

Monitoring

☑ Enable Enhanced monitoring
    Enabling Enhanced monitoring metrics are useful when you want to see how different processes or threads use the CPU

Granularity

60 seconds   ▼

Monitoring Role

default   ▼

Clicking "Create database" will authorize RDS to create the IAM role rds-monitoring-role

Log exports

Select the log types to publish to Amazon CloudWatch Logs

☐ Error log
☐ General log
☐ Slow query log

Figure 6.3 – Enable Enhanced monitoring and Log exports

Here, we have three options:

- **Error log**: This is a log that contains every error that comes out of the database activities.

- **General log**: This configuration contains all types of information; from access information to error logs and other types of logs that capture activities in the database.

- **Slow query log**: This configuration captures every SQL query that took longer than the expected time. It varies from one database technology to another.

> **Important note**
>
> A slow query log in a database is a SQL query that takes longer than an expected time. This invariably makes the application connecting to the database slow to respond to users' requests. In MySQL, a query that takes longer than 0.1 seconds is termed a slow query and is automatically logged by the MySQL server.

With that, we have activated the Performance Insights page. It takes a couple of minutes for the RDS instance to become available. The RDS console gives us some basic metrics for the RDS instance that has been created. These metrics include CPU, DB connections, memory, and storage space. To view this dashboard, navigate to the database that has been created. In that database, click on the **Monitoring** tab. This will reveal the metrics that I stated initially, as shown in the following screenshot:

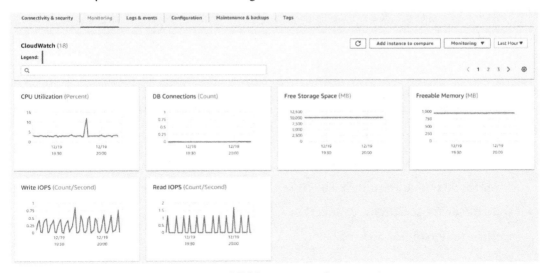

Figure 6.4 – RDS Instance metrics – page 1

This information is helpful for getting basic insights into the RDS instance that has been created. Some of the most interesting information in this dashboard includes the number of database connections that have been made to the RDS instance. There are situations where another application might not be able to connect to the database anymore. You can find this out by checking the default number of connections that have been assigned to the database, as well as the current number of used connections to the database.

Let's navigate to the **Performance Insights** page. To do that, navigate to the side menu of the RDS console and click on **Performance Insights**. On the **Performance Insights** page, click on the dropdown with the value *Select a DB instance to view the metrics* and select the instance that was created so that you can view the Performance Insights metrics. This can be seen in the following screenshot:

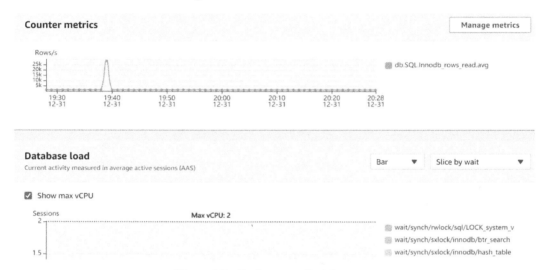

Figure 6.5 – Performance Insights page

The preceding screenshot shows the **Database load** section, which is a combination of a couple of metrics that can be found on the side of the graph. These are as follows:

- **wait/synch/mutex/sql/LOCK_plugin**
- **wait/synch/sxlock/innodb/btr_search**
- **wait/synch/sxlock/innodb/hash_table**
- **wait/io/socket/sql/client_connection**
- **wait/io/table/sql/handler**
- **CPU**

These metrics are combined to form the **Database load** metric, which gives us a quick, holistic view of the performance of the database. This makes it easy for database managers, DevOps engineers, and system administrators to get quick insights and information on the behavior of the database. Some of the metrics mentioned in the preceding list may be slightly different from database to database, but the AWS RDS team has carefully selected the most important metrics that will always form the aggregated **Database load** metric.

There is more. The database's Performance Insights data can also provide us with other information about the waits, SQL statements, and hosts in the RDS instance, as well as the database's users and databases. The following screenshot shows the most used SQL statement that our application is always sending to the database:

> **Important note**
> A wait is an interlude that occurs in a computer processor when it is trying to access a third-party device. It is the round-trip time it takes the processor to for something and get a response from the third-party resource. An example of a resource could be memory or any other external device. Wait can also be associated with different things, such as I/O wait, CPU wait, and SQL wait.

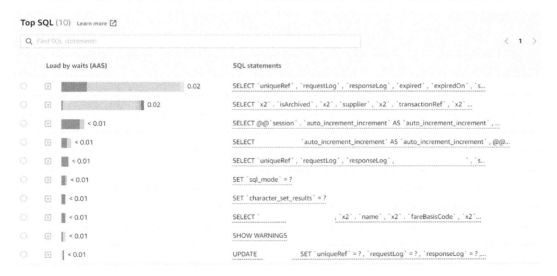

Figure 6.6 – Top operation metrics

Here, we can see the top SQL statement, meaning the most used queries by the application connecting to this database. We can also see other important information regarding **Calls/sec**, **Avg latency (ms)/call**, and **Rows examined/call**.

So far, we have only been talking about aggregated metrics. What about the logs? In *Figure 6.3*, we showed where we can activate logging in our RDS instance. By default, all the logs that are generated will eventually precipitate at Amazon CloudWatch Logs. So, let's navigate to CloudWatch Logs to see the logs our application has generated:

1. Go to the AWS console and navigate to **CloudWatch** from the **Services** top menu bar.

2. Click on the **Logs groups** link, just below the **Logs** link in the Amazon CloudWatch console.

3. For the different log groups, search for the logs group with the name of the RDS instance that you created. It is usually in the form of /aws/rds/instance/ db-instance-name/log-type, where db-instance-name is the name of the RDS instance you have created and log-type represents the log type, which could be an error log. Clicking on that link will take us to the log stream(s). Then, click on the stream to view the logs.

4. The logs will be displayed like so:

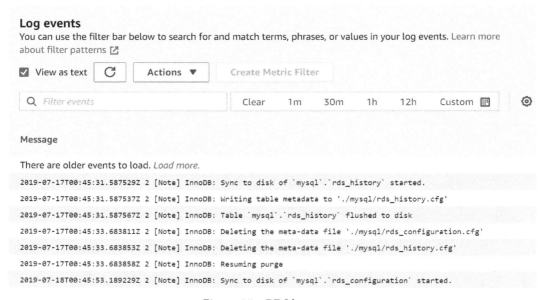

Figure 6.7 – RDS log events

With these logs, you can easily spot issues with the database that might not be visible on the database performance dashboard. Metrics can also be created from these logs to reduce the workload of having to look for a specific term or work in the logs. We learned how to create custom metrics from huge logs so that we can easily pinpoint a specific metric in *Chapter 3, CloudWatch Logs, Metrics, and Dashboard*, in the *Metrics and CloudWatch metrics* section.

It is also good to note that CloudWatch generates an automated RDS dashboard that has an aggregate of specific metrics too, just like the dashboard shown in *Figure 6.4*. You could create a more unique dashboard from that too within CloudWatch, to help you streamline the kind of dashboard you want to view from time to time and the metrics you want to set alarms on.

With that, we are fully covered in terms of understanding what is going on with our RDS database at any time, by using either the automated dashboard provided by CloudWatch or by setting up our own Performance Insights. It also important to note that, at the time of writing, Performance Insights for RDS is not supported for all RDS databases. Follow this link to learn what database engines and instance types are supported: `https://docs.aws.amazon.com/AmazonRDS/latest/UserGuide/USER_PerfInsights.Overview.html#USER_PerfInsights.Overview.Engines`.

Now that we are done with RDS instance monitoring, let's move on to something in the NoSQL department. In the next section, we will look at how to monitor Amazon DynamoDB

Logging operations in Amazon DynamoDB

We have already established that DynamoDB is a serverless NoSQL database engine. This service is proprietary to AWS, although you can get it as a **Docker** image here: `https://hub.docker.com/r/amazon/dynamodb-local`.

> **Important note**
> Docker is a containerization tool used to package applications, services, and operating systems to make deploying and running the same application in different operating systems much easier and faster.

The architecture of NoSQL databases is quite different from the relational database management system. For DynamoDB, AWS has abstracted a lot of the operational things that we should be worried about, so our focus on the metrics will be more on the database layer than the infrastructure running the database. In DynamoDB, one of the most critical metrics to watch out for is the database's read and write capacities. These determine the behavior and the availability of your DynamoDB tables. They are measured in **Read Capacity Units (RCU)** and **Write Capacity Units (WCU)**. The higher the RCU and WCU, the more money that's paid for the DynamoDB table. Apart from monitoring the table for availability, you could also monitor it to understand the money that's been spent and save more on costs by adjusting capacity provisioning accordingly.

Like every other service in AWS that requires monitoring, Amazon CloudWatch generates an automated dashboard. The following screenshot shows these dashboards:

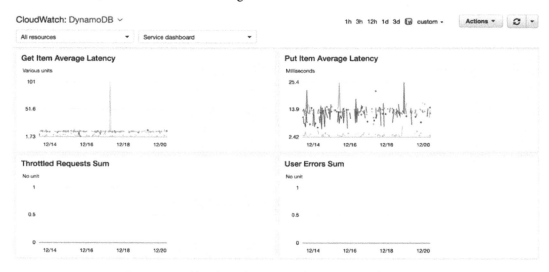

Figure 6.8 – CloudWatch automated DynamoDB dashboard

These graphs show the activities on the DynamoDB table and how it has been impacted over a certain period of time. A period of 1 week has been selected to show the different table activities.

One of the metrics shown here is called **Put Item Average Latency**. It is an operation in DynamoDB that is synonymous to INSERT INTO in SQL. It is the action of creating new data in the table. Data in DynamoDB is called an **item**. This metric measures the average time it takes (in seconds) to write a particular data or item into the DynamoDB table. The graphs shown in the preceding screenshot show that it takes about **25.4** milliseconds to write data into the DynamoDB table. This depends on the table it is writing to. The right-hand side of each graph shows a legend of the tables, and **Put Item Average Latency** varies from table to table. This metric can be helpful in finding out which tables are taking time to write to and configure an alarm based on a specific threshold. If any **Put Item Average Latency** operation takes more than 30 milliseconds to run, this means there is a problem, because this could impact the speed of the response of the application.

Another metric I would like us to talk about is **Consumed Write Capacity**. When a DynamoDB table is created (follow this documentation to learn how to create a DynamoDB table: https://docs.aws.amazon.com/amazondynamodb/latest/developerguide/getting-started-step-1.html), the WCU is configured, and this is the limit of the write capacity that the table can handle. This metric helps show the amount of WCU that has been consumed based on what has been configured. If the WCU that's been consumed is more than what was allocated, this will affect the performance of the DynamoDB table.

The graph in *Figure 6.8* shows the write capacity that's been consumed for different DynamoDB tables. The highest of them all is about **24**. This should be one of the tables with the -customer label on it. This graph can help you know when you are consuming high WCU and on which table, and help you plan for it accordingly to avoid downtime in the application while writing to the DynamoDB table. It can also be a deciding factor regarding whether you should use capacity autoscaling.

With this, we have entered the NoSQL space of databases. There is another service that is also in this space, known as the caching database. In the next section, we will learn how to monitor it. Like the other NoSQL databases, it does not use SQL queries to perform **CRUD** operations. But anyway, let's learn how to perform monitoring on this Amazon ElastiCache service.

Monitoring events in ElastiCache

Caching is an important aspect of any application. It helps improve the performance of the application by offloading certain database **I/O** operations to the cached database's storage. Just as we need to understand what is going on with the main database, we must also understand what is going on with our cache from time to time. We need to be able to carry out both proactive and reactive monitoring on our cache database engine. Our focus will be on the Redis option for ElastiCache.

Important note

I/O is an acronym for **Input/Output**. It is used to measure the communication of the input and output operations in a computer. I/O is primarily used in disks, where **I** means the **Input of information** and **O** means the **Output of information**. There is a metric called **IOps**, which means **Input/Output per second**. It is used to measure the speed at which data is written to a hard disk and received from the hard disk.

Just like other managed services, AWS handles the underlying infrastructure that hosts the Redis or Memcached database. Due to this, we will not be looking at monitoring the virtual machine that hosts the Memcached engine directly. Instead, we will look at a mix of the host metrics and the Memcached engine metrics. This is what will form the graph for the ElastiCache engine. Let's go through the steps of how to view the dashboard for an ElastiCache (use the following link to set up an ElastiCache cluster: `https://docs.aws.amazon.com/AmazonElastiCache/latest/mem-ug/Clusters.Create.CON.Memcached.html`):

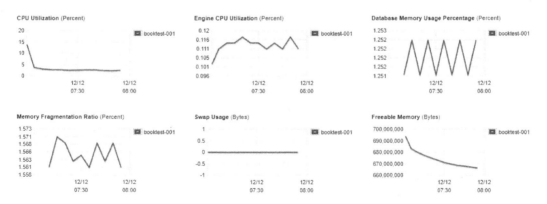

Figure 6.9 – ElastiCache monitoring dashboard

From the graphs in *Figure 6.9*, we can see that there are various metrics on this dashboard. Each metric gives us different types of insight into the behavior of the ElastiCache engine. The major resource that's used in the ElastiCache engine is memory. We also talked about a cache storing data in its memory, which makes it faster to perform I/O operations than the traditional relational or NoSQL database engines.

Based on this, we can conclusively say that one of the key metrics to always watch out for in ElastiCache is memory. From the preceding graph, we can see that there are various memory metrics that we can look at and get insights from. Ensuring that you keep a close eye on the metrics will help mitigate data loss. **Database Memory Usage Percentage** is the most basic of all metrics to watch out for. The consumption measure is shown as a percentage and tell us the total amount of memory that's used.

Another metric to watch out for is the **CPU Utilization** metric. Now, ElastiCache performs other background operations such as creating snapshots (making a backup of the current running database) that could be memory intensive in some situations, so it is wise to keep an eye on this and configure alarms to know when the numbers are going off the roof. Alarms can also be configured for **Database Memory Usage Percentage**, so that we know when it has gotten to, say, 80% utilization. In addition to memory, it is also important to monitor the number of connections that are being made to your cache database from time to time. If the connections are too high, it will impact the application(s) connecting to it that need to perform any kind of read or write operations.

Last but not the least, we have the **Events** section of the ElastiCache console. This serves as the auditor for your ElastiCache cluster. It gives us details of every event that has occurred in the cluster over time. It is a good source of information for what has happened external to the database engine itself. All the other monitoring has been on a dashboard that picks its data from the cache engine internally, but this is more of an external activity on the cluster. The following screenshot shows an example of the type of events that occur outside of an ElastiCache database:

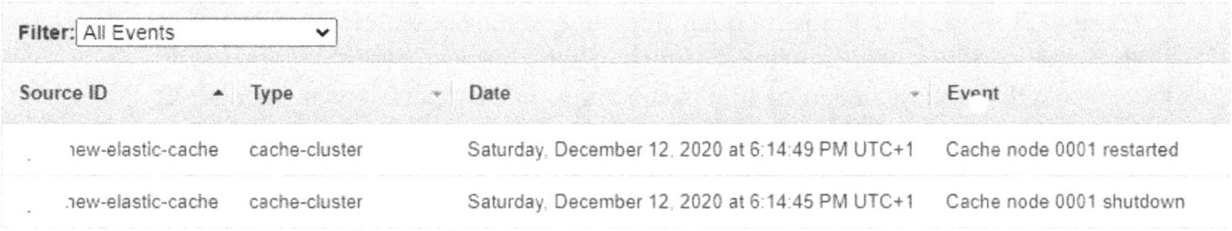

Filter: All Events			
Source ID ▲	Type ▼	Date ▼	Event
new-elastic-cache	cache-cluster	Saturday, December 12, 2020 at 6:14:49 PM UTC+1	Cache node 0001 restarted
new-elastic-cache	cache-cluster	Saturday, December 12, 2020 at 6:14:45 PM UTC+1	Cache node 0001 shutdown

Figure 6.10 – Events page in the ElastiCache console

The preceding screenshot shows that one of the nodes was shut down and restarted. This events also takes an audit of scaling information. If, for instance, a new node is added or deleted from the ElastiCache cluster, that activity is captured in this list. This is not information you can find on the monitoring dashboard of ElastiCache.

Now we know and understand the various important metrics for components that need to be monitored in ElastiCache; that is, memory, CPU, current connections, and the events of the ElastiCache cluster. Now, we will look at Redshift and Amazon DocumentDB. Let's learn how monitoring works before corroborating what we've learned.

Monitoring Redshift and Amazon DocumentDB cluster status

In this section, we will merge two services: Redshift, an AWS warehousing solution, and Amazon DocumentDB, a service for document databases that are also NoSQL databases. Redshift is mostly used for running big data and report workloads. Because of the huge amount of data it works with, it requires a unique type of technology, even though it comes from the relational SQL technology and has had some tweaks made to it to make it more efficient for querying terabytes to petabytes of data.

The ability to understand the performance of your Redshift cluster is as important as using the cluster to run those massive queries. If the queries are taking too long to respond, it is good to identify that in time and fix it accordingly. It is quite important to note this so that these issues can be spotted and resolved accordingly.

Amazon DocumentDB is like an RDS database in terms of setup and configuration. The Amazon DocumentDB service is compatible with MongoDB, which means that this is an AWS-managed MongoDB server. Due to this, it has all the features of the normal MongoDB database technology. This time, it is a managed service running in the AWS cloud, so it is made up of compute and storage resources from the user's AWS account. Let's look at how to use the default monitoring service and configure additional monitoring in our DocumentDB cluster.

> **Important note**
> MongoDB is one of the most popular document database technologies out there. MongoDB stores data in JSON format, which is also called documents. It is a NoSQL database, meaning that performing CRUD operations in MongoDB is not done through SQL statements. MongoDB has its own query language for performing CRUD operations in a Mongo database.

Monitoring Redshift

Redshift, being a **data warehouse** solution, has a lot of unique functionalities that are not common to the normal database engine.

> **Important note**
>
> A data warehouse is a large pool or collection of data that is collected from various sources within an organization. It helps business leaders and managers make more informed decisions. A data warehouse can also be used to collect a wide range of customer data so that we understand customer behavior and help sales personnel perform better due to having a better understanding of the customer.

Unlike a normal database, which is connected directly to an application and is where read and write operations are performed regularly, a data warehouse performs more read and fewer write operations. Complex queries are also run in the data warehouse in order to retrieve information from the huge amount of data that has been written to it. They are also used to generate different kinds of reports and are connected to business intelligence and other analytics tools to produce charts and graphs.

There are two major components of a Redshift cluster that need proper monitoring: *cluster performance* and *query monitoring*. First, let's look at cluster performance in detail.

Cluster performance

This is focused more on the infrastructure that is running the Redshift cluster. This performance is what determines the behavior of the queries and the Redshift engine itself. If any of the metrics in cluster performance have any anomalies, this will cascade into the Redshift engine and affect the queries that are running in Redshift. The main metrics in cluster performance are CPU utilization, percentage disk space used, database connections, health status, query duration, and auto vacuum space freed.

The following screenshot shows the cluster performance dashboard of a Redshift cluster. All these metrics are important to monitor. A good practice would be configuring the alarm threshold on all these metrics to ensure that you are pre-informed of them:

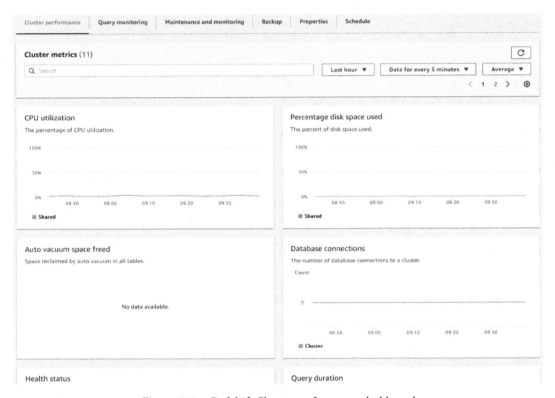

Figure 6.11 – Redshift Cluster performance dashboard

Now, let's look at query monitoring and see how it differs from cluster performance monitoring.

Query monitoring

The performance of a system is directly proportional to the code it is given. Understanding which queries are taking longer than normal is important in helping to optimize and rewrite faster and more efficient queries.

One more thing we must mention is Redshift's events and event subscription. This is a good way to get alarms sent to you when anything happens to your Redshift cluster. But what is wonderful about Redshift events is that they can send both information and error notifications. This means you can streamline the notification to receive an error notification so that you are only alerted by Redshift when something negative happens to your Redshift cluster. The events that are monitored by Redshift events are put into five major categories: management, monitoring, security, configuration, and pending. Let's create an event subscription that will send us an SNS notification when there is a security issue of some sort:

1. Log in to the AWS management console and navigate to Redshift.

2. In the Redshift console, click the **Events** icon on the left-hand side of the screen to reveal a list of clusters that have been created in Redshift (follow this link to create a new Redshift cluster: `https://docs.aws.amazon.com/redshift/latest/gsg/rs-gsg-launch-sample-cluster.html`):

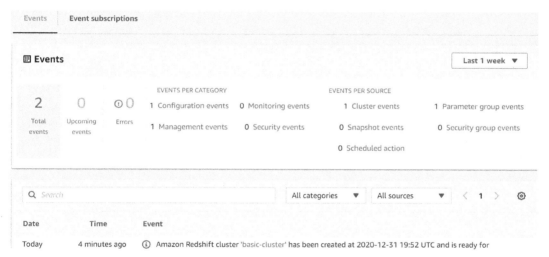

Figure 6.12 – Redshift Events page

3. Click on the **Events subscriptions** tab to see a list of events subscriptions and where we can also create an event subscription. Click on the **Create event subscription** button.

4. Fill in the form by writing the name of the event subscription. Then, select the source type. For our example, we will use **All**. For the categories, select the option management from the drop-down list.

5. Under **Subscription Actions**, choose the **Enable** option to enable this subscription and select the SNS topic you wish to use to receive notifications from. If you do not have an SNS topic created initially, use the following link to create a topic that sends emails: `https://docs.aws.amazon.com/sns/latest/dg/sns-email-notifications.html`.

6. After selecting the SNS topic, click on the **Create event subscription** button.

7. This will create the subscription in the list, and if any of those security events occur in the Redshift cluster, you will be notified accordingly.

You can get more metrics and graphs when you go to the CloudWatch console and go to the Redshift automated dashboard. Now, let's look at Amazon DocumentDB and see how monitoring works there.

Monitoring an Amazon DocumentDB cluster

Amazon DocumentDB is a managed service, so we are not so concerned with the underlying infrastructure running the DocumentDB cluster, but more about the metrics and graphs displayed to us on the AWS console. This dashboard contains default fundamental metrics such as CPU utilization memory and disk utilization. But our focus here will be on a new set of metrics that are peculiar. We can also view the metrics and graphs for these by performing the following steps:

1. Log in to the AWS management console and navigate to Amazon DocumentDB.

2. Click on the DocumentDB that already exists or go to `https://docs.aws.amazon.com/documentdb/latest/developerguide/get-started-guide.html#cloud9-cluster` to create a sample DocumentDB.

3. Then, click on the **Monitoring** tab, which is part of the options when you click on a running DocumentDB cluster (follow this [] to see how to create a DocumentDB cluster), just after the **Configuration** tab. Here, you can view the different graphs for that DocumentDB cluster, as shown in the following screenshot:

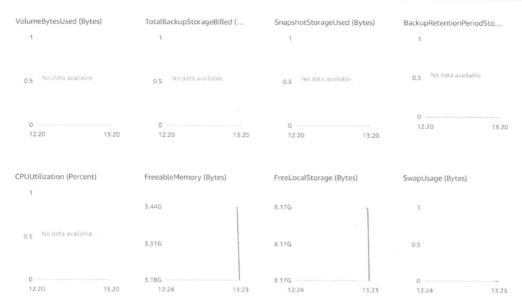

Figure 6.13 – Amazon DocumentDB dashboard

4. This shows us the common CPU and memory metrics we have been talking about in different databases in this chapter. Scrolling down a little more will take us to more graphs that are specific to Amazon DocumentDB, as shown in the following screenshot:

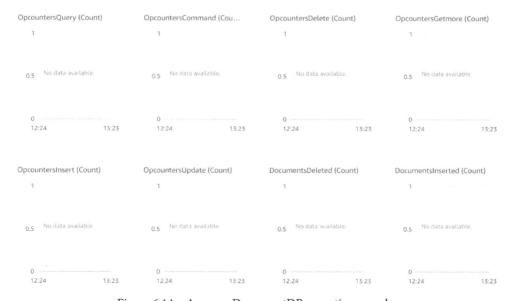

Figure 6.14 – Amazon DocumentDB operations graphs

Here, we can see the operations graphs for DocumentDB. These are specific metrics showing the behavior of the read and write operations of your DocumentDB cluster. It also shows you information about documents that have been deleted and a count of what has been inserted into your DocumentDB.

You can also enable logging for your DocumentDB while creating the DocumentDB cluster. If the DocumentDB instance is already created, no problem. Use the following steps to activate logging on the DocumentDB instance. Select the DocumentDB cluster and click on the **Modify** button to apply these changes. Then, scroll down to the **Log exports** section, as shown in the following screenshot:

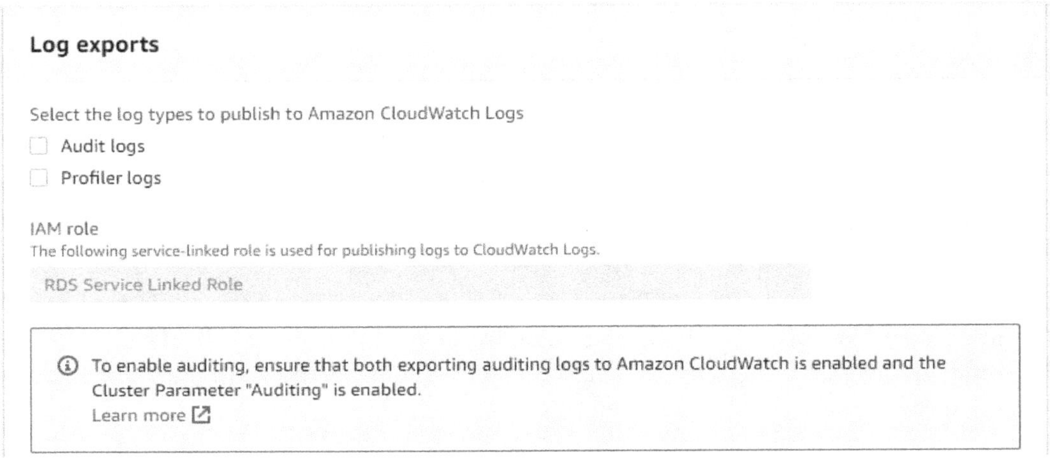

Log exports

Select the log types to publish to Amazon CloudWatch Logs

☐ Audit logs

☐ Profiler logs

IAM role
The following service-linked role is used for publishing logs to CloudWatch Logs.

RDS Service Linked Role

ⓘ To enable auditing, ensure that both exporting auditing logs to Amazon CloudWatch is enabled and the Cluster Parameter "Auditing" is enabled.
Learn more ↗

Figure 6.15 – Activating Log exports in DocumentDB

Click the checkboxes for **Audit logs** and **Profiler logs** to activate them. Note that, by default, this will send the logs to Amazon CloudWatch logs. When you're done, click **Continue** (if you are modifying an existing DocumentDB cluster) or **Create cluster** (if you are creating a new cluster).

With this, we have learned how to configure logging for our DocumentDB cluster, as well as how to monitor the cluster with the graph that is generated from the DocumentDB console. You can view more metrics in the CloudWatch automated dashboard for DocumentDB. Navigate to CloudWatch and select **DocDB** from the list of services in the CloudWatch management console to do so.

Case study on monitoring an RDS database

Johnson, who is the solutions architect of ABC enterprise, has finished a meeting with the engineering manager. That day was Black Friday, and many of the users coming to the website are going there for the first time, so there are going to be a lot of login operations connecting to the RDS database. They are observing a lot of funny things happening in production, including huge memory consumption in the RDS database. You have been able to confirm that there are lots of database connections, but you are not sure why, although the memory consumption from the dashboard also shows that there is a huge use of memory. How can you figure out, from the SQL queries alone, the most used queries and recommend a re-architecture of the application to help improve the reliability of the system?

Solution

To figure out what is wrong, we need to pull up the Performance Insights page of the database. With that, we can view the top SQL queries that are being sent to the database. Since it is Black Friday, and most customers are new, there is a chance that there will be lots of login operations going on with the database. Now, RDS databases do not perform very well when the login operation is at that level, so a good recommendation would be to move that to a cache database such as Amazon ElastiCache, which will handle that amount of login load and run other, more transactional operations on the RDS database.

Summary

Databases are the source of truth for every application. The availability of your database to be able to receive both write and read requests determines the life of your application. Losing data in any aspect of your database for reasons such as unavailability is unacceptable at all levels. Monitoring your database helps you understand the behavior of your database from time to time. We have spent time in this chapter looking at the different database technologies that exist; that is, the relational database management system and the NoSQL database system. We have also spent time looking at how these categories have related AWS services, such as RDS and DynamoDB, ElastiCache, and Redshift.

We also went further and looked at how monitoring works for each of these components. We looked at the DB load, which is the main metric in RDS, and we established that it is an aggregate of different metrics but gives you a bird's-eye view of the database's performance. We also looked at key metrics that determine the behavior of your DynamoDB table.

Next, we looked at ElastiCache, which is a type of cache database, and we also looked at the graph in *Figure 6.9* and analyzed the importance of the memory metric on the ElastiCache database. Lastly, we talked about Redshift monitoring and what to look for when we need to understand the behavior of our Redshift cluster.

We hope this chapter has been able to equip you with the right knowledge and skills to understand the behavior of your database at any point in time, and to know where to look when monitoring the different database technologies in your AWS workload. Note that managed databases are made up of three major parts that must be monitored: the compute resource, the storage resource, and the database's performance and response to applications connecting to it.

In the next chapter, we will be looking at monitoring from another perspective, which is from the angle of serverless applications. We will explore AWS services such as Lambda and step functions and learn how to monitor applications built with those services.

Questions

1. What metric is the most important in RDS for measuring database performance?

2. Which database technology matches with a NoSQL database?

3. How do you monitor DynamoDB tables?

4. There are CPU or database operations that require some delay before they can complete. What is the technical name for this delay?

Further reading

Please refer to the following links for more information on the topics that were covered in this chapter:

- DynamoDB with Boto3: `https://www.packtpub.com/product/rds-postgresql-and-dynamodb-crud-aws-with-python-and-boto3-video/9781838649722`

- Introduction to AWS RDS: `https://www.packtpub.com/product/aws-masterclass-databases-in-the-cloud-with-aws-rds-video/9781789539127`

- Why Redis?: `https://www.packtpub.com/product/mastering-redis/9781783988181`

- Getting Started with DynamoDB: `https://www.packtpub.com/product/mastering-dynamodb/9781783551958`

- Introduction to NoSQL in Azure CosmosDB: `https://www.packtpub.com/product/guide-to-nosql-with-azure-cosmos-db/9781789612899`

- Introduction to MongoDB: `https://www.packtpub.com/product/mongodb-essentials-a-complete-mongodb-guide-video/9781789952438`

7
Monitoring Serverless Applications

The previous chapter exposed to us the different ways of monitoring different AWS database technologies. We went from relational to non-relational databases, also called NoSQL databases. We then moved on to the cache database, and for that, we worked with Amazon ElastiCache, Redshift, and Amazon DocumentDB, and saw the different graphs that are generated automatically and the important metrics in these graphs that we should pay close attention to.

This chapter is going to take us on a new ride. We will be introducing the concept of serverless and talk about monitoring on some select AWS serverless services. We shall clarify the difference between serverless and managed services, which can be confusing in a lot of cases, but we shall demystify that in this chapter. Then, we shall introduce endpoint monitoring, which we talked about in *Chapter 1, Introduction to Monitoring*. It is a type of reactive monitoring that responds after a failure has occurred. We shall configure the monitoring using a CloudWatch Synthetics canary.

We shall move further to look at other serverless services, such as **Simple Notification Service (SNS)**, **Simple Queue Service (SQS)**, and Amazon Step Functions, which are serverless services used to develop different types of applications for different use cases.

We will cover the following topic in this chapter:

- Introduction to serverless
- Differentiating between serverless and managed services
- Monitoring Lambda function metrics with Amazon CloudWatch
- Endpoint monitoring for API Gateway and other applications
- Monitoring SQS and SNS on Amazon CloudWatch
- Monitoring Step Functions using CloudWatch alarms
- Case study on Lambda tracing with Amazon X-Ray

Technical requirements

To be able to accomplish the technical tasks in the chapter, you will need to have the following technical pre-requisites:

- A working AWS account (you can opt for the free tier, which will cost $0/month for 1 year)
- Basic knowledge of serverless (https://aws.amazon.com/serverless/)
- Basic understanding of messaging and queues (https://aws.amazon.com/sqs/)
- Basic understanding of state machines (https://docs.aws.amazon.com/step-functions/latest/dg/amazon-states-language-state-machine-structure.html)

Check out the following link to see the Code in Action video:

https://bit.ly/30vPJ4b

Introduction to serverless

As much as it is a buzzword, the term serverless has been used in more ways than you can imagine. But what is serverless? Why would anyone want to go serverless? Before we talk about something being serverless, let's understand what a server is. In *Chapter 4, Monitoring AWS Compute Services*, we talked about monitoring compute services, so an example of a server is an EC2 instance. In the EC2 scenario, you will be in charge of performing operating system updates, security patches, network security, scaling of applications deployed in EC2 instances, and every other operation you need to perform to keep the application up and running.

What serverless means is that you do not have to worry about all the operational work involved in managing the server. In serverless computing, you focus only on the application that has been built and deployed. You do not have to worry about scaling the server; the serverless design performs the scaling based on the traffic that the application has and does it on demand. Serverless can scale up during load and scale down when the traffic has dropped. This makes serverless a go-to service for start-ups and large enterprises alike, as it cuts down on the **Operational Expense (OpEX)** by almost 90% and also ensures that your applications that are deployed in a serverless architecture are reliable, available, and highly efficient.

Apart from serverless compute, there is also serverless storage. The concept of not having to manage any storage infrastructure also comes into play here. In serverless storage, you do not have to manage the underlying infrastructure that stores data. You also do not have to worry about scaling the storage of data. In some cases, you can have almost unlimited storage. Amazon S3 is a serverless storage service that can be used to store any kind of file/object data. S3 has no limit to the amount of data it can store. Terabytes to exabytes of data can all be stored in Amazon S3, and you never get a sense of it getting filled up. You also do not have to worry so much about the integrity of the data stored in S3.

This same concept of serverless and off-loading operational complexities from the user is the whole goal behind serverless. With this model, software engineers, system administrators, and DevOps engineers can focus more on the reliability and availability of the application more than focusing on both the application and the infrastructure when you oversee hosting and managing the full setup end to end.

Some of the most popular AWS serverless services are as follows:

- AWS Lambda
- Step Functions
- Amazon S3
- Amazon **Elastic File System (EFS)**
- DynamoDB
- Aurora Serverless for MySQL/PostgreSQL
- Amazon Kinesis
- AWS Glue
- Amazon Sagemaker
- Amazon QuickSight
- All the AWS machine learning services

Each of these services is used for various cases from application hosting and database storage to network and object storage, **extraction, transformation, and loading (ETL)** for data engineering, and machine learning and **artificial intelligence (AI)** services.

Since we now understand what serverless is, let's try to debunk a confusion that looms around the tech world that could also be confusing in this book. The next section is going to clearly explain the difference between a managed service and a serverless service.

Differentiating between serverless and managed services

We have been talking about the concept of managed services in this book. In the previous chapter, we discussed the different database services in **Relational Database System (RDS)**. In a managed service, though you do not have direct access to the infrastructure hosting the service, you are given the liberty to configure the scaling needs and to perform system patch updates yourself. You also have to learn how to configure, manage, and maintain replication in the database.

In a serverless database, you have no such worries about how it is going to be scaled. You configure the initial capacity units you need for the application. As the demand for more database infrastructure units is needed, the serverless database scales automatically without the user having to make any application code changes.

While in a managed system, a change or upgrade from the current version to a new version could lead to downtimes of almost 8–10 minutes before the new changes or upgrades. You are also in charge of security patches that need to be applied to the database, which could also take a couple of minutes for the new update to be applied to the database.

In serverless, you do not have to worry about security patches and updates to your database. All of this is managed automatically for you by AWS, hence cutting off downtime during upgrades and allowing the AWS team to make modifications and changes to the database with no downtime noticed in the database.

In a nutshell, the scaling of application requests and security of the services is what serverless gives, but for managed services, you might have to perform some operational work to get the database up and running again.

We now understand the difference between serverless services and managed services. The next step is to look at the monitoring of applications deployed in a serverless compute service. We shall begin by looking at monitoring in an AWS Lambda function.

Monitoring Lambda function metrics with Amazon CloudWatch

AWS Lambda was the first serverless application service built by AWS. When developers build an application, the next thing they need is a server provisioned for them with some specifications for CPU, memory, and disk at least. Now, the system administrators and DevOps engineers are tasked with ensuring the infrastructure that has been provisioned is enough to keep the application running. If for any reason more resources are needed, then the onus is on AWS to provide that infrastructure to avoid any downtime on the application running within the server that has been provisioned.

This has made operations teams grow larger because the more customers and users the company acquires for the application, the more engineers will need to be employed to manage the scale of the application, both from the development and operations perspective. It requires operations engineers that understand how to design and plan for an application that scales from hundreds to thousands of users and understand how to handle failures effectively, as well as operating system upgrades, patches, and strategies to increase resources without causing downtime for the users of the application.

> **Important Note**
>
> Operations engineer is the general term used for engineers who manage, secure, scale, and set up software infrastructure. Operations engineers are system administrators, security engineers (application, network, and infrastructure), database administrators, DevOps engineers, infrastructure engineers, DevOps analysts, and more. Their role is quite different from the software engineer/software developer.

This could be a lot of skills required for a single person or team. Hence, the AWS Lambda service cuts down these operational complexities by 70–80%. When using Lambda to deploy and run applications, you do not have to worry about managing any servers or scaling infrastructure. All you need to do is deploy the written application into the Lambda function and the services take care of the rest. Although you might need to allocate the amount of memory your application will need to run, that is the only major resource that needs to be configured. The rest is history. You sit back and relax, and AWS takes care of the rest of the operational work involved in operating patching, security, and scaling. This reduces the workload on the operational team.

Hey, before we get caught up in all the beautiful things we can do with Lambda, our book is focused on monitoring, so let's switch gears here. Now, monitoring is part of the operational tasks for the operations engineers. But Lambda functions are quite different from the other compute services we discussed in *Chapter 4, Monitoring AWS Compute Services*, and *Chapter 5, Setting Up Container Insights on Amazon CloudWatch*. This also means that monitoring for Lambda functions will be different. We do not have access to the server used in Lambda because it is serverless. But we still need to monitor our application to know what is going on from time to time and configure metrics and alarms that will help give insights and send a notification when any kind of anomaly is discovered in the application behavior.

Lambda, in conjunction with Amazon CloudWatch, has a rich set of methods for monitoring the behavior of your Lambda application. You are also able to view both the application logs of the application running as a Lambda function and the logs of the service itself running the application. The reason it is called a **function** is that that is the basis for which the application runs. The application starts from a function that we call the **handler**. This starts the application. Lambda functions run for a short period of time and give a response within that period. The maximum time a Lambda function can run for now is 15 minutes. When a function starts, it is called an **invocation**. Functions are triggered by various means: EventBridge, API Gateway, AWS IoT, application load balancer, CloudWatch Logs, CodeCommit, DynamoDB, Kinesis, Amazon MQ, MSK, S3, SNS, and SQS.

The most basic metric in a Lambda function is the invocation count. This is the count of the number of invocations made by the function. This means how many times the application has run. Remember that Lambda does not run on its own; it needs to be triggered to run the application code that has been deployed to it. The Lambda console in the AWS management console has a monitoring tab for every function that is created.

To view the basic metrics of a function, use the following steps:

1. Log in to the AWS management console and navigate to Lambda. This will take us to the Lambda console.

2. Click on the function if you already have one. You can create a simple Lambda function with the following guide: `https://docs.aws.amazon.com/lambda/latest/dg/getting-started-create-function.html`.

3. Click on the **Monitoring** tab, just after the **Permissions** tab. This will show the graphs and metrics for your Lambda function, as in the following screenshot:

Figure 7.1 – Lambda function monitoring console

Looking at the preceding screenshot, we can see a couple of metrics and graphs that can help give us some insight into the characteristics of the Lambda function. The first graph has the label **Invocations**. This is the number of invocations that your function has made since its creation. This is a count of the number of times the function has been triggered or called.

We already mentioned that a Lambda function has a maximum of 15 minutes to run a function. The next metric shows you how long a function is taking to run. Now, one thing that makes this metric important is to know how long a task is taking so that the code could be optimized to reduce the time if it is taking too long. You might want to increase the time to the maximum, which is 15 minutes. But when your application needs to either read/write to a DynamoDB table, it should not take that long. So, this graph can show us if a function is taking too long to run and we can figure out what could be causing the problem.

The next metric is **Error count and success rate**. This graph/metric is an extra step up from the invocation count. Every Lambda trigger leads to the function code running. So, either the code runs successfully or the code has a bug and it fails. This metric helps you to know the number of times the function ran successfully or failed. The rate of error or success is measured in percentage, so you can easily spot the percentage of failure or success your Lambda function has attained. When there is a failure, you can dig deeper from the failure in the graph into the logs of the application.

Lambda sends the logs of your application to Amazon CloudWatch and aggregates them neatly into CloudWatch log groups with the format /aws/lambda/[name-of-function], where [name-of-function] represents the name of the Lambda function that has been created. When you click on the log group, you will be able to see the log stream (each stream contains the day in which the log has been collected), and clicking on the log stream will eventually show the log data for the function. The following screenshot is an example of a log from an AWS Lambda function:

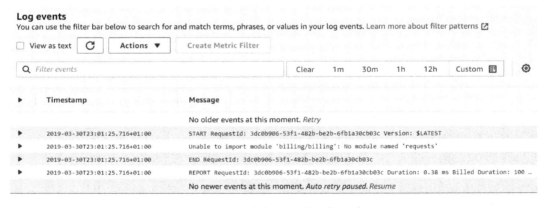

Figure 7.2 – Lambda logs in CloudWatch Logs

The preceding screenshot is a sample of a log from Lambda. The actual log to look at is the second line, which states **Unable to import module 'billing/billing': No module name 'requests'**. That is the actual application log. For an application running in production, there is going to be a long list of logs. Logs being created here does not necessarily mean that the function failed but depends on how the developer decides to configure logging in the application. Most times, the default logging function is used for the programming language, or a print to send the output. The CloudWatch logs serve as the stdout for the programming language.

> **Important Note**
> **stdout**, also known as **standard output**, is the default output where messages and information are made visible to the user in the Unix/Linux terminal. Whenever an `echo` command or `print` command is used either in Linux Bash or Python programming, that signal is sent to the stdout, which is what makes it visible to the user.

There are many ways to understand what is going on with your application running in AWS Lambda. We have talked about the graphs/metrics and showed where we can find the logs of the function. The last concept that is used to understand the behavior of your Lambda function is called **observability**. Observability comes from the word observe. This is the senior brother of monitoring. Now, from the beginning of this book up to this point, we have been showing you how to monitor what is going on in your application after it has happened, which is what logs and metrics are doing for you. What about seeing what is going on with your application in real time and quickly reacting to it before it becomes logs that you have to react to after it has happened?

Let me introduce you to observability. Observability of your application is being able to follow your application as it is working and see things as they happen, the ability to see the internal states and workings of your application during run time. It is built on these three pillars:

- Tracing
- Metrics
- Logs

With these three concepts, you can understand deeper what is going on with the system from the inside. The AWS service that makes this possible is AWS X-Ray. This service can trace requests moving across the different application services or Lambda functions that are running. By embedding the X-Ray SDK in your application, you can get a map of the application architecture and trace the path of every request made to the application. This makes it easy and fast to locate failure across a route of requests. AWS X-Ray can show the request coming from the user/customer and how it moves from function to function and the destination.

Lambda Insights is another method that can be used to monitor your function. It is a feature that was recently launched in CloudWatch. It gives deeper insights than the previous graphs you have seen in the Lambda console. If you need to get an understanding of what each Lambda function is costing and easily isolate performance problems, then Lambda Insights is the best tool to use.

We have learned about logging, graphs, and metrics in CloudWatch for Lambda functions. We have also seen the different ways of monitoring and observing our Lambda functions. We have also used the medium to introduce observability and understood what makes it different from monitoring.

It is time for us to talk more about a part of monitoring we introduced in *Chapter 1, Introduction to Monitoring*, when we talked about types of monitoring. Let's go to the next section and talk about endpoint monitoring and see how it can be configured for not just API Gateway but any application running on the HTTP protocol.

Endpoint monitoring for API Gateway and other applications

We have been talking about metrics, logging, and being able to see what happens, and configuring alarms based on the logs and metrics generated from the logs. This method of monitoring is good but could take a while to configure and get up and running. There is another type of monitoring that gives an immediate response to the availability of your system. While logs and metrics give you internal information, endpoint monitoring gives you external feedback based on what users and customers are experiencing. It is very possible for your application to be running smoothly, with no logs and no bugs, yet your users and customers will not be able to use the application because they cannot access it.

Endpoint monitoring is the technique of sending pings intermittently to your application URL or endpoint to get feedback about whether it is up and running. This technique, on a basic level, rides on the HTTP protocol status codes.

> **Important Note**
>
> **HTTP** is an acronym for **HyperText Transfer Protocol**. It is the protocol used to transmit text, images, video, and other multimedia content over the TCP/IP protocol or the internet. It comprises a request/response scheme. The request is sent by an application to a server and receives a response. The application could be a web browser requesting a website; the response is received from the server and the website is displayed in the browser.

The HTTP status codes are a way of knowing whether a request was sent successfully or not. We have established that HTTP is a request/response paradigm. But not every request sent comes back successfully. When the response is returned, it comes with certain information that makes us know what caused the failure of our request. These issues have been categorized into a set of status codes. The following table shows the HTTP status codes and the codes that mean success and the ones that mean failure:

Status Code	Technical Meaning	Literal Meaning
200, 201, 202	Success	Everything is working fine.
301, 302	Temporary/Permanent Redirect	Everything is working fine.
401	Unauthorized Access	You do not have the right access.
404	Not Found	Application has a problem, a specific file/path is not found.
501, 502, 503	Server Error	Something is wrong with the web server.

Table 7.1 – HTTP status codes

This can be used as a reference to know whether a request is successful or it has failed. These response status codes are not visible to the user in the browser; instead, they are injected in the HTTP header payload. The following screenshot shows HTTP response headers:

▼ General

Request URL: https://ssl.gstatic.com/gb/images/a/99be7c5086.png

Request Method: GET

Status Code: ● 200

Remote Address: 216.58.223.227:443

Referrer Policy: origin

▼ Response Headers

accept-ranges: bytes

age: 198498

alt-svc: h3-29=":443"; ma=2592000,h3-T051=":443"; ma=2592000,h3-Q050=":44
3"; ma=2592000,h3-Q046=":443"; ma=2592000,h3-Q043=":443"; ma=2592000,quic
=":443"; ma=2592000; v="46,43"

cache-control: public, max-age=31536000

content-length: 4608

content-type: image/png

cross-origin-resource-policy: cross-origin

date: Wed, 23 Dec 2020 14:43:06 GMT

expires: Thu, 23 Dec 2021 14:43:06 GMT

last-modified: Tue, 22 Oct 2019 18:15:00 GMT

server: sffe

vary: Origin

x-content-type-options: nosniff

x-xss-protection: 0

Figure 7.3 – HTTP response payload

This understanding of HTTP status codes is what we are going to use to explain how the endpoint monitoring service in AWS works. This service is called **AWS CloudWatch Synthetics canaries**. It is part of the Amazon CloudWatch service. What Synthetics canaries do is perform intermittent HTTP calls to your application and get a response.

If it receives the 200 status code from calling your application, then it means the application responded appropriately. If there is any other status code that is not around 2xx (200, 201, 202), then it means the application/server did not respond well, meaning something is wrong with it.

> **Important Note**
>
> Endpoint is a generic name used for a **Universal Resource Locator** (URL) or website name. It is usually used for the paths that are associated with an **Application Program Interface** (API). But it can be used as a generic term for any URL whether it uses HTTP protocol or not. For example, the endpoint/URL for the Packt Publishing website is www.packtpub.com.

Synthetics is able to do this via a schedule and a Lambda function configured inside of it. In that way, it sends HTTP requests to your URL or endpoint and does this based on the schedule that has been configured for it. The service is fully serverless; there is no server management or crontab configuration for scheduled operations. There are different kinds of canaries, but we shall be setting up a basic canary that will monitor the official website of Packt Publishing, which is www.packtpub.com. To create a canary to monitor the uptime of that URL, we shall use the following steps:

1. Log in to the AWS management console and navigate to **CloudWatch**.

2. In the CloudWatch console, go to the bottom-left sidebar and click on **Canaries** under the **Synthetics** option, as shown in the following screenshot:

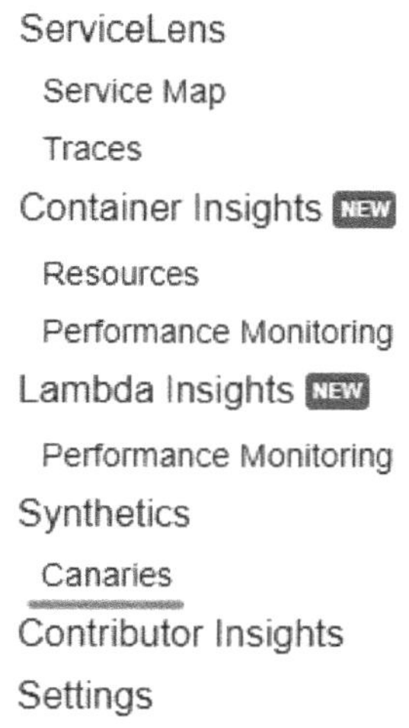

ServiceLens

  Service Map

  Traces

Container Insights [NEW]

  Resources

  Performance Monitoring

Lambda Insights [NEW]

  Performance Monitoring

Synthetics

  Canaries

Contributor Insights

Settings

Figure 7.4 – Navigating to Synthetics canaries

This will take you to the **Canaries** dashboard.

3. Click on the **Create canary** button on the screen to create a new canary. There are various options for creating a canary. We shall stick to the first option, which states **Use a blueprint**. We shall also be doing Heartbeat monitoring.

4. The next step is to enter the name we want to call the canary. For our example, we shall use the name `monitoringpacktsite`.

5. The next box asks for the application or endpoint URL. We shall put the URL for the Packt Publishing website, which is `packtpub.com`. Please note that you can put any URL here that you wish to monitor:

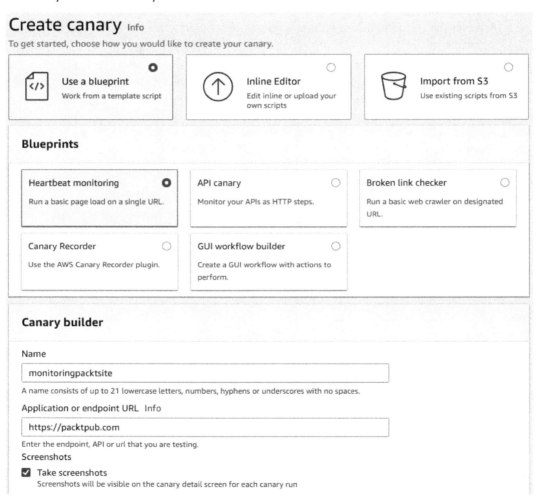

Figure 7.5 – Creating a canary

6. By default, the canary takes a screenshot of the page, so we shall leave that default option. Scrolling down shows the Lambda function that the Synthetics canary will be using to ping the endpoint. The next option scrolling down is the schedule. The default schedule is 5 minutes, which means that the website will be called every 5 minutes to check whether the status code returns 200. To help figure things out faster, the time can be reduced to 1 minute.

7. We shall leave the other options and scroll to the bottom and click the **Create canary** button.

    A canary takes a while before it is created. When it is created, it will need to send requests to the endpoint for a while to receive data that it can show in the canary dashboard.

    The following screenshot is the canary dashboard for the one we just created:

Figure 7.6 – Canaries dashboard

8. In the preceding screenshot, we can see that the canary has run for a couple of hours, and the results say **Passed**, meaning that the website is up and running and has returned HTTP status code 200 over that time. We could go deeper and see more interesting information. So, I will click on the **monitoringpacktsite** canary name to view more information. On the details page, click on the **Monitoring** tab to view monitoring details about the canary:

Figure 7.7 – Canary monitoring metrics

The screenshot shows more details about the canary. There are lots of metrics here, but the two graphs/metrics take quite a lot of the attention here. First is **Duration**, which shows us how much time in seconds it takes the web page to load completely. This metric is important for frontend engineers and website designers so that they can know how to optimize the website to load faster. The time showing here is about **19.8** seconds.

The second is the **Ok (2xx)** metric, which is the metric that shows the count of status 2xx status codes that have been received. 2xx, by the way, is used to represent any status codes in the range of 200–299, which are all deemed to be successes in the definition of HTTP status codes.

Endpoint monitoring with Synthetics canaries makes it easy to configure monitoring for APIs and HTTP endpoints. It is also quite easy to configure for any URL. This means that a Synthetics canary can be used to monitor the availability of a website and can go further to tell you how long it takes your website to load. The next step is to look at the monitoring of other serverless services. We shall look at how to monitor and know when our messages do not send in **SNS** and learn about queues in **Amazon SQS**.

Monitoring SQS and SNS on Amazon CloudWatch

SQS and SNS are similar services used generally as messaging services. SQS is mostly used for application messaging while SNS is mostly used for application-to-device messaging. In most cases, it can be confusing for users to know when to use which service. So, when you want to perform an asynchronous task in an application, SQS is the right service. But when you need to send an email, SMS or request to a HTTP endpoint, SNS is the right option to choose.

> **Important Note**
>
> An asynchronous task is one that does not give feedback immediately. It is usually used when performing batch processing or a huge number of transactions. Those transactions are queued in a messaging system and the transactions/requests are processed intermittently. An example is in the payment of staff salaries; the payment does not come in immediately for everyone, but instead it comes in batches.

SQS is a distributed message queuing service for storing transactional messages to be processed asynchronously. It is a managed service, meaning that AWS is in charge of scaling and securing the service. But to ensure that SQS is running efficiently, we need to monitor it and be able to know when there are issues with our SQS service.

When you create an SQS queue, the service automatically generates a dashboard based on the instance of the SQS service that has been created. To view monitoring metrics for the queue, click on the queue itself to view the standard graphs and metrics created by AWS automatically.

Click on the **Monitoring** tab to view the graphs. You can create a simple SQS queue here, `https://docs.aws.amazon.com/AWSSimpleQueueService/latest/SQSDeveloperGuide/sqs-configure-create-queue.html`, with a Lambda trigger that will consume the messages entering the SQS queue with this link: `https://docs.aws.amazon.com/AWSSimpleQueueService/latest/SQSDeveloperGuide/sqs-configure-lambda-function-trigger.html`.

The following is an example of graphs from an SQS queue:

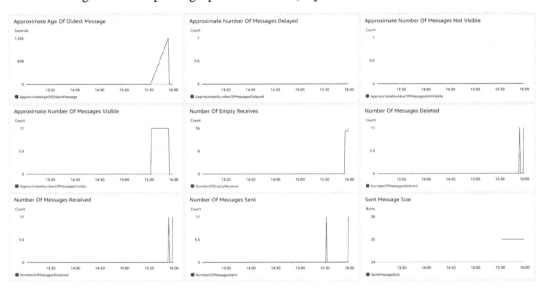

Figure 7.8 – SQS monitoring console

In the preceding screenshot, we can see different graphs showing the state of messages that have been sent to the queue and received and deleted. This is a proper view to always know the status of messages going in and out of the queue. This serves as the dashboard in knowing whether a message sent to the queue arrived, or whether the message has been deleted. You are also able to see the size of the message that has been sent in kilobytes.

SNS does not have a console for monitoring; instead, you will have to navigate to CloudWatch to view the metrics generated by the SNS topic. It is automatically generated by the CloudWatch automated dashboard when an SNS topic is created. The following screenshot is a sample of the graphs and metrics generated by an SNS topic:

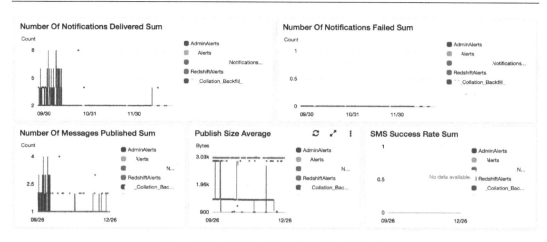

Figure 7.9 – SNS dashboard on CloudWatch

The preceding screenshot with graphs is able to give us a summary of different metrics based on the SNS topic and the messages that have been delivered in total.

With this, we now see how to monitor and track activities in both SQS and SNS services. It is easier to know the status of messages in the SQS queue from the dashboard and act accordingly, while the SNS dashboard provided by CloudWatch shows information about failed notifications for which alarms can be configured.

Next, we will look at how monitoring works in another interesting AWS service called Step Functions. We shall define step functions, talk about use cases, and see how to monitor step functions.

Monitoring Step Functions using CloudWatch alarms

When you have a step-by-step workflow and you need to coordinate it using a service, then AWS **Step Functions** is the service for that. Step Functions makes it easy for non-engineers to be able to set up a step-by-step workflow using a state machine. Say, for example, you want to create a flow that receives customer information, sifts through the data and collects emails, and sends feedback to the customer based on information found in the biodata. Let's assume we want to find out whether a customer's age is eligible for the service. This is a flow that has four stages:

1. Collect customer/user information.
2. Get the email from the customer data.

3. Check for information about the age of the customer to see whether it is over the eligible age.

4. Send back an email notifying the customer of whether they are eligible or not.

This is a step-by-step workflow of being able to filter those who are eligible for a service or not. Step Functions has a rich **user interface** (**UI**) for creating a workflow for a scenario like this. It uses state machines to achieve its workflow design.

> **Important Note**
> A state machine is a collection of states or tasks and the relationships that exist between those states with their inputs and outputs. The output of a state determines the input of the next state and it goes on and on until the process is complete.

Step Functions usually works in conjunction with AWS services. You can connect Step Functions to a couple of Lambda functions. If you have some Lambda functions created and you want them to run a specific coordinated manner or pattern, then Step Functions is the tool to coordinate that. A list of AWS services that Step Functions integrates seamlessly with is as follows:

- Lambda
- AWS Batch
- DynamoDB
- Amazon ECS
- Amazon SNS
- Amazon SQS
- AWS Glue
- Amazon SageMaker
- Amazon EMR
- Step Functions
- AWS CodeBuild
- API Gateway
- Amazon EKS
- AWS Fargate

Step functions are made up of events that give us information on the states of each state in the workflow. We are looking at monitoring our step functions to find out whatever happens when the step function is running. The events in a state machine are as follows:

- **Execution started**: This is the state in which the execution of the step function has started.

- **Execution succeeded**: This means that the execution process of the step function was successful.

- **Execution failed**: This means that the step function failed either at a particular task or step.

- **Execution timed out**: This means that the step function started execution but for some reason spent too much time executing a particular step and had to come to a halt.

- **Execution aborted**: This means that the execution process was abruptly interrupted.

These events can be monitored by **Amazon EventBridge** and the appropriate feedback mechanism triggered appropriately as we did in *Chapter 4*, *Monitoring AWS Compute Services*, and *Chapter 5*, *Setting Up Container Insights on Amazon CloudWatch*. For this setup function, we shall configure an EventBridge event pattern that will notify us when a step function fails. This is quite important as it will notify us without having to go to the console to get such information. Let's assume we have created a step function with the name `compressimage`. This step function receives an event from an S3 bucket, validates that the file received is an image, compresses the image with a Lambda function, stores the image in another bucket, creates a thumbnail from the compressed image, and writes the update back to a DynamoDB table. We need to know whenever this step function fails or times out.

To use Amazon EventBridge to monitor that, we shall create it with the following steps:

1. Log in to the AWS management console and navigate to **Amazon EventBridge**.

2. Click on the **Create rule** button to create a new rule.

3. Fill out the form with the following information:

   - **Name**: `compressimageevent`

   - **Description**: An event listener for the `compressimage` step function

   - **Define pattern | Event pattern**

   - **Pre-defined pattern by service**

- **Service provider: AWS**

- **Service name: Step Functions**

- **Event type: Step Functions Execution Status Change**

- **Specific status(es): FAILED**

- **Specific state machine ARN(s)**

Define pattern

Build or customize an Event Pattern or set a Schedule to invoke Targets.

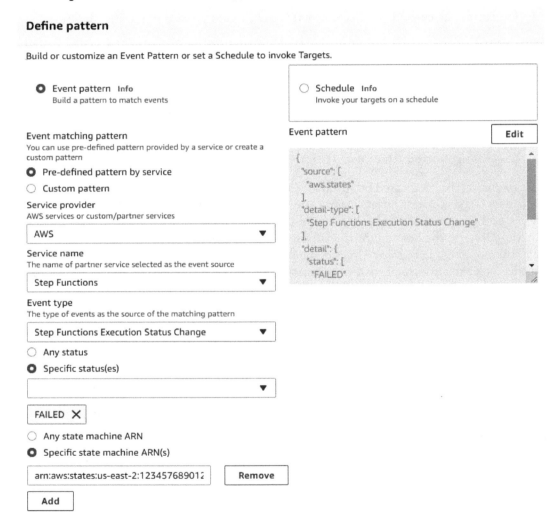

Figure 7.10 – Configuring Amazon EventBridge for a step function

4. For the target, choose the SNS topic that has been created. Ensure that you have created an SNS topic, else you can create one with this link: `https://docs.aws.amazon.com/sns/latest/dg/sns-create-topic.html`.

5. Click on the **Create** button to create the rule.

From the configuration, this rule simply sends a trigger to the SNS topic based on a **FAILED** state that occurs in a specific step function that we have. The step function is triggered by a file to an S3 bucket. If for any reason the function fails, EventBridge is triggered and we get a notification of the failure.

Apart from reading events of **Success**, **Failure**, **Abortion**, or **Timeout**, step functions also generate logs to give more details of the status of the function. Like every other service, the logs of a state machine are sent to *Amazon CloudWatch Logs*. The first point of call here is the Step Functions console. The console gives you a list of state machines, and when you click on a particular state machine, you can see some basic information about past executions. See the following screenshot for more details:

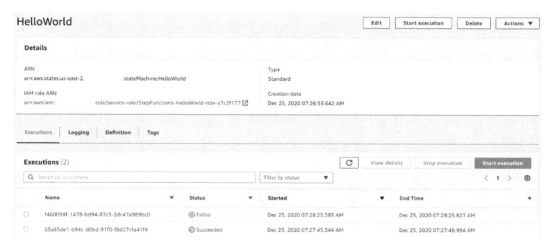

Figure 7.11 – The Step Functions console showing details of a state machine

From the preceding screenshot, we can see the **Executions** section, which shows some executions: one showing **Failed** and the other **Succeeded**. This is the first level of monitoring of the state machine, to know when an operation fails or whether it is successful. We can go further by clicking on the **Logging** tab to view more logs and the activities of the execution. But for this logging to work, it needs to be enabled during the creation of the step function:

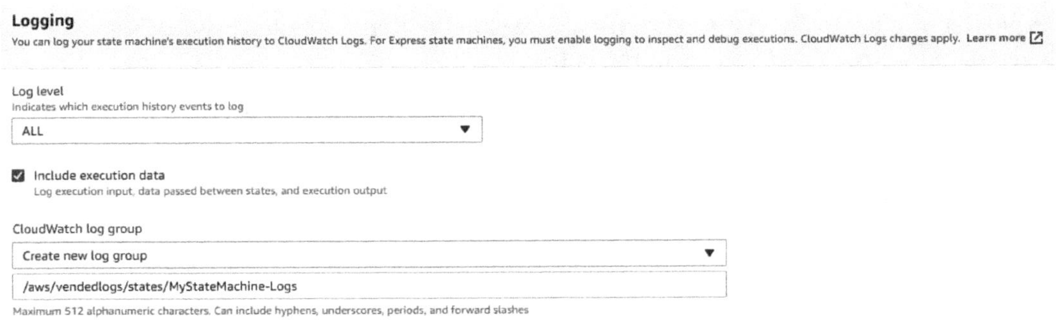

Logging

You can log your state machine's execution history to CloudWatch Logs. For Express state machines, you must enable logging to inspect and debug executions. CloudWatch Logs charges apply. Learn more

Log level
Indicates which execution history events to log

ALL ▼

☑ Include execution data
  Log execution input, data passed between states, and execution output

CloudWatch log group

Create new log group ▼

/aws/vendedlogs/states/MyStateMachine-Logs

Maximum 512 alphanumeric characters. Can include hyphens, underscores, periods, and forward slashes

Figure 7.12 – Enabling logging in the step function

The logging has various options of log level; it could either be **ALL**, **ERROR**, **FATAL**, or **OFF**, which means logging is totally disabled. For this scenario of logging, **ALL** has been activated, which means the logs will contain all the log levels. The following screenshot shows the logs from the state machine:

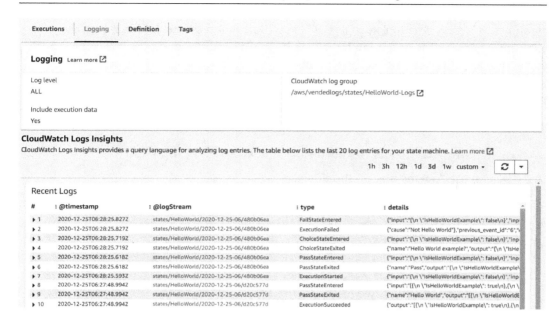

Figure 7.13 – Logging in the step function state machine

The **Logging** dashboard shows us some details of the logging, which includes the log level that was configured, and CloudWatch log groups too. We can go to the CloudWatch log groups to see this log group. But something is quite unique here. It brought the logs here to our doorstep. Looking down a little bit, you can see the CloudWatch Logs insights and below that, the logs of the executions made with the different states, date and time, and more details. We can expand each line to see more details. See the following screenshot:

Figure 7.14 – Expansion of a log for a state machine

This shows more information, such as the input information under **details.input**, the output message after the execution has run, which is **@message**, and other relevant information about the execution that you need to understand what happened to an execution.

We can use the following steps to create a CloudWatch alarm for the step function, which sends an alarm when a step function is aborted:

1. Log in to the AWS management console and navigate to **CloudWatch**.

2. Click on the **Alarms** link on the sidebar.

3. Click on the **Select metric** button to choose the metric to configure an alarm for.

4. Click on the **States** option on the page that shows different metrics.

5. Click on **Execution Metrics** to show the different execution metrics for state machines.

6. The list shows the different execution metrics for the state machine. Click on the item with the metric name **ExecutionsAborted**.

7. Click on the **Select metric** button. This will lead us to the alarm configuration page.

8. For the **Statistic** option, delete **Average** from the box and choose the **Maximum** option.

9. Scroll to the bottom and in the **Conditions** section, inside the box labeled **than…**, enter 0. This means if there is an aborted execution, this alarm should be triggered. Click **Next**:

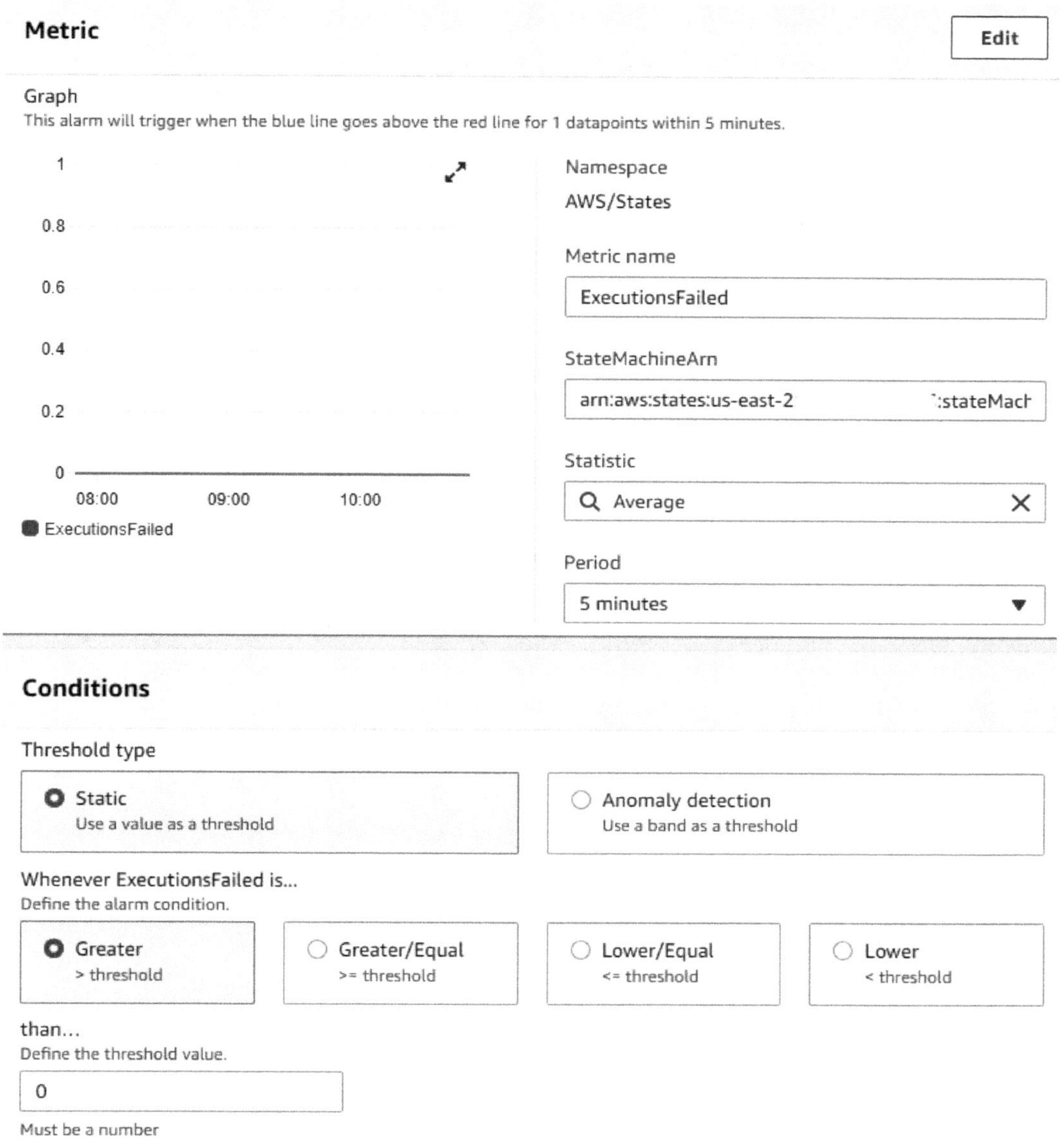

Metric

Edit

Graph

This alarm will trigger when the blue line goes above the red line for 1 datapoints within 5 minutes.

1

0.8

0.6

0.4

0.2

0

| 08:00 | 09:00 | 10:00 |

■ ExecutionsFailed

Namespace

AWS/States

Metric name

ExecutionsFailed

StateMachineArn

arn:aws:states:us-east-2   ':stateMach

Statistic

Q Average   ✕

Period

5 minutes   ▼

Conditions

Threshold type

● Static	○ Anomaly detection
Use a value as a threshold	Use a band as a threshold

Whenever ExecutionsFailed is...

Define the alarm condition.

● Greater	○ Greater/Equal	○ Lower/Equal	○ Lower
> threshold	>= threshold	<= threshold	< threshold

than...

Define the threshold value.

0

Must be a number

Figure 7.15 – Configuring an alarm threshold for the step function

10. Choose an SNS topic for the notification or click on **Create new topic** and enter the email that will receive the notification. Click on the **Create topic** button to create the topic. Then, click **Next**.

11. Enter the name of the alarm, for example, `stepalarm`, and the description, which could be optional. Then, click **Next**.

12. Confirm all the information from the preview page and click **Create alarm** when everything is confirmed.

> **Important Note**
> Ensure that you confirm the email notification sent to your email before you can start receiving notifications.

With this, we have a CloudWatch alarm that sends us notifications whenever the step function we created gets aborted.

Step functions are quite amazing for different consecutive workflows. We have also seen how to monitor them to ensure we are aware when our workflow fails or is successful at any given time. We do not want to assume that everything will always work fine, even if step functions are serverless, because anything could go wrong, so monitoring to get feedback is crucial to the proper workings of our step function.

Let's take a case study for this chapter and see how what we have learned can be connected to a real-life scenario.

Case study on Lambda tracing with Amazon X-Ray

The software engineering team just started using Lambda functions. For them, it is exciting to be able to deploy applications easier, due to the automated pipeline you have created for them using Amazon CodePipeline. So, deployments are smooth and fast. They also have access to the logs of the application in the CloudWatch console, so they can view the logs of each Lambda function. But they notice that data does not move from one function to the other. A particular Lambda function is supposed to call another Lambda function in succession, about six of them call each other in that manner. What service and feature will you use to show the path of the request from the first Lambda function to the last function?

Solution

It is obvious that the challenge they are facing is the inability to trace a request from one Lambda function to another. The service that can help with this is AWS X-Ray. The features in X-Ray are both service maps and traces. This will show how the request is moving from one Lambda function to the other and will help identify the failure or where the request stopped during its journey.

Summary

In this chapter, we have seen monitoring from a whole new perspective. We worked on the methods used to monitor a Lambda function, starting with the Lambda infrastructure metrics and graphs, and then receiving the application logs from the Lambda function in CloudWatch log groups.

We introduced the concept of observability and how tracing plays a role in making observability a reality. Then, we moved on to endpoint monitoring, where we configured a simple canary that we used to monitor the Packt Publishing website. Then, we saw how to monitor the SQS and SNS services to know when things are not working correctly in those services. We rounded things off with the last option in the workflow, which is on monitoring step functions. We want to be able to know when a function/step fails and easily fix it and test again. All this information is available in both the Step Functions console and the CloudWatch console for step functions.

In the next chapter, we shall be looking at monitoring in the context of big data. We shall first introduce the concepts of big data to aid with better understanding monitoring and metrics with big data.

Questions

1. What is another name is given to a Lambda function?

2. What runs within the Synthetics canary to perform the intermittent endpoint checks?

3. When there are groups of functions, what service enables you to trace a transaction across these functions?

4. Are step function logs stored in CloudWatch?

Further reading

Refer to the following links for more information on the topics covered in this chapter:

- Introduction to API Gateway: `https://www.packtpub.com/product/building-a-scalable-serverless-application-on-aws-video/9781788476065`

- Simple Notification Service with Boto3: `https://www.packtpub.com/product/working-with-sqs-and-sns-aws-with-python-and-boto3-series-video/9781838642297`

- Learning about AWS Lambda: `https://www.packtpub.com/product/learn-aws-serverless-computing/9781789958355`

- Error tracking in server: `https://www.packtpub.com/free-ebook/serverless-design-patterns-and-best-practices/9781788620642`

8
Using CloudWatch for Maintaining Highly Available Big Data Services

The last chapter was focused on talking about serverless applications and how to monitor them. First, we explained the meaning of serverless and deciphered the differences between managed services and serverless services. We then looked at a couple of serverless services in the AWS suite. We explained them and some use cases for the different serverless services that were defined. We then moved on to X-Ray and saw how to monitor these services. We also talked about how Synthetics canaries in CloudWatch can be used for endpoint monitoring.

In this chapter, we will be looking at the monitoring of AWS big data services. But first, we need to understand the concepts of big data and the value big data brings to the table. We shall look at the different aspects that make up the practices of big data. We will also connect all these practices and see how they are all interdependent to achieve one goal. Then, we will extrapolate the value of monitoring in all these practices.

We shall see how monitoring plays a vital role in achieving great success as a big data engineer. This is possible when we have a proper understanding of the technology and its components, which components we need to keep an eye on, and how they impact big data operations. We will look at ways to mitigate these issues if they ever occur during our work as big data engineers. We shall also see how monitoring helps us to improve the performance of data pipelines and reduce the operations cost of running big data pipelines to perform big data operations.

In conclusion, we shall take a case study of a scenario and see how what we have learned can come into play in a near real-world scenario.

Let's get this show started!

We will cover the following topics in this chapter:

- Introduction to big data
- Aspects of big data
- Monitoring Amazon Kinesis agent/service
- Analyzing Amazon CloudTrail with Amazon Athena
- CloudWatch alarms for AWS Glue jobs
- A case study

Technical requirements

To be able to accomplish the technical tasks in the chapter, you will need to have the following technical pre-requisites:

- A working AWS account (you can opt for the free tier, which will cost $0/month for 1 year)
- Basic knowledge of managed services
- A basic understanding of data and data engineering
- An understanding of database management systems, types of data structures, data types, and fundamentals of SQL
- Knowledge of at least one operating system, be it Windows or Linux, but Linux is preferable
- An understanding of EC2 instances, **Amazon Machine Image** (AMI), and general knowledge of **Infrastructure as a Service** (IaaS) in AWS

Check out the following link to see the Code in Action video:

`https://bit.ly/3qwxkPq`

Introduction to big data

Man has been generating data for quite a long time. The method of storing data has changed from physical to electronic. But as the method of storing data changes, man still continues to store data in different forms and tell stories in different ways, across different geographies, cultures, beliefs, and traditions. From words to symbols and figures to represent data, we have been storing information for thousands of years. We usually only used to reference this data in the future if we needed to go back to something or validate something that we had stored in the past. It could also be used to gain a knowledge of things in the past. But storing data was done for various reasons.

Just before the digital age arrived, we started seeing this data life cycle in another light. Mathematicians could take numbers and data and create some interesting interpretations and draw interesting perceptions based on the data collected and how it is represented. Fast-forward to the 21st century, where computers and other computing devices are used to create and store data.

Properties of big data

There are four properties that classify data that is called big data. You might have a huge amount of information, but it might not be classified as **big data**. So, for a dataset to fit the criteria of being called big data, it must have the four Vs. They are as follows:

- **Volume**: The data must be exceptionally large.
- **Velocity**: The data must be generated continuously from single or multiple sources.
- **Variety**: The data should not be on just one thing, but different, unrelated things.
- **Veracity**: The data must have quality.

Let's now look at the aspects and different activities in the big data ecosystem, the different operations that the data must go through for it to be able to tell stories and give better insight. We shall look at the theories and then further look at the AWS tools and how monitoring plays a key role in the whole setup.

Overviewing the aspects of big data

In the big data ecosystem, there are different activities, some of which form job roles, and some are regular tasks that need to be embarked on to ensure relevant data is churned for other teammates to work with. These activities are in two broad categories, one of which involves collecting the data from various sources and bringing out what is necessary and what will make sense for the other team to use to draw out insights. The second involves the people involved in telling the stories with the data that has been prepared. The task of creating graphs and charts and telling stories is the role of data analytics experts. In some situations, they are also referred to as business intelligence experts. They can take data that has been prepared in a particular form and draw out very meaningful insights for applications, systems, and businesses in the general sense. The aspect on which the expert is focused is what usually determines what label they are given.

The data is prepared by another expert called a **data engineer**. This person is tasked with ensuring that the data that will be used by the data analytics expert is devoid of any type of **noise**. Noise usually makes data inaccurate and creates outliers and strange anomalies when representing data in a chart or graph.

> **Important note**
> Noise in data means a part of the data that is corrupted or twisted in some form that does not conform to the other existing datasets. Most times, if a dataset follows a certain pattern and for some reason one item in the dataset does not conform, that item is deleted and is categorized as noise, which could make the distribution skewed to a different interpretation.

A data engineer is usually someone who understands some software engineering programming languages, such as Python or Scala, and understands the different structures of data. We already explained different data structures in *Chapter 6, Performance Insights for Database Services*, in the section called *Introduction to database management*. So, data engineers deal with a lot of data structures, but mostly around structured and semi-structured data, trying to bring them together to form a holistic combination of all the data that has been gathered. These operations are generally known as the **ETL process**. ETL is an acronym that stands for **extraction, transformation, and loading**. We will learn about these three processes in detail in the following subsections.

Extraction

This is the process of pulling or collecting data from a particular data source or from various data sources. It could be data that is dumped out of a relational database system or logs of an application, or data generated from Google Analytics or any other location. The data engineer's task is to collect this data and store it in a particular location.

This location serves as the temporary storage of the data. In some situations, this location is called the **data swamp**. There are a number of AWS services used for the extraction process, one of which is Amazon Kinesis (this is a family name for a grouping of four services, which are **Amazon Kinesis Data Streams, Amazon Kinesis Data Firehose, Amazon Kinesis Data Analytics**, and **Amazon Kinesis Video Streams**).

Kinesis is mostly used to extract data from virtual machines and applications, and the services are used for the real-time streaming of data from one source to another destination. There are also other services used for extracting data from different sources.

During the extraction process, every activity needs to be monitored to ensure that the process is working as it has been designed or configured to work. Each of these services has various monitoring metrics and dashboards that make it easy to understand what is going on during the ETL process at any point in time.

Transformation

This process involves putting the data in the right format or order to be used by the data analyst or machine learning engineer. In the transformation process, data that is not needed is removed and, in some cases, new data is added from the existing dataset or from another dataset to form a larger dataset. Transformation could also include some form of data compression to compress the data to be in a format that is more optimized for running queries. All of this is what happens during the transformation process, which is the second stage of the ETL process. There are various AWS services that can be used for data transformation, which are Amazon **Elastic MapReduce** (**EMR**), AWS Glue, and AWS Lambda.

Loading

When the data has been extracted and transformed, it needs to be stored in a location before it can be accessible to perform analytics or other kinds of data operations with it. The loading operation is the last stage of sending the data that has been extracted and transformed to a proper storage location. This storage needs to be a very secure, scalable, and highly available storage service or engine.

Data scientists, machine learning engineers, data analysts, and business intelligence experts will need to work with this data, so the data engineer needs to ensure that the loading process is always top-notch and the data loaded is appropriate and sufficient for other engineers to carry on with their activities. In data engineering, the technical term for the location that serves this purpose is called the **data lake**.

Amazon S3, **Amazon S3 Glacier**, **AWS Lake Formation**, **Amazon Redshift**, and **Amazon Elasticsearch** are all locations where the loading of data can be done. Each of these services has monitoring in different forms. We already covered monitoring for Amazon Redshift in *Chapter 6, Performance Insights for Database Services*. We shall talk more about Amazon S3 in *Chapter 9, Monitoring Storage Services with Amazon CloudWatch*, where we talk about monitoring storage services with Amazon CloudWatch.

This process is called a **data pipeline**. A data pipeline in data engineering is a step-by-step process of architecting a system used to prepare data in a format that is more meaningful and useful for further analysis, analytics, and machine learning purposes. The major operation in a data pipeline is the ETL process.

The following diagram is a schematic of an end-to-end ETL process with some AWS services:

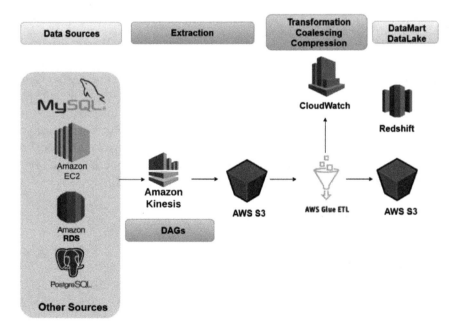

Figure 8.1 – Data pipeline showing an ETL process

Figure 8.1 shows the process of ETL where the destination is the (**DataMart/DataLake**). The service for extraction at this point is Amazon Kinesis while the service used for transformation is **AWS Glue ETL,** it is used for extracting and loading the data into **Amazon S3.**

Now that we understand what data engineering is about and the ETL process of it is clearer to us, let's look at one extraction service in AWS. Let's see how to monitor our extraction workloads in AWS to ensure the high availability and scalability of our data pipelines.

Monitoring Amazon Kinesis agent/service

We introduced Amazon Kinesis in the previous section, but we did not really look into it in depth. Amazon Kinesis is a data streaming family of services made of Kinesis Data Streams, Kinesis Firehose, Kinesis Analytics, and Kinesis Video Streams. Our focus in this section will be on Kinesis Data Streams and Kinesis Firehose. These two services are used to stream data from various sources and various activities can occur after the extraction process. Kinesis Data Streams allows you to use the **Kinesis Producer Library**, also known as the **KPL**, to read data from a source and send it to the Kinesis service. It serves as an agent to collect information and forward the data collected to the Kinesis service in the AWS console. You can see how to create a simple Kinesis data stream here: `https://docs.aws.amazon.com/streams/latest/dev/tutorial-stock-data-kplkcl2-create-stream.html`.

In some cases, data is collected as it is generated and sent to other systems for real-time analysis. An example is Sonos. Sonos is a speaker manufacturer that uses Amazon Kinesis Data Streams to collect various information as you use their speaker to listen to music. See details here: `https://youtu.be/-70wNNrxf6Q`.

Kinesis Data Firehose is somewhat like Kinesis Data Streams. It is also used to collect data and the data can be streamed. But the difference with Firehose is that you need to configure a specific destination where the data is going to be stored. For example, when configuring Kinesis Data Firehose, you are required to specify the destination that the data will be written to. You can see how to create Kinesis Data Firehose here: `https://docs.aws.amazon.com/firehose/latest/dev/basic-create.html`. This destination could be an Amazon S3 bucket or an Amazon Elasticsearch domain. You also have the option of putting a Lambda function as a transformation step before the data eventually gets to the destination. This makes Kinesis Data Firehose not just a tool that extracts data, but in conjunction with AWS Lambda, it is able to transform in some cases to perform analytics on the data and eventually write the data to Amazon S3 or any other destination configured for it.

Kinesis is made up of two parts: the agent and the service. The agent is what is installed in an EC2 instance or configured in your application that collects or extracts data from a system. It is usually called the KPL. This library is configured to send the data it has extracted to the Kinesis service, which is the one that is created in the AWS console. Kinesis Data Streams has a **Kinesis Client Library** (**KCL**), which is used to consume data from the Kinesis service, but in the case of Kinesis Firehose, there is no need for a KCL, because all the data sent to Kinesis Firehose has a destination already configured for it.

Amazon CloudWatch has a default method to easily monitor your Kinesis data streams. There is deep integration with every stream created in the Kinesis Data Streams console. There are different dashboards and metrics that are created on CloudWatch when a Kinesis data stream is created by default, but there are a couple of notable graphs and metrics that are key. The following is a summarized chart that shows certain graphs and metrics that are key to how Kinesis Data Streams works:

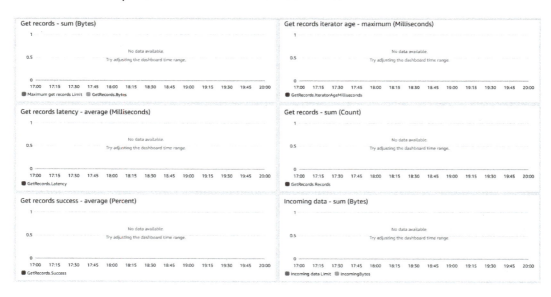

Figure 8.2 – Sample Amazon Kinesis dashboard

The preceding screenshot contains some important metrics/graphs. The first graph gives information about the number of records it has collected, with the metric name **Get records**, and it is measured in bytes. This can help you to know whether the KPL is pulling data as it should, how much data is it pulling, and even whether the number of shards configured for the Kinesis stream has enough capacity compared to the data it is transmitting.

We also have **Get records latency**, which tells us the latency or time lag on average that it takes for it to receive data from the KPL. This can increase in count when the KPL is restarted while it is sending data to Kinesis.

The other metrics are **Incoming data - sum (Bytes)**, **Get records - sum (Count)**, and **Get records Iterator age - maximum (Milliseconds)**; they are all ways to monitor the flow of data through the stream and get feedback on the behavior of the stream. A good practice is to configure an alarm on the **Get records - sum (Bytes)** metric to trigger when the number of bytes is getting close to the number of bytes configured for the stream. The number of bytes capacity for the stream is determined by the number of shards that has been configured for it. This can be configured via the CloudWatch console.

We have looked at collecting data with Kinesis. These different metrics are used to measure the availability and scalability of our Kinesis stream by configuring an alarm when the records are going above what was configured. Next, we will be looking at monitoring the full AWS account by collecting logs and analyzing those logs using another serverless service in AWS.

Analyzing Amazon CloudTrail with Amazon Athena

Our monitoring scope has been focused on a particular service, getting logs from the service and analyzing those logs, using the autogenerated metrics from **Amazon CloudWatch** or creating our own custom metrics. This monitoring is based on what is going on within the service itself. There are external activities that also go on outside the service. When an EC2 instance is created in the AWS console, that activity can be monitored to know who created the instance, when it was created, and other relevant information about the EC2 instance that has been created. The service that keeps this type of information and more about any service creation or update or deletion is called **AWS CloudTrail**. CloudTrail serves as the auditor to your AWS account(s). It captures a trail of every activity that goes on within the AWS console. Most of the information it collects is through API calls to the different AWS services.

> **Important note**
> **API** is the acronym for **application program interface**. It is a standard interface that usually uses the HTTP protocol for communication and is used for communication on the web. When two different systems (developed with different languages and architecture) need to communicate, an API is the standard way with which both systems will communicate.

The API calls could be directly working with the AWS management console, which involves activities creating, viewing, updating, or deleting resources. It could also be working through the AWS **Software Development Kit (SDK)**, or through raw API requests sent to the AWS backend services. All these requests are logged by AWS CloudTrail. With the number of logs and information stored in CloudTrail, it means that there's going to be hundreds to thousands of logs and pieces of data in there. It could be like finding a needle in a haystack to start searching for something. The question could also be *what will I be looking for in that haystack of information?* Monitoring is not only done to make an application highly available and scalable; there is also security monitoring. One reason you should check your CloudTrail logs is to audit security activities and to do a security audit in the case of a security event or incident. To be able to sift through this huge amount of data, we need to turn to a service that can do this swiftly and efficiently. **AWS Athena** is a service in the AWS ecosystem that can be used.

> **Important note**
> The AWS SDK is the official AWS programming plugin or module that allows software engineers to use a particular programming language to communicate with the AWS API service. The AWS SDK is designed and managed by AWS and the SDK is available for different programming languages, such as Java, Python, JavaScript, C#, C++, Ruby, Java, Go, and PHP.

Athena is a serverless query service that is used to query a flat file of data (JSON, CSV, Parquet, or ORC) and different database sources via federated queries. The data analyzed by Athena resides in an Amazon S3 bucket. The configuration involves creating a connection from the Athena service to an Amazon S3 bucket. The federated queries can connect to a lot of other data sources, such as Amazon CloudWatch Logs, Amazon CloudWatch metrics, Amazon DocumentDB, Amazon Redshift, MySQL, and PostgreSQL. For most big data workloads, Athena is used to query the data that has been written into an S3 bucket as part of the loading process in the ETL pipeline. **Athena tables** need to be created to allow Athena to query data from its data source (primarily Amazon S3).

For this scenario, we shall be using Athena to query the data in CloudTrail to be able to pinpoint activities/events that have occurred in my AWS account. For this to be possible, we need to create a particular CloudTrail trail. CloudTrail by default has a lot of events because it is a list of all the API activities in the AWS account, so we need to streamline it to a certain group of events we want to collect and store in S3 and eventually query with Athena.

The first stage is to create the trail to collect specific information that we shall eventually query with Athena. Use the following steps to create a trail in CloudTrail:

1. Log in to the AWS management console and navigate to **CloudTrail**.

2. On the CloudTrail console, there is a **Create trail** button. Click on the button to create a new trail.

3. Fill in the form that appears as shown in the following screenshot:

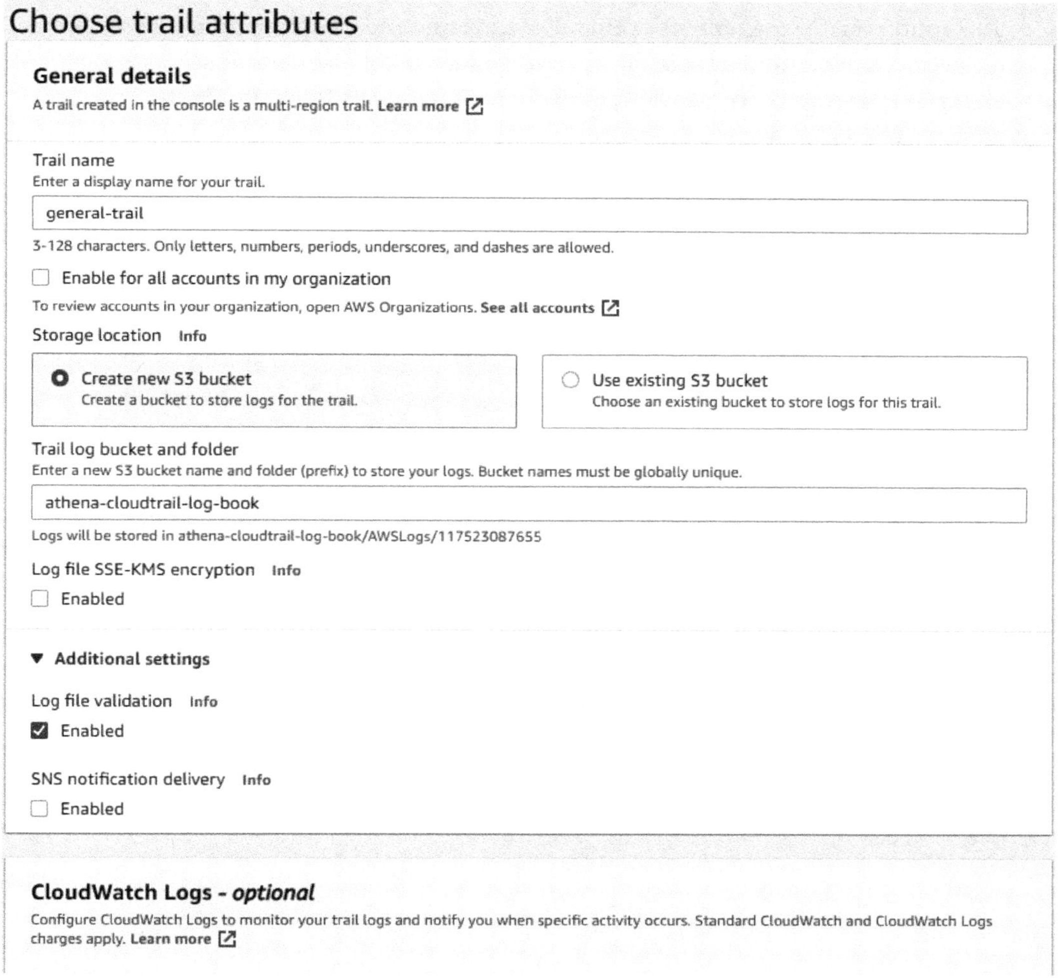

Choose trail attributes

General details
A trail created in the console is a multi-region trail. **Learn more** [↗]

Trail name
Enter a display name for your trail.

> general-trail

3-128 characters. Only letters, numbers, periods, underscores, and dashes are allowed.

☐ Enable for all accounts in my organization

To review accounts in your organization, open AWS Organizations. **See all accounts** [↗]

Storage location   Info

○ **Create new S3 bucket**
Create a bucket to store logs for the trail.

○ Use existing S3 bucket
Choose an existing bucket to store logs for this trail.

Trail log bucket and folder
Enter a new S3 bucket name and folder (prefix) to store your logs. Bucket names must be globally unique.

> athena-cloudtrail-log-book

Logs will be stored in athena-cloudtrail-log-book/AWSLogs/117523087655

Log file SSE-KMS encryption   Info
☐ Enabled

▼ **Additional settings**

Log file validation   Info
☑ Enabled

SNS notification delivery   Info
☐ Enabled

CloudWatch Logs - *optional*
Configure CloudWatch Logs to monitor your trail logs and notify you when specific activity occurs. Standard CloudWatch and CloudWatch Logs charges apply. **Learn more** [↗]

Figure 8.3 – Creating a trail in AWS CloudTrail

In the screenshot in *Figure 8.3*, we have entered the name of the trail, which is `general-trail`. We shall update the bucket name, which we will use to collect the logs. The bucket name has been edited to `athena-cloudtrail-logs`. By default, **Log file SSE-KMS encryption** is enabled, but in this scenario, we have disabled it. The bottom part of the screenshot shows **CloudWatch Logs** as an option, which notes that CloudTrail logs can also be sent to CloudWatch Logs. Scroll to the bottom and click the **Next** button to continue.

4. The next step will involve selecting the type of events we want to see in the logs. The options are **Management events**, **Data events**, and **Insights events**. By default, it selects **Management events**, so we shall go for that. It also asks which activities under **Management events** we want. By default, it selects **Read** and **Write**. We shall go with that. Click **Next** to continue:

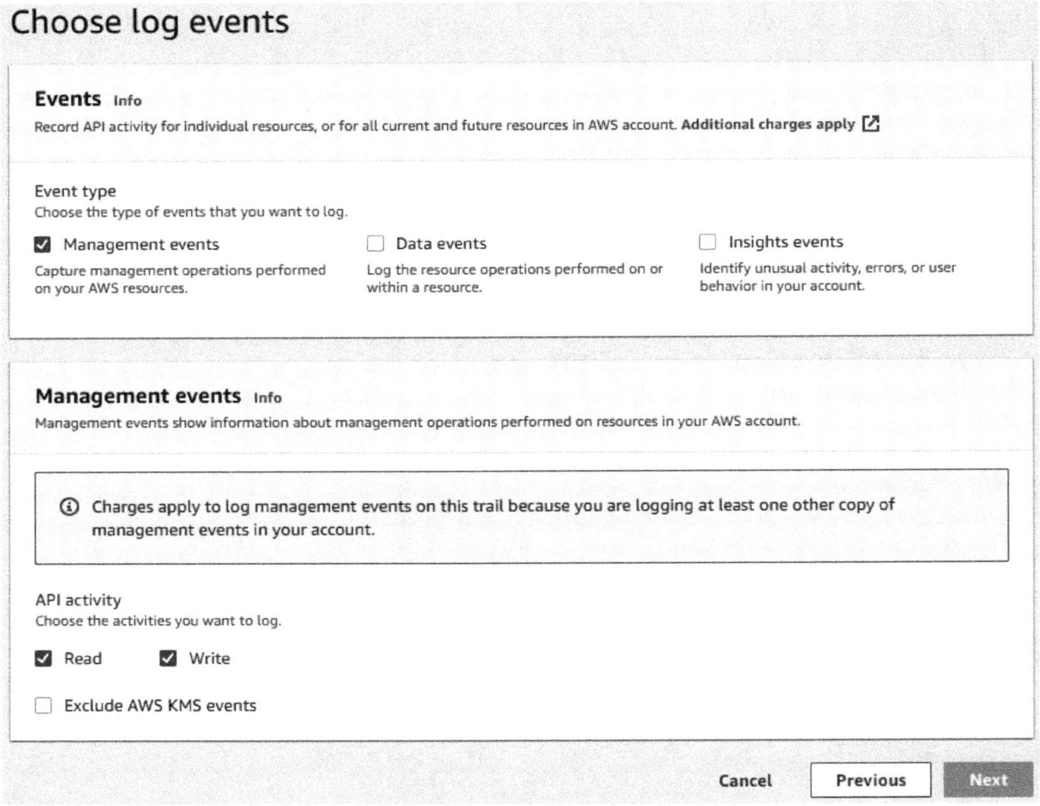

Choose log events

Events Info
Record API activity for individual resources, or for all current and future resources in AWS account. **Additional charges apply** ⧉

Event type
Choose the type of events that you want to log.

☑ Management events

Capture management operations performed on your AWS resources.

☐ Data events

Log the resource operations performed on or within a resource.

☐ Insights events

Identify unusual activity, errors, or user behavior in your account.

Management events Info
Management events show information about management operations performed on resources in your AWS account.

> ⓘ Charges apply to log management events on this trail because you are logging at least one other copy of management events in your account.

API activity
Choose the activities you want to log.

☑ Read   ☑ Write

☐ Exclude AWS KMS events

Cancel   Previous   Next

Figure 8.4 – Selecting events in the CloudTrail trail configuration

5. This is the last stage to review and create. When the configuration is reviewed, scroll to the bottom and click the **Create trail** button:

Figure 8.5 – Created trail actively logging in to Amazon S3

This concludes the creation of the trail for CloudTrail. This means that data is being written to the S3 bucket that has been configured for it. The next stage is to create an Athena table to be able to query the data. These are the steps:

1. On the same CloudTrail console, go to the left-side menu and click on the **Event history** link.

2. On the **Event history** page, there is a button called **Create Athena table**. Click on it.

3. This will show a pop-up dialog. In the dialog, select the S3 (`athena-cloudtrail-log-book`) storage location, which we already created in the previous steps.

4. Click the **Create table** button to create the Athena table that will enable us to query the logs in S3:

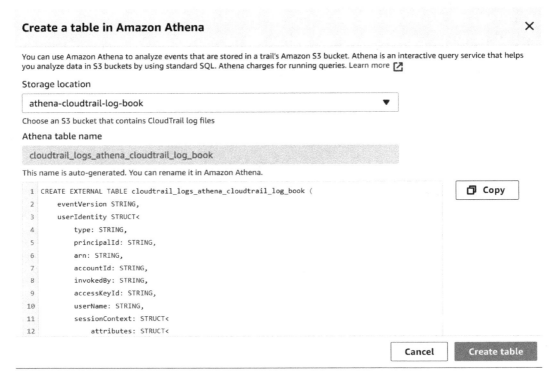

Figure 8.6 – Creating an Athena table for the CloudTrail trail

5. Navigate to Athena via **Services | Athena** from the CloudTrail console.

6. If this is your first time using Athena, the query result location needs to be configured. Use this link to set up the configuration: `https://docs.aws.amazon.com/athena/latest/ug/querying.html`.

7. The data and table are highlighted by default on the left-hand side of the screen, so let's write a simple SQL query to show the `ListBuckets` events that have occurred in the AWS account.

8. Enter the following query in the Athena console:

```
SELECT * FROM default.cloudtrail_logs_athena_cloudtrail_
log_book WHERE cloudtrail_logs_athena_cloudtrail_log_
book.eventname='ListBuckets'
```

9. Click the **Run query** button to run the query displayed in *Step 8*. This will show the result of that activity, as shown in the following screenshot:

eventtime ▼	eventsource ▼	eventname ▼	awsregion ▼	sourceipaddress ▼	useragent ▼
2020-12-30T21:54:05Z	s3.amazonaws.com	ListBuckets	eu-west-1	212.102.40.67	[AWS Console Glue, aws-internal/3 aws-sdk-jav
2020-12-30T11:47:54Z	s3.amazonaws.com	ListBuckets	eu-west-1	66.115.177.134	[AWS Console Glue, aws-internal/3 aws-sdk-jav
2020-12-30T11:47:53Z	s3.amazonaws.com	ListBuckets	eu-west-1	66.115.177.134	[AWS Console Glue, aws-internal/3 aws-sdk-jav
2020-12-30T11:47:54Z	s3.amazonaws.com	ListBuckets	eu-west-1	66.115.177.134	[AWS Console Glue, aws-internal/3 aws-sdk-jav
2020-12-30T11:47:53Z	s3.amazonaws.com	ListBuckets	eu-west-1	66.115.177.134	[AWS Console Glue, aws-internal/3 aws-sdk-jav
2020-12-30T13:30:36Z	s3.amazonaws.com	ListBuckets	eu-west-1	66.115.177.139	[AWS Console Glue, aws-internal/3 aws-sdk-jav
2020-12-30T13:30:36Z	s3.amazonaws.com	ListBuckets	eu-west-1	66.115.177.139	[AWS Console Glue, aws-internal/3 aws-sdk-jav
2020-12-30T13:30:43Z	s3.amazonaws.com	ListBuckets	eu-west-1	66.115.177.139	[AWS Console Glue, aws-internal/3 aws-sdk-jav
2020-12-30T13:30:37Z	s3.amazonaws.com	ListBuckets	eu-west-1	66.115.177.139	[AWS Console Glue, aws-internal/3 aws-sdk-jav
2020-12-30T11:48:59Z	s3.amazonaws.com	ListBuckets	eu-west-1	66.115.177.134	[AWS Console Glue, aws-internal/3 aws-sdk-jav
2020-12-30T11:49:00Z	s3.amazonaws.com	ListBuckets	eu-west-1	66.115.177.134	[AWS Console Glue, aws-internal/3 aws-sdk-jav
2020-12-30T11:48:59Z	s3.amazonaws.com	ListBuckets	eu-west-1	66.115.177.134	[AWS Console Glue, aws-internal/3 aws-sdk-jav
2020-12-30T21:54:04Z	s3.amazonaws.com	ListBuckets	eu-west-1	212.102.40.67	[AWS Console Glue, aws-internal/3 aws-sdk-jav
2020-12-30T21:54:05Z	s3.amazonaws.com	ListBuckets	eu-west-1	212.102.40.67	[AWS Console Glue, aws-internal/3 aws-sdk-jav
2020-12-30T21:54:04Z	s3.amazonaws.com	ListBuckets	eu-west-1	212.102.40.67	[AWS Console Glue, aws-internal/3 aws-sdk-jav
2020-12-30T21:43:00Z	s3.amazonaws.com	ListBuckets	eu-west-1	212.102.40.67	[AWS Console Glue, aws-internal/3 aws-sdk-jav

Figure 8.7 – Results from the CloudTrail log

This is a basic query used to show an activity, when it happened, who performed the activity, and other relevant information about that event. This could be useful in tracking a malicious login or activity by a user or an application that has the credentials to communicate with AWS services within the account.

This section has shown us that monitoring not only covers application and infrastructure availability and scalability, respectively, but being able to audit security events in your infrastructure is also key, and we have shown how we can perform a timely security audit in our AWS account. CloudTrail insight events are another good way to identify unusual activities and unusual user activities in your AWS account, and then store them in your CloudTrail events.

The next section will introduce AWS Glue jobs and we'll see how we can configure monitoring and how CloudWatch integrates with AWS Glue.

Monitoring AWS Glue jobs with CloudWatch alarms

AWS Glue is a serverless service used to perform ETL operations in AWS. Glue connects to multiple data sources to retrieve and transform data into different structures and formats. AWS Glue is easy to use and makes it faster to perform a transformation using Python or Scala, which are the two main options within Glue. Glue also has a very deep integration with Athena. The tables in Athena can be read within Glue and used for further ETL processes.

We shall do a simple example of transforming the data we queried previously in Athena: using a CloudTrail trail. We will create a Glue job that transforms the original data, compresses it to a different data format (Parquet), and writes it to another S3 bucket. Then, we can see the logs and activities and the different metrics used to measure the success or failure of a Glue job. These are the steps to create a Glue job:

1. Navigate to **Services | Glue** in the AWS management console.

2. In the AWS Glue console, click the **Jobs** link on the left-hand side.

3. On the **Jobs** page, click the **Add job** button.

4. Fill in the form as shown in the following screenshot. For the IAM rule, use this link to create a role: `https://docs.aws.amazon.com/glue/latest/dg/create-an-iam-role.html`. Click **Next** to continue:

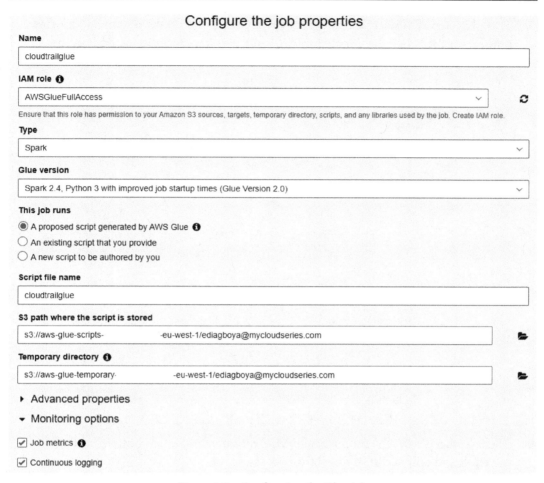

Figure 8.8 – Configuring the Glue job

5. Select the data source, which will be **cloudtrail_logs_athena_cloudtrail_log_book**, which we created in the previous section. Then, click **Next** to continue.

6. For the transform type, leave the default option selected, which is **Change schema**. Click **Next** to continue.

7. This next step is to select the target to which Glue will send the output. So, for this option, we shall click the **Create table in your data target** option and fill in the form as in the following screenshot:

Figure 8.9 – Configuring an AWS Glue data target

8. This option creates the bucket in the **Target path** location. Click **Next** to continue.

9. The last stage shows the output schema definition. Scroll to the bottom and click **Save job and edit script** to finish the process.

This will finally create the job. With the script, click on the **Run job** button to run the job for the first time. To view log and metric information, click the **X** button in the top-right corner of the screen. Click on the job on the **Jobs** dashboard and click on **View additional metrics**. This will show us the metrics/dashboard. The following screenshot shows a sample dashboard for Glue jobs:

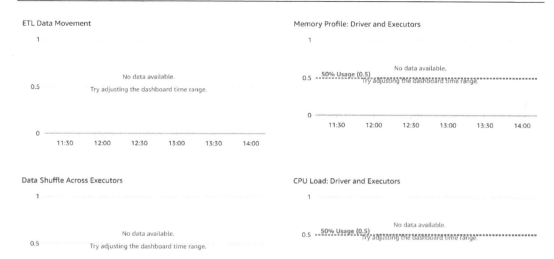

Figure 8.10 – Glue job dashboard/metrics

With this dashboard, we know what is going on in terms of the ETL activity in the job that has just been created, as well as other metrics, such as the CPU and memory load used during the process of running the job.

There are also other touch points in AWS Glue to be able to monitor jobs and understand when they fail and how they are performing, or whether the job ran at all.

Case study on monitoring a Kinesis stream

The data engineering team has been using an AWS EC2 instance with a custom plugin to extract data generated from the Apache server. For some reason, they noticed that it is taking time for the KCL to receive information being sent to it. The instance is restarted and the KPL is restarted, and they notice that the problem persists. What should have been done or configured to ensure that the team is alerted when this sort of incident occurs?

Solution

When the Kinesis stream is created, head on over to the Amazon CloudWatch console and configure an alarm with a specific threshold for the **Get records latency** metric, to ensure that the team is alerted via an SNS email or SMS notification.

Summary

The concept of big data is continually expanding in conjunction with data engineering. We have spent time explaining what big data is and the different aspects of big data, as well as how these aspects intertwine, from the role of a data engineer who helps to sanitize data and make it more friendly and usable by business intelligence experts, to that of data scientists, machine learning engineers, data analysts, and more. Understanding the process of making this data clean is important and monitoring plays a key role in that. We also explained the concept of ETL, which is one of the fundamental concepts of data engineering. Then, we talked about the AWS tools that are used for ETL work: Kinesis for extraction, Glue for transformation, and S3, where the data is stored or loaded.

Lastly, we introduced one important aspect of monitoring in the AWS ecosystem, which is AWS CloudTrail. We then moved on to explain the importance of CloudTrail, how to use the CloudTrail console, and how to use CloudTrail with Athena to get deeper insights, faster. We also saw how to navigate the huge amount of data generated by CloudTrail with the help of Amazon Athena, which can be effective in monitoring and checking for anomalies and any malicious activity going on in the AWS account.

The next chapter shall be focused on storage, which we already touched on a little bit here, but in the next chapter, we shall have a whole conversation around storage monitoring in AWS.

Questions

1. Where is the standard location where AWS Glue jobs store their logs?

2. When data is extracted and transformed, what is the next stage of the process?

3. When CloudTrail is created, where is the data stored before it can be analyzed by Amazon Athena?

4. What metric in Kinesis Data Streams helps you to know the number of bytes of data a stream can handle?

Further reading

Refer to the following links for more information on the topics covered in this chapter:

- Introducing big data: `https://subscription.packtpub.com/book/application-development/9781788995092/1/ch01lvl1sec11/introducing-big-data`

- Handling unstructured data: `https://www.packtpub.com/product/big-data-analysis-with-python/9781789955286`

- Amazon EMR: `https://www.packtpub.com/product/aws-certified-big-data-specialty-certification-video/9781800563773`

- Why big data? `https://www.packtpub.com/product/big-data-architect-s-handbook/9781788835824`

- What is AWS EMR? `https://www.packtpub.com/product/learning-big-data-with-amazon-elastic-mapreduce/9781782173434`

9
Monitoring Storage Services with Amazon CloudWatch

Big data was what drove our monitoring conversation in the previous chapter. First off, we introduced the concept of big data and different areas thereof, including ETL and data analytics. Then we talked about the AWS services that are used for big data work and data analytics. Then we drilled down into the core focus, which is monitoring for these services and the major metrics we should always keep our eyes on when using these services. We talked about storage a little bit, but did not go into detail. This chapter will help us do just that.

Switching gears into storage and explaining a number of concepts relating to storage is what this chapter will be focused on. To be able to understand how to monitor storage services, we first need to understand the fundamentals of storage and storage in the cloud. Then we will look at the different storage technologies in the AWS ecosystem. We will look at how the different storage technologies match with their corresponding AWS services. We will examine some real-life scenario examples of cases where monitoring and understanding the metrics of the storage service can affect cost and, in certain cases, the performance of the information stored within that storage service.

We will cover the following topics in this chapter:

- What are storage services?
- Amazon EBS volume metrics
- Performance metrics of Amazon EFS on CloudWatch
- Monitoring Amazon FSx
- CloudWatch alarms on Amazon S3
- Case study of a consolidated EBS volume dashboard

Technical requirements

To be able to accomplish the technical tasks in the chapter, the following technical prerequisites are necessary:

- A basic knowledge of managed services
- Knowledge of at least one operating system, be it Windows or Linux, but preferably Linux
- An understanding of EC2 instances, AMIs, and a general understanding of IaaS in AWS

Check out the following link to see the Code in Action video:

```
https://bit.ly/3ezOk5b
```

Understanding storage devices

In the world of computing, there is a very essential part that can never be underrated. Once all the mathematical and computational operations are done, this information needs to be stored in a location for easy reference, archiving, and audit purposes. Storage devices were invented for this very task.

Storage devices are designed to keep data that can be retrieved at any time it is needed. However, there are other parameters to consider when we look at storing information. We need to ensure that the information is stored in the proper format, and we need to ensure that the information retains its integrity. This means that if we store *A* and want to retrieve it at a later date, we should get it exactly how it was stored. The *A* we get at a later date should be no different to the *A* we stored previously.

The security of the information we store is also crucial. The durability of the storage device is extremely critical. This will give us confidence that the integrity of the data is maintained. Lastly, there is the question of accessibility; how easily can the data be accessed when it is needed? Does it take an exceedingly long time to access or can we get it in milliseconds? These are some of the key points we should always consider when storing information in any kind of storage medium.

AWS has a vast array of storage services that satisfy all of these concerns. These storage devices are designed for various use cases, application scenarios, and industry specifications. We will be introducing these services in the following subsections and talk about the use cases of each of them.

EBS

EBS is an acronym for **Elastic Block Storage**. It is also known as Amazon EBS. It is an AWS scalable storage service used in association with EC2 instances. In simple terms, EBS is like the hard disk of your EC2 instance, in the same way a laptop or desktop has a hard disk. We talked about the different components that make up an operating system in *Chapter 4*, *Monitoring AWS Compute Services*, under the *Understanding disks in IaaS* section. There, we introduced the concept of disks and talked about the **Input/Output Per Second** (**IOPS**) metric for measuring write and read operations in the operating system. This time, we will go deeper into other important metrics of an EBS volume in AWS, things to look out for to understand the behavior of your EBS volume.

There are different types of EBS volumes. These are designed for various purposes and workloads. There are certain applications that require extremely high throughput in terms of response time. This means that the speed of I/O on the EBS volume must be higher than normal. Those types of applications require a unique type of EBS volume to produce such kinds of throughput. There are other applications that do not require so much throughput, just a standard amount to run application workloads. There are also applications that do not require the information to be used all the time, just intermittently, and do not require quick retrieval of the data. This leads us to the different types of EBS volumes:

- General Purpose SSD (gp2)
- General Purpose SSD (gp3)
- Provisioned IOPS SSD (io1)
- Provisioned IOPS SSD (io2)
- Cold HDD (sc1)

- Throughput Optimized HDD (st1)

- Magnetic (standard)

These different types of storage serve various purposes. Provisioned IOPS SSD (io1 and io2) is the fastest, and is used for high throughput systems and applications. Most applications use the General Purpose SSD (gp2 and gp3) for databases and application services.

EBS volumes serve as storage for your EC2 instance, so web applications, mobile application backends, and machine learning projects using EC2 instances will require an EBS volume attached to the EC2 instance. It is also possible to attach multiple EBS volumes to an EC2 instance. This depends on the operating system. For Windows, each new EBS volume is seen as a new drive represented by a drive letter, and for Linux, each new EBS volume is seen as a mount, represented by a unique mount path. The number of EBS volumes that can be mounted on an EC2 instance is determined by the operating system and the instance type. Next, let's talk about another AWS storage technology, called S3.

S3

This is an object-based storage option in the AWS ecosystem. **S3** is an acronym that stands for **Simple Storage Service**. It is a store for keeping different types of **objects**. Objects in this context mean files, such as image files, PDF files, Word files, and video files, basically, any type of file. The files are stored in logical locations called S3 buckets. In each S3 bucket, files can be uploaded and folders can be created within the buckets. S3 has no limit in terms of the number of files that can be stored in it. S3 does not serve as a storage service alone; it can also be used to host and serve **static websites**. S3 also has huge applications in big data and machine learning workloads because of its reliability and durability in keeping objects. Data stored in S3 can be stored in different files and folders and can be accessed either via an S3 **Uniform Resource Identifier** (**URI**) or via an HTTP URL, which gives access to view or download the file.

S3 also has a robust security suite, which is used to ensure that the files stored within the buckets are secure. The security in S3 ranges from giving access to a specific object to someone who needs it to ensuring that sensitive data is extremely hard to delete within the S3 bucket. S3 also boasts replication, meaning that any data stored within S3 is replicated in at least three AWS availability zones. This means that the data is properly backed up and, in case anything happens to one of the regions, the data is available in other regions. S3 also falls into the category of managed services, which means you do not have to worry about server provisioning, scaling, and the security of the underlying infrastructure that is used to run the Amazon S3 service.

> **Important note**
> Static websites are websites that are built with HTML, CSS, and JavaScript.
> They do not have a server-side part for processing database connections and
> other complex application resources.

In AWS, there is a principle called the **Shared Responsibility Model**. This model explains the shared security of responsibility binding both parties, which are the user (you) and the vendor (AWS). The model explains that AWS is responsible for the **Security of the Cloud**, while you, the user, are responsible for **Security in the Cloud**. This means that all the hardware security, physical location security, cooling systems, power, and everything else that it takes to keep the cloud environment up and running is the responsibility of AWS. But you, the user, are responsible for any resources running within the cloud infrastructure.

Breaking it down, this means that if there is a security breach in your AWS instance due to a poor configuration undertaken by you, or a malicious application got into any of the resources within your AWS account, you, as the user, are responsible for that breach or malicious activity in your AWS account. AWS is going to be available to give support and professional technical advice on best practices in terms of how to avoid it, but AWS will not assume responsibility for that type of incident.

The next service we will be talking about is Amazon EFS. Let's first understand what it is, along with some of its real-world applications.

EFS

Amazon **Elastic File System** (**EFS**) is an easy-to-use NFS storage service. **NFS** is an acronym for **Network File Storage**. It is a unique type of storage that requires expertise to set up, manage, and scale. It uses a computer network to store files. It can store anything from terabytes of data up to exabytes of data. Being able to set up and manage data at that scale can be very daunting and expensive to run. AWS has taken care of all of those operational complexities and made it easier, faster, and more efficient with the EFS service. Just like the EBS volume, EFS needs to be mounted in an EC2 instance before the storage can be accessed.

EFS can also be attached to your on-premise instance via a VPN or **AWS DirectConnect**. However, there is a difference between an EBS and EFS service; while a single EFS can be mounted on multiple EC2 instances, EBS volumes can only be mounted on a single EC2 instance at a time. The maximum size you will find in an EBS volume is a 16 TB (terabytes) storage capacity, but EFS can be as much as 8 EB (exabytes) of storage capacity, which is 8,000,000 terabytes. But this is the catch; writing to EBS volumes is faster than writing to EFS because an EBS volume is directly attached to the EC2 instance, while EFS is connected via the network, meaning that there is some latency when data is written in an EFS volume, unlike the EBS volume. Amazon EFS is only supported on the Linux operating system.

> **Important note**
> AWS DirectConnect is a managed service from AWS that allows you to connect your data center directly to the AWS global infrastructure. It is usually used by companies who do not want to connect via the public internet, but create an exclusive consistent connection to the AWS global infrastructure, for security, compliance, and network efficiency purposes.

EFS is very suitable for big data and machine learning workloads, which do not require a **strong consistent read**. EFS can also serve as database storage for big data database engines such as **Elasticsearch**, **Apache Spark**, and **Hadoop** type workloads. They can also be used as persistent storage for containers deployed in Kubernetes or any other type of container orchestration service/tool.

Other storage services are available within AWS, such as Storage Gateway and AWS Backup, but these three mentioned are the major storage services you will find being used for the majority of workloads within the AWS ecosystem. Since we now have a basic understanding of these services, let's now move on to see how monitoring works for each of these services. We will start with the EBS storage service.

Monitoring Amazon EBS volume metrics

IOPS is a measure of the speed at which a disk can read and write information. The full meaning of **IOPS** is **input/output per second**. This means that the speed of the read and the write is measured in seconds. The speed at which data is read and written to the EBS volume determines the speed at which the data will be received by the application running within the EC2 instance, thereby impacting the experience that users using the application will receive. IOPS is one of the many metrics we monitor to keep track of the behavior of an Amazon EBS volume. Amazon EBS volume has a dashboard of various metrics and data that is captured to enable us to understand other behaviors of our EBS volume. We already mentioned previously that an EBS volume is irrelevant without an EC2 instance, meaning that the behavior of the EBS volume will be directly proportional to the metrics we find within the EBS volumes (*all things being equal*).

On a basic level, when an EBS volume is created (EBS volumes are created during the process of creating an EC2 instance; sometimes, they can be created independently from an EC2 instance; refer to the following instructions at https://docs.aws.amazon.com/AWSEC2/latest/UserGuide/ebs-creating-volume.html), it provides some metrics on the EBS volume dashboard. The most basic metric we should know about is whether our EBS volume is **Okay**. This means that the EBS volume we have created has no defects or problems running. This can be ascertained in the **Status Checks** tabs of the EBS volume, as shown in the following screenshot:

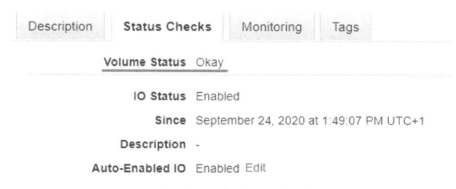

Figure 9.1 – Status checks for EBS volumes

The preceding screenshot also contains other relevant information pertaining to the EBS volume, including **IO Status**, **Since**, **Description**, and **Auto-Enabled IO**. This is the starting point in terms of monitoring the status of our EBS volume. With this, we know when it was created, and we can also see that **IO Status** is **Enabled**.

The next step is to go deeper into more meaningful and useful metrics for measuring the performance and behavior of our EBS volume. To do that, we will navigate to the EBS volumes page. Then we will click on the **Monitoring** tab, which is an option that comes with every EBS volume that is created, which is located within the EC2 management console. To get to the EBS volume and then the **Monitoring** tab, perform the following steps:

1. Launch the AWS management console and navigate to **EC2**.

2. On the EC2 dashboard, go to the side-bar navigation and locate **Elastic Block Store** (which is the same as EBS). Click on the **Volumes** link.

3. If you have volumes already created, you will see the list of volumes that have been created. Click on one of the volumes and then click the **Monitoring** tab just below the list. If you do not have any volumes, use the following link to create an EBS volume: https://docs.aws.amazon.com/AWSEC2/latest/UserGuide/ ebs-creating-volume.html.

4. This will show all the basic metrics of an EBS volume, as shown in the following screenshot:

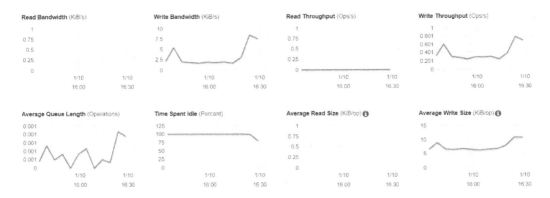

Figure 9.2 – EBS volume metrics

From the preceding screenshot, we can identify that there are a couple of metrics for the EBS volumes. These metrics include **Read Bandwidth, Write Bandwidth, Read Throughput, Write Throughput, Average Queue Length, Time Spent Idle, Average Read Size**, and **Average Write Size**. Each of these metrics explains different behaviors of the EBS volume. The read/write bandwidth means how much data has been read and written in terms of kilobytes per second. From the screenshot, we can see that there has been some write activity that has occurred.

Another important metric to look at is **Average Queue Length**. There is a standard that needs to be maintained for an EBS volume; this standard is an **Average Queue Length** (**AQL**) of at least one per minute. From the graph in the preceding screenshot, we can see that the AQL is less than one per minute, which means that everything is running fine with the EBS volume. The read and write throughput also gives you an idea of the read/write speed of the EBS volume.

However, there is a metric that is not visible in this dashboard, even when you try to view this dashboard of the EBS volume in CloudWatch. That metric is the percentage of disk space consumed. This metric can only be obtained when the Unified CloudWatch agent is installed in the EC2 instance where the EBS volume is attached. Then, that metric is activated during the installation and is sent to CloudWatch. Most of the time, it is impossible to know when the disk space is filled up because, by default, there is no dashboard for that. We explained how to configure the Unified CloudWatch agent in *Chapter 4, Monitoring AWS Compute Services*, in the *Collecting custom metrics on EC2* section. In that section, in Table 4.1, we also identified a list of metrics that can be captured by the Unified CloudWatch agent, among them `disk_used_percent`, which is stored as a metric in the CloudWatch metrics, as shown in the following screenshot:

Instance Nam... ▲	ImageId	InstanceId	InstanceType	device	fstype	path	Metric Name
Monitoring_Instance	ami-00514a528eadb	i-0d7	t2.small	xvda1	ext4	/	disk_used_percent
Monitoring_Instance	ami-00514a528eadb	i-0d7	t2.small	tmpfs	tmpfs	/dev/shm	disk_used_percent
Monitoring_Instance	ami-00514a528eadb	i-0d7	t2.small	devtmpfs	devtmpfs	/dev	disk_used_percent
Monitoring_Instance	ami-00514a528eadb	i-0d7	t2.small	xvda1	ext4	/var/lib/docker	disk_used_percent

Figure 9.3 – EBS volume custom metrics in CloudWatch

Clicking on the first metric will generate a graph that shows the percentage of disk space that has been used on the EBS volume, as shown in the following screenshot:

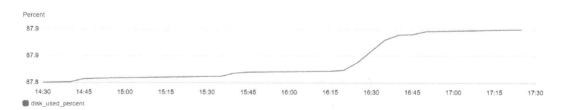

Figure 9.4 – Graph showing the percentage of disk space used

This graph shows that approximately 87% of disk space has already been used. We can take this further and create an alarm based on this metric to send an email when the disk space has peaked at 80%. This can help you know when the disk space is almost getting exhausted to enable you to swing into action and either increase the EBS volume size or delete unnecessary data causing the disk to get filled up.

We explained how to create an alarm from a metric in *Chapter 7*, *Monitoring Serverless Applications*, in the *Monitoring step functions using CloudWatch alarms* section. You can use that template to create an alarm for the `disk_used_percentage` metric, so you are always aware when the EBS volume disk capacity is almost used up.

Identifying the key metrics to look out for in EBS volumes is what we have done and what to do when we have identified them. The next storage service we will be looking at now is Amazon EFS, which we have already explained earlier. This time, we will look at how monitoring works within this service.

Understanding the performance metrics of Amazon EFS on CloudWatch

Throughput is measured in MB/s, meaning the number of megabytes written or read per second. This metric is generally used to measure the speed of a read/write operation. Amazon EFS is a storage system, hence, this metric also counts within it. EFS is also unique, as mentioned previously, in that it is a network attached storage service. This means that information sent to write to EFS is via a network. So, any network latencies or deficiencies will have a grave effect on the throughput of an EFS instance.

Being that EFS is a network thing, this means that the number of clients connecting to the EFS storage service matters a lot. EFS has a way of monitoring the number of connections performing any type of I/O operations on it. Remember that EFS can be mounted on multiple EC2 instances, as well as on-premise virtual machines. So, knowing the number of client connections is another important metric that is captured by EFS. The other metrics captured by Amazon EFS can be obtained from the EFS monitoring dashboard within EFS. To view the dashboard, click on an EFS instance that has been created previously (see how to create a simple EFS instance here: `https://docs.aws.amazon.com/efs/latest/ug/creating-using-create-fs.html`). The following screenshot shows a sample of graphs and metrics for an EFS instance:

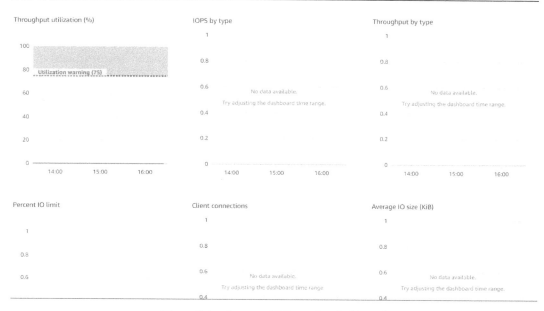

Figure 9.5 – Amazon EFS metrics dashboard

The preceding screenshot shows a couple of graphs and metrics measured by Amazon EFS. These are baseline metrics that are quite helpful in understanding the behavior of the EFS instance. This graph will show the number of client connections made to the EFS service. The number of client connections is usually proportional to the number of EC2 instances that the EFS service is mounted on. There is also **Average IO size**, measured in kilobytes, which means the average input/output size of data in kilobytes.

As with every other metric, you can view more options and details via Amazon CloudWatch Console. When a mount is successfully done on an EC2 instance (see how to mount an EFS on an EC2 instance here: `https://docs.aws.amazon.com/efs/latest/ug/mounting-fs.html`), you can perform other monitoring operations on the EFS that has been mounted on the EC2 instance. To do that, you need to install the Amazon EFS client called `amazon-efs-util-package` (use the following link to install in Amazon Linux: `https://docs.aws.amazon.com/efs/latest/ug/installing-amazon-efs-utils.html` and use the following link for other Linux distributions: `https://docs.aws.amazon.com/efs/latest/ug/installing-other-distro.html`). This helps us to send logs from the Amazon EFS service, which becomes available in CloudWatch Log groups, in the `/aws/efs/utils group`. The log stream in the log group contains the name of the EC2 instance(s) where the EFS service is mounted.

EFS is a network attached storage and we have seen the various key metrics to always watch out for when using Amazon EFS for our various workloads. Moving on to the next storage service in the AWS, we have Amazon FSx. We will first have a little introduction to Amazon FSx, understand what it can be used for, and then look at the different metrics that help to understand the behavior of an Amazon FSx instance.

Monitoring of Amazon FSx

This is the EFS version for Windows. It is a storage filesystem that can be attached to your Amazon EC2 Windows instance. FSx is a distributed filesystem and comes in two flavors – **Amazon FSx for Windows File Server** and **Amazon FSx for Lustre**. The first is strictly used for Windows servers and has an integration with **Microsoft Active Directory**. This means that governance and security measures can be easily implemented via the Active Directory part for the file server when it is mounted on the Windows Server operating system. It also has support for SSD and HDD storage options, depending on your storage needs and requirements.

> **Important note**
> Microsoft Active Directory is a group of services used in Windows Server operating systems for managing users and devices within a network. It is usually used to manage the privileges and authorizations that users and devices have within a network to ensure that the right users have the right permissions to the right resources and services.

Due to its speed and high efficiency, FSx can be used for workloads that require speed and high performance. FSx can be used for various workloads, such as **high-performance computing (HPC)**, video processing, and financial modeling workloads. FSx is quite easy to set up and get up and running. To set up an FSx instance, perform the following steps:

1. Log in to your AWS management console and navigate to **FSx**.

2. In the FSx management console, click on **Create file system**.

3. This will display the two options to choose from, as shown in the following screenshot. Click on the **Amazon FSx for Lustre** option. Then click **Next** to continue:

File system options

○ Amazon FSx for Windows File Server

**Amazon FSx
for Windows File Server**

◉ Amazon FSx for Lustre

**Amazon FSx
for Lustre**

Amazon FSx for Lustre

Amazon FSx for Lustre makes it easy and cost effective to launch and run the world's most popular high-performance file system. Use it for workloads where speed matters, such as machine learning, high performance computing (HPC), video processing, and financial modeling.

- Allows your workloads to process data with consistent sub-millisecond latencies, up to hundreds of gigabytes per second of throughput, and up to millions of IOPS.
- POSIX-compliant, so you can use your current Linux-based applications without having to make any changes, providing a native file system interface that works as any file system does with your Linux operating system.
- Supports multiple deployment options for short-term and long-term data processing.
- Seamlessly integrated with Amazon S3 (connect your S3 data sets to your FSx for Lustre file system, run your analyses, write results back to S3, and delete your file system), Amazon SageMaker, Amazon Elastic Kubernetes Service (EKS), and AWS ParallelCluster.
- Accessible from on-premises over Direct Connect and VPN connections.
- File system data is automatically encrypted at-rest and in-transit.

Cancel   Next

Figure 9.6 – Creating an FSx filesystem

4. Fill the form that displays next. Type the name of the filesystem (for example, sample) and enter the storage capacity you require. It takes a minimum of 1.2 TiB. Leave all configurations as their default settings and then click **Next** to continue.

5. The following page shows a review of everything that has been configured for your confirmation. When everything is confirmed, click the **Create file system** button to create the new filesystem.

It takes a couple of minutes before the filesystem is available. Once it is available, you can then attach it to an EC2 instance as a mount path. The following screenshot shows instructions on how to mount an FSx filesystem to a Linux instance:

▼ **Attach instruction - using the default DNS name**

1. Open a terminal

2. Create a new directory on your EC2 instance, for example /fsx

   ○ `sudo mkdir` /fsx

3. `sudo mount -t lustre -o noatime,flock fs-0ba21b576287763b3.fsx.us-east-1.amazonaws.com`@tcp:/hkt3bbmv /fsx

Figure 9.7 – Mounting FSx to Amazon EC2

By following the instructions in the preceding screenshot, we will be able to attach the FSx filesystem to our EC2 instance. Now that we have our FSx instance, how do we monitor its behavior and activities? FSx has a dashboard that helps us do just that. We should be able to know when our disk capacity is getting used up. This and other relevant information is available on the FSx monitoring dashboard. To get there, click on the FSx filesystem that we have created, and then click on the **Monitoring** tab just after the **Network & security** tab. This will give us the monitoring dashboard as shown in the following screenshot:

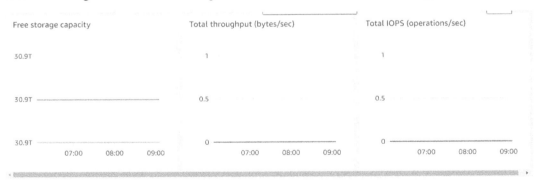

Figure 9.8 – FSx monitoring dashboard

The preceding screenshot is a snapshot of an FSx service. The dashboard provides metrics such as **Free storage capacity**, which helps us to know how much of the provisioned capacity is in use and how much is free. There is also **Total throughput**, which is the rate that measures the speed of the disk in bytes per seconds. Lastly, there is **Total IOPS**, which is the measure of I/O operations on the disk, also measured per second.

A good practice is to go to Amazon CloudWatch and configure an alarm on the free storage capacity to ensure that when it gets to a particular threshold, it sends an alarm or triggers a Lambda function that scales up the size to something higher to avoid any incident that will make it impossible for the FSx filesystem to perform I/O operations.

We have seen how to monitor our FSx filesystem via the FSx monitoring dashboard, which provides some good metrics and graphs on the behavior of the filesystem that we have created. The same monitoring can be done for both the **Amazon FSx for Windows** and the **Amazon FSx for Lustre** filesystems. Let's now move on and look at monitoring from the block storage standpoint, seeing how CloudWatch monitors Amazon S3 and its resources.

Understanding CloudWatch metrics on Amazon S3

In the introductory section of this chapter, we talked about storage devices. One of the storage devices mentioned was Amazon S3. We discussed that Amazon S3 is an object store that can store almost any number of files uploaded to it. Amazon S3 is exceptionally durable, with an SLA of 99.999999999%. This number, according to the uptime.is SLA calculator, means that there is zero downtime daily, weekly, monthly, quarterly, and even yearly. In this kind of service, you might not be monitoring for the availability of your files since AWS has promised that zero downtime will occur.

In S3, you might not find the fancy metrics and dashboard that are used to analyze and understand the performance of the system. Instead, S3 offers a more unique way of observing what needs to be monitored and measured. For every S3 bucket, there is a **Metrics** tab that shows just two graphs:

- **Total bucket size**
- **Total number of objects**

This is demonstrated in the following screenshot:

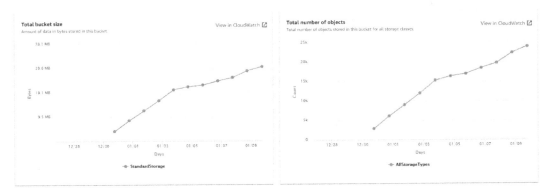

Figure 9.9 – S3 metrics dashboard

To be able to view these metrics, click on any bucket that has been created (follow this link to learn how to create an S3 bucket: https://docs.aws.amazon.com/AmazonS3/latest/gsg/CreatingABucket.html). On the tabs that are shown, click on the **Metrics** tab. This will instantly show the bucket metrics for the specific bucket. Different buckets will have different graphs to show, based on the activity within that bucket.

From the preceding screenshot, we can see the two metrics we already mentioned previously represented in graph form. The first, which is **Total bucket size**, specifies the size (in bytes) of all the objects in the bucket. This gives an estimate for you to know how much data is stored in the bucket. For our example, the bucket is holding 29.1 MB of data. The next metric is **Total number of objects**, which is a count of the number of objects that exist within the bucket. From our graph, the total number of objects in this bucket is approximately 24,000.

These are straightforward metrics to have an overview of the objects that are stored within the bucket. However, you can also access other more detailed information regarding your bucket, such as logs, which are the way in which the different objects are being accessed. By default, server access logging is disabled for S3 buckets, but this can be enabled for a bucket if the need arises. These are the steps to enable server access logging in S3:

1. Log in to your AWS management console and navigate to **S3**.

2. On the S3 management console, click on any bucket that exists on the list.

3. On the tabs within the bucket, click on **Properties**, just after the **Objects** tab.

4. Scroll down to the section called **Server access logging**. Click on the **Edit** button on the far right-hand side.

5. Click the **Enable** radio button and then fill out the bucket where the logs generated will be sent (ensure that the bucket already exists).

6. Click **Save changes**.

Whenever any object is accessed on this bucket, that activity will be logged immediately on the configured S3 bucket. This information can be analyzed further using **Amazon Athena** to gain more insights into the access patterns of the objects within the S3 bucket.

The last metric captured by S3 is the request metric, which is available at one-minute intervals following some latency to process.

With this, we have seen that monitoring in S3 is quite different to monitoring in other services, such as database and compute services. Due to its high durability, what needs to be monitored is much more reduced. To wrap this up, let's look at a case study for EBS volumes.

Case study regarding a consolidated EBS volume dashboard

You have been hired as the system administrator for a company that just migrated to AWS. This company has been running an on-premise service for the past decade, and they are planning a massive migration. This migration involves about 30 virtual machines all running different operating systems, with different configurations and disk spaces. The CTO is worried about monitoring the disk usage of the servers in the long run, as the disk usage of about 10 virtual machines that have been migrated as EC2 instances is not visible in CloudWatch. You have been hired as an expert in cloud monitoring, particularly AWS, to handle this. The CTO wants to have a single dashboard to be able to see the disk usage for every virtual machine/EC2 instance that has been migrated so that the CTO can know when the disk is getting used up and plan for more space or perform optimization operations to delete some of the cache data within the EBS volumes. How do you go about this?

Solution

The first step is to configure the CloudWatch unified agent to be able to pull the disk percentage metrics from all the EC2 instances. The next step involves setting up widgets for each of the metrics and showing the disk consumption in a chart. This widget is then executed for every single EC2 instance that has been migrated. Then, a CloudWatch dashboard is created with all these widgets added to it. This gives a unified dashboard of all the disk percentage consumption for all the EC2 instances that have been migrated.

Summary

The storage ecosystem in AWS is really a remarkably interesting section of AWS cloud computing. We have spent time defining the different types of storage techniques and the technologies in AWS. We talked about Amazon S3 being object storage that can be used to store any amount of data. We talked about EBS volume, which is block storage and works closely with EC2 instances for storing information. We also looked at key metrics to watch out for in an EBS volume. We also mentioned EFS, FSx, and large-scale storage, and covered configurations and key metrics relating to these services that should be monitored for better performance and cost effectiveness.

In the next chapter, we will be looking at monitoring as it is associated with network services in AWS. We will look at the different networking services in AWS and how CloudWatch integrates with all of them.

Questions

1. What metric tells you if the speed of your EFS filesystem has reached its peak and requires the mode to be changed?

2. Apart from the **Bucket Size** and **Number of Objects** metrics in S3, are there other metrics that exist in Amazon S3?

3. An EBS volume monitoring dashboard displays a lot of metrics relating to the performance and availability of the EBS volume. However, there is one important metric that is not readily available in the EBS monitoring dashboard, but which is essential in knowing whether there is enough space in the EBS volume. What metric is this?

Further reading

For more information on the topics covered in this chapter, refer to the following titles:

- *Features of Amazon S3*: https://www.packtpub.com/product/amazon-s3-essentials/9781783554898

- *Basic Concepts of Amazon S3*: https://www.packtpub.com/product/amazon-s3-essentials/9781783554898

- *Getting Ready for AWS EBS*: https://www.packtpub.com/product/aws-masterclass-storage-cdn-aws-s3-aws-cloudfront-video/9781788992930

- *Introduction to AWS EFS*: https://www.packtpub.com/product/aws-masterclass-storage-cdn-aws-s3-aws-cloudfront-video/9781788992930

10

Monitoring Network Services

The last chapter focused on the monitoring of storage devices. We spent time explaining the different storage services in the AWS ecosystem. We talked about Amazon S3, **Amazon EFS**, and **Amazon FSx** and the different ways they can be applied in different workloads. We then looked at how monitoring works in each of these services and how to look at key metrics to get a better understanding of what is going on from time to time.

In this last chapter on the monitoring of AWS services, we shall be looking at the monitoring of networking services. We will start by looking at the basics of computer networks, the different components, and the terms associated with computer networking. Then, we shall look at the different networking services in AWS and see a brief summary of what each of them is designed for and the purpose they serve as part of the networking stack in the AWS ecosystem.

Then, we shall be looking at the monitoring architecture for some of the essential services and understand the key metrics to always watch out for when using these services. They usually generate lots of graphs, metrics, and logs, so the ability to know the right metrics and graphs to focus on is key in being a monitoring and observability expert.

We will then look at a case study, which is a real-life scenario that will require an understanding of network monitoring, and we will see how to solve the problem and question that will be posted in the case study.

We will cover the following topics in this chapter:

- Introduction to computer networking
- Monitoring Amazon VPC flow logs
- Understanding the behavior of a load balancer with status metrics
- Application observability with App Mesh and Cloud Map
- Configuring logging in Amazon Route 53
- Case study on VPC analysis

Technical requirements

To be able to accomplish the technical tasks in this chapter, you will need to have met the following technical pre-requisites:

- A working AWS account (you can opt for the free tier, which will cost $0/month for 1 year)
- A basic understanding of **Domain Name System** (**DNS**)

The code files for this chapter can be downloaded from `https://github.com/PacktPublishing/Infrastructure-Monitoring-with-Amazon-CloudWatch/tree/main/Chapter10`.

Check out the following link to see the Code in Action video:

`https://bit.ly/3vbCWCe`

Introduction to computer networking

The idea of making two computers able to talk is fundamental to networking. A single computer can contain valuable information; for that information to be available to another computer or computers, there needs to be a connection between the computer with the information and the computer that needs that information. The process of making these computers communicate to share information is called **networking**.

Computer networking can be classified into two major categories:

- **Local Area Network (LAN)**: A LAN is a small network of computers within an enclosed environment. The network of computers within an office or within a school premises all fall under LAN. A LAN can be either a wired or a wireless network. Wired means that a network cable is used to connect the computers and other network devices together. Wireless means that the computers can communicate wirelessly without the need for network cables. That is made possible through a wireless hub or hotspot that all the computers connect to. Now, because they are connected to that single source, they can then communicate via that source as that's what binds them. Just the way our phones are connected to masts and cell towers.

- **Wide Area Network (WAN)**: This is the senior brother of LAN and is used for wider area coverages and reaches. A network that connects buildings within a city or across a country is known as a WAN. Based on that concept, this means that the internet is the largest WAN in the world. The AWS global infrastructure is an example of a WAN. This infrastructure network is an Amazon-dedicated network that connects all its availability zones within a country, and the availability zones are connected to other availability zones in other countries around the world. A WAN comprises both wired and wireless networks. In some cases, fiber optic cabling is used and in other cases, telecommunication masts serve as the medium for transmitting information.

Now that we understand the two basic types of networking, let's talk about some common networking terms that we shall be using in this chapter that we should know about, to help us get a better understanding of the monitoring infrastructure we shall be talking about subsequently.

Understanding a few common networking terms

To have a better understanding of this chapter, we shall start by introducing a few common networking terms. These terms are not directly connected to AWS networking but are used as umbrella terms in both cloud computing and on-premises networking. They are essential to have at your fingertips before having any engagement or conversation on anything concerning networking. They are discussed in the following subsections.

IP address

When the post office needs to send a letter or parcel, there needs to be a destination address or delivery address with the house number, street number, and other relevant information needed to send the message or parcel to its destination. In networking, a message is called packets. For these packets to get to their destination, there needs to be an address tied to them. This address is called an IP, which stands for **Internet Protocol**. An IP address is a number set used to uniquely identify a device in a network. Network devices range from phones to laptops, desktops, servers, and network devices. Each of these devices needs to have an IP address for them to be identified. No two devices within a network can have the same IP address; if for any reason this happens, it causes what is called an **IP conflict**. In most cases, IP addresses are allocated dynamically via a technology called **Dynamic Host Control Protocol** (**DHCP**). This service ensures that two devices on the network do not get any type of IP conflict. An example of an IP address is 10.198.211.3.

Subnets

This is a logical method for dividing and separating a large network. Subnets are used to create subgroups from a larger network, which is used for security and compliance configurations. A large network could a subnet for application servers and another subnet for a database server that might not need internet connectivity. Each of these subnets will have further unique security and **firewall** configuration. Subnets are used in AWS networks. Subnets are created under a **Virtual Private Cloud** (**VPC**) and are used as the infrastructure backbone for **Elastic Compute Cloud** (**EC2**), **Relational Database Service** (**RDS**), **Elastic Container Service for Kubernetes** (**EKS**), **Elastic Container Service** (**ECS**), and other AWS services that require network infrastructure to run.

Important Note

A firewall is a hardware device or software used to control network access. Firewalls are made of rules that open and close specific network ports and protocols to allow/deny access to and from other devices to ensure the network is secured.

This network division is done via a notation called CIDR notation. **CIDR** stands for **Classless Interdomain Routing**. This notation is used to define the groupings and divisions of a network. The CIDR notation is usually represented with the IP address, a forward slash, and a number that represents the CIDR notation. An example of a CIDR notation is 10.197.212.4/16. The following table is a sample of the group of devices that a CIDR block can take. The devices are represented by the IP address range column:

CIDR Notation	IP Range	Number of Devices
1.0.0.0/8	1.0.0.0 - 1.255.255.255	16,777,216
1.0.0.0/16	1.0.0.0 - 1.0.255.255	65,536
1.0.0.0/24	1.0.0.0 - 1.0.0.255	256

Table 10.1 – Table showing the group of devices that a CIDR block can take

The preceding table shows a list of CIDR notations, IP ranges, and a number of devices that a particular CIDR ranges.

Internet gateway

The internet gateway is a service that gives a subnet access to the public internet. Networks generally do not have any form of internet access when configured by default. The only way the network can have access is when an internet gateway is attached to it.

Network interface

A network interface is a device that is attached to a phone or computer to give it the ability to join a network. Network interface devices are also called network cards on laptops and desktops. There are network interface devices for a wired network and for wireless networks. A wired network interface is visible, but a wireless one is usually invisible. The network interface is available on all mobile phone devices, which is why they can connect to Wi-Fi and data networks, because of the network interface device that is configured within the mobile device.

Now that we understand some common networking terms, let's look at networking services in AWS and have a basic understanding of what they do.

Exploring AWS networking services

In the previous section, we just talked about various networking terms that encompass all types of networking infrastructure. In this section, we shall drill down into specific networking services offered by AWS. We shall give a basic definition of what they are, how they work, and where they are applied when setting up cloud infrastructure.

The networking services used in AWS are discussed in the following subsections.

VPC

VPC is an AWS service that is used to create network connectivity infrastructure. Without a network configuration, EC2 instances cannot be created or configured in AWS. The underlying network infrastructure that makes EC2 instances run is VPC. When you sign up for AWS for the first time, a default VPC is created across all the regions of your AWS account. VPC also has other features, such as internet gateways, NAT gateways, subnets, transit gateways, **Virtual Private Network (VPN)**, AWS Network Firewall, security groups, and **Network Access Control Lists (NACLs)**. They are used for various network configurations, from dividing the network into subnetworks to creating a VPN for secured networking communication. There are also security groups and NACLs that are used to configure security policies on the network. VPC is the bedrock of **Infrastructure as a Service (IaaS)** within the AWS ecosystem.

CloudFront

The speed of your website will determine whether users stay or leave. Hence, it is essential to ensure the website loads as fast as possible. The problem with this is twofold. When a user visits a website, the site pages get downloaded into the user's browser. Modern browsers have a way of storing some data so that when the page loads again, it becomes faster. This same technology exists within the AWS cloud; it uses an **Edge location** to store a website that has been loaded previously, and that website is distributed across all the Edge locations.

> **Important Note**
> An Edge location is a special kind of mini data center that is used to accelerate application delivery and performance. Edge locations are set up close to where customers are located to reduce the latency of the application and improve the speed to give customers and users the best experiences.

This further improves the speed of the website as it will be delivered via the Edge location where all the website information has been cached.

Load balancing

This is a feature that is used to improve the availability of an application that is **scaled horizontally**. Load balancers are used to route traffic across various EC2 instances that are configured behind them.

> **Important Note**
>
> Horizontal scaling is a technique used to maintain the high availability of an application. It involves adding more servers or EC2 instances to an existing server to share the load that one server carries. A load balancer is set up in front of these servers to act as the router of the traffic across the servers that are configured behind the load balancer. There is also vertical scaling, which involves increasing the resources of a single virtual machine to handle the load of traffic hitting that server. Vertical scaling is not used often to scale an application because it leads to system downtime and does not give the system high availability, hence engineers turn more to horizontal scaling for high availability.

The load balancer and EC2 instances must be within the same network VPC to allow traffic routing between these EC2 instances. AWS has three types of load balancers. They are as follows:

- A classic load balancer, which is used for both HTTP and TCP requests.

- An application load balancer, which is used strictly for application routing. This falls under the HTTP protocol, which is the seventh layer of the OSI model.

- A network load balancer is the last type of load balancer, which is designed strictly for TCP networking and is Layer 4 of the OSI model.

These load balancers serve unique purposes based on the application-specific network model.

Route 53

This is the AWS DNS routing and domain name registration service. Route 53 serves as a DNS manager for your domain name. You can purchase a domain name from anywhere and use Route 53 to route requests to applications and services. Route 53, like any other DNS manager, supports all the basic DNS records types, such as the following:

- **A record**, used for IPv4 network routing

- **MX record**, used for configuring email servers

- **TXT record**, mostly used for domain name validation

- **AAAA record**, used for IPv6 network routing

- **CNAME record**, usually used for website subdomain routing

- **CAA record**, used to validate a domain for issuance of SSL/TLS certificates

Route 53 also has some unique features that make it different from normal DNS managers, one of which includes the unique routing policies that can be configured when any of the record types are being configured. These routing policies are as follows:

- Simple routing policy
- Weighted routing policy
- Geolocation routing policy
- Failover routing policy
- Multivalue answer routing policy

These routing policies determine how traffic is routed from the user sending the DNS request to the service configured in the DNS manager.

Lastly, Route 53 has a domain name registration feature that can be used to purchase a domain name. Domain names are also called the website name. For example, `packtpub.com` is a domain name and was purchased and is owned by Packt Publishing. When the name is bought, a DNS manager such as Amazon Route 53 is used to point the domain name to the IP address of a server, and within that server an application has been built and is running. When the user types that domain name, it automatically sends the user to the server that contains Packt Publishing's website content, and the server shows the user the page. This process of getting a website from the DNS is called **DNS resolution**.

This last section has helped us understand the different AWS networking services and what they are used for. The next section is going to focus on one of the services mentioned, VPC. We shall look at how monitoring works in the Amazon VPC service.

Monitoring Amazon VPC flow logs

The previous section explained the importance of Amazon VPC as it is the underlying infrastructure that other AWS services need to run efficiently – services such as EC2, RDS, EKS, ECS, Lambda, **Elastic MapReduce** (**EMR**), Elastic Beanstalk, Batch, Elasticsearch Service, Amazon Redshift, and ElastiCache. Due to this fact, it will also be important to know how to monitor what is going in the network infrastructure that these services run on.

VPC has a feature that allows this to be possible, called **flow logs**. A flow log is a combination of all the traffic data going through the VPC, which is a combination of all the subnets within the VPC, be it a private or public subnet. Flow logs make it possible to know the size of the data being sent or received, whether a network request was accepted or rejected, the source and destination port of a request, the source and destination IP address of a request, the network interface ID, the subnet ID, and much more information that is used in understanding the different requests and responses going through the VPC network.

This information can be collected in the form of logs, and these logs can be sent to either Amazon S3 or Amazon CloudWatch Logs, making it easy to view and analyze them to get insight into the activities in a specific VPC and all the components connected to that VPC. The logs sent to Amazon S3 can be analyzed using either the **Amazon S3 Select** feature in Amazon S3 or Amazon Athena, which uses SQL to query through data. The data in CloudWatch Logs will go into specific CloudWatch streams and can be viewed in the streams, or can also be analyzed using CloudWatch Log Insights.

Let's look at how to create a flow log from a VPC, send these logs to Amazon CloudWatch, view the logs, and explain the information we see in the VPC flow logs.

These are the steps to create a flow log:

1. Navigate to the VPC management console in the AWS management console.

2. In the VPC management console, click on **Your VPCs** on the left-hand side of the screen to show the VPCs that exist.

3. In the list of VPCs that show, click on the VPC you want to create the flow log on. For our example, we will click the **default** VPC in the list. This will give more details at the bottom of the screen, as shown in the following screenshot:

Figure 10.1 – VPC details

4. From the details page of the VPC that has been selected, click on the tab labeled **Flow logs**.

5. Click on the **Create flow log** button:

Figure 10.2 – Creating a VPC log

6. Fill out the VPC flow log form to configure the flow log. First is the name of the flow log, which is options. For this case, we shall set the name of the flow log as defaultfl. The next option is **Filter**. Leave the default option, which is **Accept**. The next option is **Maximum aggregation interval**, which means the maximum interval of time during which a flow of packets is captured. For this option, select **1 minute**. The next option is **Destination**. For this, there are two options: **Send to CloudWatch Logs** or **Send to an Amazon S3 bucket**. For this example, we shall send the flow log data to CloudWatch, so we will leave the default, which is **Send to CloudWatch Logs**.

7. Still filling in the form, the next option is to select the destination log group. To be able to select a log group, one first needs to be created. Use the following link to create a log group: https://docs.aws.amazon.com/AmazonCloudWatch/latest/logs/Working-with-log-groups-and-streams.html. When the log group is created, select it from the list or click the **Refresh** button to repopulate the list and select the log group.

8. The next step is to select the **Identity and Access Management** (**IAM**) role that will authorize VPC to write flow logs into the CloudWatch log group that has just been selected. We need to create an IAM role that allows this. To do that, use the guide on how to create an IAM role shown in *Chapter 2, CloudWatch Events and Alarms*, under the *Configuring a basic CloudWatch agent* section. But for this scenario, this is the policy to be used:

```
{
    "Version": "2012-10-17",
    "Statement": [
        {
```

```
        "Effect": "Allow",
        "Action": [
            "logs:CreateLogGroup",
            "logs:CreateLogStream",
            "logs:PutLogEvents",
            "logs:DescribeLogStreams"
        ],
        "Resource": [
            "arn:aws:logs:*:*:*"
        ]
    }
  ]
}
```

9. We will need to update the trusted entity to give the VPC access to write to
    CloudWatch log groups. To do that, click on the role that we created in the previous
    step, then click on the **Trust relationships** tab, and then click on the **Edit trust
    relationship** button. This will show the policy document for the trust relationship.
    The next step is to update it with the following policy:

```
{
  "Version": "2012-10-17",
  "Statement": [
    {
      "Effect": "Allow",
      "Principal": {
        "Service": [
          "ec2.amazonaws.com",
          "vpc-flow-logs.amazonaws.com"
        ]
      },
      "Action": "sts:AssumeRole"
    }
  ]
}
```

10. Click the **Update Trust Policy** button to save the changes we have made. This will update the trusted relationship and add VPC as a trusted entity, as shown in the following screenshot:

You can view the trusted entities that can assume the role and

Edit trust relationship

Trusted entities

The following trusted entities can assume this role.

Trusted entities

The identity provider(s) ec2.amazonaws.com

The identity provider(s) vpc-flow-logs.amazonaws.com

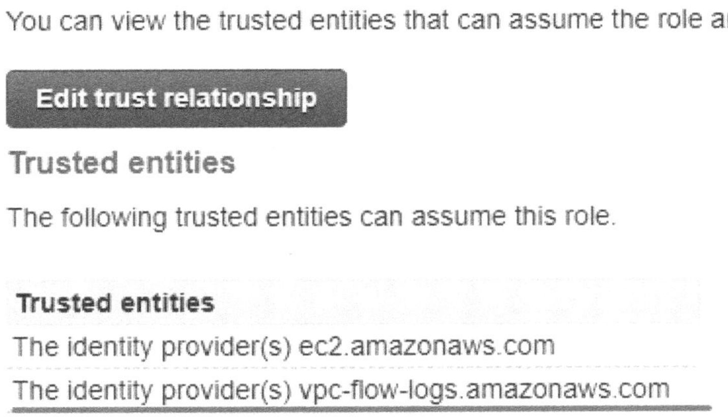

Figure 10.3 – Editing trusted entities

11. Going back to the VPC flow logs page, we can refresh and select the IAM role that has just been edited.

12. The next option is **Log record format**. This means the format in which the logs will be generated. There is a default, but it can also be customized to have more information. The default format contains information such as `version`, `accountid`, `interface-id`, `srcaddr`, `dstaddr`, `srcport`, `dstport`, `protocol`, `packets`, `bytes`, `start`, `end`, `action`, and `log-status`. There are other parameters that can be used when configuring custom logs, but we shall use the default for this setup.

13. Finally, the tags can be left, and then click on the **Create flow log** button.

14. It takes a few minutes before the logs are available, but to check them, we navigate to the CloudWatch console, then **Log groups**. Then, click on the log group that was created initially. You should find a log stream identified by a network interface, for example, `eni- 123a51fbc45e3g76-all`. Click on the stream to view the logs. This will show the logs. The following screenshot is an example of what the logs look like:

```
2 1          5 eni-0          3b92 74.82.47.21 172.31.46.198 38715 17 17 1 29 1611401350 1611401386 REJECT OK
2 1          5 eni-0          3b92 221.131.165.119 172.31.46.198 15969 22 6 14 2782 1611401350 1611401386 ACCEPT OK
2 1          5 eni-05         3b92 172.31.46.198 221.131.165.119 22 15969 6 12 2417 1611401350 1611401386 ACCEPT OK
2 1          5 eni-05         b92 194.26.25.118 172.31.46.198 54480 1050 6 1 40 1611401350 1611401386 REJECT OK
2 1          eni-05           b92 194.147.140.105 172.31.46.198 49287 32869 6 1 40 1611401350 1611401386 REJECT OK
2 1          5 eni-05         b92 194.26.25.118 172.31.46.198 54480 3361 6 1 40 1611401350 1611401386 REJECT OK
2 1          5 eni-0          b92 194.26.25.118 172.31.46.198 54480 7096 6 1 40 1611401350 1611401386 REJECT OK
2 1          eni-0            b92 34.64.73.76 172.31.46.198 54346 22 6 14 1449 1611401399 1611401446 ACCEPT OK
2 1          5 eni-05         b92 172.31.46.198 34.64.73.76 22 54346 6 12 2349 1611401399 1611401446 ACCEPT OK
```

Figure 10.4 – VPC flow logs in Amazon CloudWatch Logs

Each item in the screenshot of *Figure 10.4* represents the parameters that we used as defaults. The first is the version, which is **2** in the screenshot. The next is the AWS account ID, which is blurred. Then is the network interface ID (also called the elastic network interface in AWS), and then is the source address, which is different from one log item to the other, but the first one is 74.82.47.21, all the way to the last column item, which is OK for the log status. This is a detailed view of the activities of all resources running under that elastic network interface, showing the network request moving from source to destination.

This is extremely helpful in debugging network activities, and since it is log information, metrics can be created from it to filter rejections or network failures, and CloudWatch alarms can be configured for it. See the *Creating a metric filter* section in *Chapter 3, CloudWatch Logs, Metrics, and Dashboard*, to see how to create a metric from the flow logs that have been collected.

Now we understand how to configure flow logs in VPC to collect logs and information on every network packet flowing across the VPC network. In the next section, let's look at how to monitor another network service in AWS, an elastic load balancer.

Understanding the behavior of a load balancer with status metrics

We already mentioned the load balancer in the introductory section of this chapter. We talked about the three types of AWS load balancers: classic, application, and network. But in this section of the chapter, we shall be focused on the monitoring of load balancers. To be able to monitor a load balancer, we need to have one running that has been created. Use the following guide to create a simple application load balancer: https://docs. aws.amazon.com/elasticloadbalancing/latest/application/create-application-load-balancer.html.

Once the load balancer is created, click on it and scroll down to view the details. This contains more information about the load balancer. On the tabs that are displayed, click on the **Monitoring** tab to show graphs and metrics about the load balancer, as shown in the following screenshot:

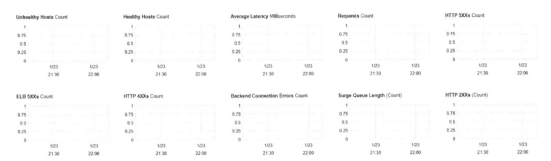

Figure 10.5 – Application load balancer graphs

The preceding screenshot shows different graphs with different metric information. We shall be talking about a few of these metrics that are very key to help you understand what is happening with the load balancer. The first graph in the preceding screenshot has the title **Unhealthy Hosts** and tells us the number of hosts that the load balancer is not connected to. We explained that a load balancer usually had servers configured behind it. AWS load balancers have a feature that does a health check to ensure that the load balancer can connect to the servers configured behind it. If it cannot connect for any reason (could be that the backend server is down or the port mapping from the load balancer to the service is incorrect), the load balancer counts the number of hosts it cannot connect to as unhealthy hosts. The next metric shows **Healthy Hosts**, which means the servers that the load balancer can connect to. The **Requests** metric is a count of the number of requests that have hit the load balancer.

There is a set of HTTP status metrics such as **ELB 5XXs**, **HTTP 4XXs**, and **HTTP 2XXs**, which are all used to know the status of the backend application. The 5XX and 4XX stand for errors. Any these found as counts in the graph data in *Figure 10.5* means that the server behind the load balancer is reachable but the application in that server has errors.

There is also the metric called **Surge Queue Length**. This metric helps in understanding the number of requests that have been queued in the load balancer and have not been served to the backend services. This is the load balancer's little way of throttling requests that have been sent to the backend server from time to time.

Now that we have seen how to get information and understand the behavior of our load balancer, let's look at how to monitor App Mesh and Cloud Map.

Application observability with App Mesh and Cloud Map

The goal of **observability** is knowing what is going on internally. In a microservice application, there are various moving parts and components of your application, so it is quite important to understand the flow of traffic within the different microservices that are interconnected. This is one of the pillars of observability called tracing. As the application grows, the number of microservices in the system grows. If there is no service mesh in the system, it becomes near impossible to understand the inner workings of the system and how traffic flows from service to service.

> **Important Note**
>
> Microservices are an architecture used to develop applications, where the application is broken down into different pieces that work independently, run independently, are developed independently, and are also deployed independently. During runtime, these systems then connect and share information via different media, APIs, message queuing, networks, and so on.

This is where AWS App Mesh shines. With App Mesh, you can understand, monitor, and control communication within your microservices. It does this by installing a sidecar for every application deployed in your container orchestration service. With that, it is able to get network information of traffic flowing in and out of the running container. When every container in the cluster has a sidecar, it gives end-to-end visibility of the logical flow of the containers running within the cluster. This concept is also known as a **service mesh**.

> **Important Note**
>
> A service mesh is a network infrastructure layer that works side by side with applications running in a microservice architecture to help with a centralized method of administering, securing, tracing, and monitoring all network service communication between the different microservices.

So, we can rightfully say that AWS App Mesh is a managed service for service mesh, allowing deeper integration of the service to be used for both Amazon EKS and Amazon ECS.

AWS Cloud Map

From the name, you can tell that Cloud Map helps you create a map of the AWS services that you are using. Most times, these services are used as separate entities and there is usually no way of understanding the changes that occur in the services when scaling operations are made, or other types of service changes. With Cloud Map, the AWS service(s) you are using are registered to it, and it can help to map the services based on what is registered to it. Since the services are registered on Cloud Map, it can automatically discover them and knows the most up to date and healthy service resources.

When a Cloud Map namespace is created in Cloud Map (a namespace is the logical way that Cloud Map groups all the services of a single application), it creates a Route 53 private hosted zone.

There are three options Cloud Map uses to discover registered services/instances:

- API calls
- API calls and DNS queries in VPCs
- API calls and public DNS queries

Each of these options will require a service instance to be registered with its IP and by sending intermittent pings as health checks, Cloud Map is able to get a sense of the different services that your application is using. Cloud Map is mostly used for **containerized** microservices workloads.

> **Important Note**
>
> Containerized means that the application is designed to run in a Docker container. See more information about Docker containers in *Chapter 5, Setting Up Container Insights on Amazon CloudWatch*, in the *Container services in AWS* section.

In AWS, the two services for running containerized applications are Amazon ECS and Amazon EKS. They can be registered and kept up to date in AWS Cloud Map. When an application is deployed in an ECS or EKS cluster, a service is created, and that service is registered with Cloud Map. With that, Cloud Map is able to help you maintain the service without using any other third-party tools.

Both App Mesh and Cloud Map are about observability and while one is helping you see the flow of traffic within application services running in your cluster using the service mesh technique, the other is helping you to register and manage the services in your container orchestration cluster, reducing the stress of deploying an open source tool and maintaining it too.

Let's move forward to see how logging is configured in Amazon Route 53 and other interesting monitoring tooling that exists in Route 53.

Configuring logging in Amazon Route 53

Route 53, like every other AWS service, has a lot of interesting services. There are many unique features in Amazon Route 53 that you might not find in other DNS services. One of them is the unique routing policies that were already mentioned in the *Introduction to computer networking* section where Route 53 was introduced.

In this section, we are looking at Route 53 in the context of monitoring. There are a couple of things that can be monitored in Route 53, from something as basic as monitoring the status of the domain registration to know whether it is complete to showing the status of a domain to know when it is going to expire. You can also send DNS query logs of the configured hosted zones to Amazon CloudWatch Logs for further analysis. The DNS query logs are supported on both private DNS- and public DNS-hosted zones.

> **Important Note**
> A hosted zone is a logical collection of DNS records that makes it easy to manage DNS records that all come from the same domain name or **Top-Level Domain (TLD)**.

Let's configure query logging for a public hosted zone. To do this, we shall use the following steps:

1. Navigate to Route 53 in the AWS management console.

2. Click on a DNS-hosted zone that has been created. If you do not have one, use the following link to create a hosted zone: `https://docs.aws.amazon.com/Route53/latest/DeveloperGuide/CreatingHostedZone.html`.

3. On the hosted zone page, there is a button named **Configure query logging**, in the top-right corner of the screen. This will take us to the page to configure the query logging:

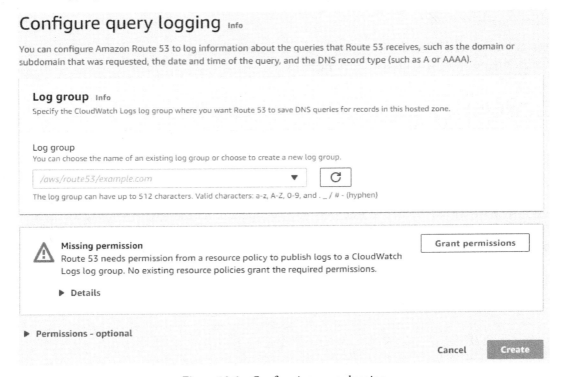

Figure 10.6 – Configuring query logging

4. Click on the dropdown with the label **Log group** to select the log group to send the log data to. There is also the option to create a fresh log group for this in the list, so we shall click that option and create a log group called /aws/route53/hzlogs.

5. Click on the **Grant permissions** button to grant Route 53 permission to publish logs to CloudWatch Log groups.

6. Click the **Create** button to activate the query logging.

   This will activate the query logging and starts sending logs to the CloudWatch log groups that we just created.

> **Important Note**
> The log group that is created automatically goes to the **N. Virginia** region of CloudWatch. So, automatically, the Route 53 logs will be sent to the CloudWatch log group that is in the **N. Virginia** region.

To view the logs, we navigate to the CloudWatch management console | **Log groups** and then to /aws/route53/hzlogs, which is the name of the log group we created from the Route 53 console. Click on the log group to view the log stream. Different log streams will be displayed. Click on any of them to view the logs. The data in the log stream will look as in the following screenshot:

▶	Timestamp	Message
		No older events at this moment. *Retry*
▶	2021-01-25T00:08:17.000+01:00	1.0 2021-01-24T23:08:17Z Z20P7P79MZ2056 mycloudseries.com A NOERROR UDP CDG3-C1 34.245.82.45 -
▶	2021-01-25T00:10:17.000+01:00	1.0 2021-01-24T23:10:17Z Z20P7P79MZ2056 mycloudseries.com A NOERROR UDP CDG3-C1 3.248.186.214 -
▶	2021-01-25T00:18:20.000+01:00	1.0 2021-01-24T23:18:20Z Z20P7P79MZ2056 mycloudseries.com A NOERROR UDP CDG3-C1 3.248.186.46 -
▶	2021-01-25T00:18:20.000+01:00	1.0 2021-01-24T23:18:20Z Z20P7P79MZ2056 mycloudseries.com A NOERROR UDP CDG3-C1 34.245.82.42 -
▶	2021-01-25T00:22:22.000+01:00	1.0 2021-01-24T23:22:22Z Z20P7P79MZ2056 mycloudseries.com A NOERROR UDP CDG3-C1 3.248.186.217 -
▶	2021-01-25T00:23:22.000+01:00	1.0 2021-01-24T23:23:22Z Z20P7P79MZ2056 mycloudseries.com A NOERROR UDP CDG3-C1 34.245.82.33 -
▶	2021-01-25T00:26:23.000+01:00	1.0 2021-01-24T23:26:23Z Z20P7P79MZ2056 mycloudseries.com A NOERROR UDP CDG3-C1 3.248.186.217 -
▶	2021-01-25T00:27:23.000+01:00	1.0 2021-01-24T23:27:23Z Z20P7P79MZ2056 mycloudseries.com A NOERROR UDP CDG3-C1 34.245.82.44 -
		No newer events at this moment. *Auto retry paused.* Resume

Figure 10.7 – Route 53 query logs on a CloudWatch log stream

These are just like CloudWatch Synthetics canaries, which are used for application health check monitoring, as discussed in *Chapter 7, Monitoring Serverless Applications*. Route 53 also has a health checker feature that can be used to monitor websites, domains, IP addresses, and services with different ports other than 80 and 443, which are the common network ports for an application. This feature can be found in the Route 53 management console on the left hand-side menu, with the name **Health checks**. Click this option, then click on the **Create health check** button. Fill in the form shown in the following screenshot:

Configure health check   ❷

Route 53 health checks let you track the health status of your resources, such as web servers or mail servers, and take action when an outage occurs.

Name	*example name* ❶
What to monitor	● Endpoint ❶
	○ Status of other health checks (calculated health check)
	○ State of CloudWatch alarm

Monitor an endpoint

Multiple Route 53 health checkers will try to establish a TCP connection with the following resource to determine whether it's healthy. Learn more

Specify endpoint by	● IP address ○ Domain name
Protocol	HTTP ▾ ❶
IP address *	*192.0.2.44 or 2001:DB8::1* ❶
Host name	*www.example.com* ❶
Port *	80 ❶
Path	/ *images* ❶

▸ Advanced configuration

URL	❶
Health check type	Basic - no additional options selected (View Pricing)

Figure 10.8 – Configuring a Route 53 health check

The next step is to create an alarm that notifies you when the health check fails. After that, click on the **Create health check** button to create the health check.

This health check is mostly used for a failover routing policy in Route53, which is how the routing policy knows that the primary backend service is down, and then routes the traffic to the secondary backend. The health check status is continually sent to the failover routing policy, which helps it to decide on and know the action to take. It also routes back to the primary backend service when the service becomes available.

Though many users are not concerned about monitoring DNS queries, if you have a private DNS configuration and there are problems with DNS resolutions, one of the steps that can be taken is to collect logs and see what is going on under the hood. There are also cases where the traffic flow might need to be audited and graphs created and used to understand the flow perfectly.

Let's look at a simple case study of how the knowledge we have gotten from this book can be helpful in a real-life scenario.

Case study on VPC analysis

You are the **Site Reliability Engineer** (**SRE**) in charge of the availability of all the applications of a media company. Your company runs a streaming service where users watch movies, TV series, and other video content. You have been receiving reports from the support team that customers are noticing a decline in the speed at which the movies are loading for watching and from time to time, the video does not stream smoothly. After checking the application, you notice that the application runs fine but the application connects to Amazon Aurora PostgreSQL and you need to check how traffic goes and returns from the application to Amazon Aurora. What actions would you take to investigate this?

Solution

The first step is to create a VPC flow log, because both the application, which will most likely will be in EC2, and the Aurora database are both running on VPCs. Analyze the logs collected in either CloudWatch Logs or Amazon S3. Check the logs where the destination address/port is the Aurora database and check the speed at which the response is returned.

Summary

This chapter was all about networking. We started by introducing computer networking and all the various components of computer networking. Then, we drilled down to looking at networking from the AWS standpoint and the different AWS services and the different areas of networking specialty that they cover.

The next stage was then to take some of the services and see how networking works for each of them. We started with Amazon VPC and understood the value of flow logs, and then we created a flow log to demonstrate how we can use it to collect logs of network activities in our VPC and subnets within the VPC. We explained the different information contained within the log and how to interpret the meaning of the logs generated by the VPC flow logs.

We then moved on to load balancers in AWS and looked at the graphs and metrics of a load balancer and what some of the metrics mean. We talked about how to configure alarms for the critical graph metric.

Then we moved on to App Mesh and Cloud Map, and the monitoring of services deployed with App Mesh and Cloud Map.

Finally, we rounded out the chapter by looking at DNS monitoring with Amazon Route 53. We configured a simple Route 53 health checker that can be used for Route 53 failover configuration or can be connected to a CloudWatch alarm to send a notification when the health check on a domain or IP address fails.

The next chapter is the conclusion of this book. We shall consolidate all we have been learning in the last 10 chapters of the book. Best practices to follow in ensuring proper monitoring and the cost of running monitoring in CloudWatch shall also be explored in the next chapter.

Questions

1. What feature in VPC is used to view networking activities from EC2 instances?

2. What are the two destinations for VPC flow logs?

3. What metric/graph in a load balancer tells you that the backend configured with the load balancer is available?

4. True or False: It is possible to configure a Route 53 health check to be able to send notifications?

Further reading

For more information on the topics covered in this chapter, refer to the following links:

- The basics of networking with AWS: https://www.packtpub.com/product/practical-aws-networking/9781788398299

- Working with Route 53: https://www.packtpub.com/product/aws-networking-cookbook/9781787123243

- Elastic load balancing: https://www.packtpub.com/product/practical-aws-networking-video/9781789349788

- AWS networking essentials: https://www.packtpub.com/product/aws-networking-solutions-video/9781788299190

11
Best Practices and Conclusion

In the previous chapter, we talked about the monitoring of networking services. We started by talking about the fundamentals of networking and all the different key aspects to understand basic networking. Then, we went further to talk about some AWS network services and then looked at monitoring for some select AWS services.

This chapter is the concluding chapter of this book. We shall be talking about best practices and techniques for monitoring. Monitoring is usually an afterthought in application development and deployment operations. But application logs and metrics become important when there are any performance issues noticed or there is downtime – everyone turns to monitoring and logging. But if there is not a proper process for how to set up monitoring in your organization, then it is going to be more difficult to have that information readily available when you need it.

In this chapter, we shall be talking about the best practices and techniques to use to ensure that we do monitoring in the right way and more consistently. This book has shown monitoring for different AWS services. In this concluding chapter, we shall talk about best practices and techniques to implement monitoring on these services. We shall also talk about how you are billed when using Amazon CloudWatch for the collection of logs, the creation of metrics, and the creation of charts.

We will cover the following topics in this chapter:

- Best methods used in monitoring
- An explanation of CloudWatch billing
- Summarizing everything learned so far

Best methods used in monitoring

As was said in the introduction of this chapter, monitoring is usually an afterthought of application development and deployment, although it is a major process and is a major part of the **Site Reliability Engineer (SRE)** role. A major purpose of this role is to ensure that systems maintain high availability and reliability. One of the pillars of making sure a system is highly available and reliable is to ensure that there is proper monitoring and observability of the system. The SRE role goes beyond configuring monitoring tools; SREs bring a lot of automation into the work being done, meaning that some programming/scripting knowledge is needed to be a good SRE.

SREs are also involved in building and designing a process for how incidents, escalations, and downtimes are handled in the system. They are the ones that work with businesses and other departments to set **service-level agreements (SLAs)**, **service-level objectives (SLOs)**, and **service-level indicators (SLIs)** for different systems and applications running within the organization, for both internal use and customer-facing systems.

This responsibility means that there must be a method for monitoring observations. The following are key points that are the best methods for carrying out monitoring.

Automate everything

The first step in ensuring monitoring is consistent is to automate the process of configuring monitoring in your systems and applications. It is usually easier for SREs and system administrators to forget monitoring and set up the infrastructure and do monitoring when the infrastructure is already set up. When monitoring is part of the setup process, then it will not be forgotten during the process. One way to ensure this is using cloud automation tools such as **Terraform** and **CloudFormation**. When the infrastructure is set up using any of these tools, monitoring can be incorporated as part of it and can be the standard in the organization for how every infrastructure is set up to ensure consistency across all services set up within the AWS environment. One basic configuration is the health monitoring of a website or application endpoint.

The following link is a simple Terraform script that can be edited to apply a Route 53 health check to any URL of an application that is deployed into the AWS environment (`https://github.com/PacktPublishing/Infrastructure-Monitoring-with-Amazon-CloudWatch/blob/main/Chapter10/terraform/route53healthchecker.tf`). To run the Terraform template, use the following instructions: `https://learn.hashicorp.com/tutorials/terraform/automate-terraform`.

Another way to automate monitoring configurations is using AWS **Simple Systems Manager (SSM)**.

Audit monitoring configurations from time to time

In fast-moving systems, there are bound to be a lot of changes, configurations, and deployments happening at the same time, and quickly. It is important that services and applications are still monitored during these changes. There are situations where after a service is created or deleted, the monitoring setup does not follow suit. You could have an EC2 instance that has been terminated and the dashboard of the custom metrics from the EC2 instance is still up. This could cost some money, especially if it is not really in use.

Performing periodic audits on the monitoring and observability infrastructure is quite essential. It could also help spot possible issues. An example is logs might stop being sent to CloudWatch Logs for one reason or another. This could be an oversight and when those logs are needed at any time, you might discover that the instance has not been sending logs to CloudWatch. With periodic auditing, this can be quickly spotted and fixed.

Measuring workload performance

Logs and metrics are not only used to know when something has gone wrong but can also be used to envisage when a problem is about to occur. In *Chapter 1, Introduction to Monitoring*, we spoke about proactive and reactive monitoring. Being proactive is knowing when something will go wrong and acting on it before your attitude to the incident becomes reactive. Being reactive means that you do not know when something occurs but react when it has occurred. Measuring workload performance could mean understanding how much time it took for a request to move around the system from start to finish. A Synthetics canary helps in pinging your website and shows you the view from the user's perspective. This is a technique that can tell you how long the website takes to load, whether there are 404 errors on the website, and many other metrics that will help you know how the system is performing. When these performance issues are identified, they can be quickly addressed before they become incidents.

Ensuring important metrics go with alarms

There are lots of logs that can be collected for CloudWatch from various services. But it is important to focus on the most important logs and create metrics for them. The next thing that should follow the metrics is threshold alarms. Now, alarms on their own can be too much and when there are too many alarms, it reduces the importance of alarms, which should indicate important incidents and draw your attention to something important. Using composite alarms in AWS is a good way to reduce the number of notifications sent by multiple alarms that have been configured. Use the following link to see how to create composite alarms in Amazon CloudWatch: `https://docs.aws.amazon.com/AmazonCloudWatch/latest/monitoring/Create_Composite_Alarm.html`.

An explanation of CloudWatch billing

With all the interesting features we have explained in this book, it is quite important to know that CloudWatch, just like every other AWS service, is not free of charge. Although, AWS has a free tier with the following features, which AWS promises will be free forever based on the free tier link (`https://aws.amazon.com/free`). The following screenshot shows what CloudWatch can give you for free every month:

Amazon CloudWatch

10

custom metrics and alarms

Monitoring for AWS cloud resources and applications.

10 Custom Metrics and 10 Alarms

1,000,000 API Requests

5GB of Log Data Ingestion and 5GB of Log Data Archive

3 Dashboards with up to 50 Metrics Each per Month

Figure 11.1 – Amazon CloudWatch free tier package

From the screenshot, we can see that you can get 10 custom metrics and 10 alarms for free. Custom metrics are metrics that you create manually from the logs that are being sent to CloudWatch Logs. This means you can create 10 of those for free. Anything more than that you will be charged for. Now, these charges vary from metrics to dashboards, alarms, logs, events, contributor insights, to canaries. The prices for these components usually vary from region to region. For example, the cost of collecting logs and sending them to CloudWatch Logs to store costs $0.50 per GB in the Ohio region, and it costs $0.76 in the Tokyo region. These prices are not usually the same from region to region for the different components. But some components are the same across all the regions. Dashboards, for example, cost $3 per dashboard per month no matter the region you are in. For more details on CloudWatch pricing, check the CloudWatch pricing page. It gives more information based on custom metrics, container insights on both ECS and EKS, Lambda insights, and more. This is the link to the CloudWatch pricing page (https://aws.amazon.com/cloudwatch/pricing/). It is quite important to understand some of these metrics as they could incur a lot of charges if not well monitored and audited from time to time as many dashboards and metrics might be needed to understand our application.

Summarizing everything learned so far

In this section, we shall do a recap of everything we have learned in the last 10 chapters of this book, going from one chapter to another:

1. *Chapter 1, Introduction to Monitoring*, was an introduction to monitoring. We looked at monitoring from its first principles and explained how it has evolved over time and taken in software and cloud monitoring. Then we moved on to the types of monitoring and the importance of monitoring in a system. Then, we introduced Amazon CloudWatch and talked about how the well-architected AWS framework is helpful as a guide in performing monitoring more efficiently in AWS.

2. For *Chapter 2, CloudWatch Events and Alarms*, we started going deeper into more monitoring concepts, such as CloudWatch Events and Amazon EventBridge, comparing them and showing the differences. We also looked at the components of an event and moved straight on to look at what a CloudWatch alarm is and how to create one.

3. *Chapter 3, CloudWatch Logs, Metrics, and Dashboard*, introduced logs and talked about how important they are in taking note of every event that occurs in a system or an application. We also introduced metrics, which are what help to make logs have a better meaning, and then dashboards are used to represent the metrics in pictorial form.

4. In *Chapter 4, Monitoring AWS Compute Services*, we started looking at monitoring in relation to different AWS services. Specifically, we focused on compute services such as EC2 and Elastic Beanstalk and practiced configuring logging to CloudWatch Logs using the CloudWatch Unified Agent.

5. In *Chapter 5, Setting Up Container Insights on Amazon CloudWatch*, we continued with compute services, but this time our focus was on containers. We introduced the concept of containers and talked about AWS services used for container orchestration. We then looked at Container Insights for monitoring on both ECS and EKS.

6. *Chapter 6, Performance Insights for Database Services*, took a turn into the monitoring of database services in AWS. We started by introducing database management, talking about the types of database technologies and different database technologies. We then looked at the different database technologies in AWS, such as RDS, Redshift, and how to configure monitoring and logging for these services.

7. *Chapter 7, Monitoring Serverless Applications*, was focused more on serverless applications. To help get a better understanding, we first explained the concept of serverless and the different serverless services in AWS. Then we went further to explain how monitoring works on each of the serverless services, such as Lambda, and introduced endpoint monitoring via CloudWatch Synthetics canaries.

8. In *Chapter 8, Using CloudWatch for Maintaining Highly Available Big Data Services*, we looked at monitoring big data services in AWS. We first identified the different operations in big data and the AWS services used for the different big data operations such as data analytics and data engineering. We then looked at how to monitor and track issues when running workloads in big data services.

9. *Chapter 9, Monitoring Storage Services with Amazon CloudWatch*, was focused on storage services and the monitoring of EBS volumes, EFS, and FSx storage services using Amazon CloudWatch to get deep insights into the behavior of the storage services.

10. *Chapter 10, Monitoring Network Services*, introduced more on monitoring network services in AWS. It started by introducing the basics of networking and the components of a computer network. Then, we did a demo on how to create VPC flow logs, which give information on the flow of network logs in and out of the AWS network. Then, we also talked about monitoring in other AWS networking services.

Next, let's get a summary of the book that corroborates all we have been learning in a nutshell.

Summary

The purpose of this book was to ensure that you have a clear introduction to every aspect of monitoring AWS services using Amazon CloudWatch. In conclusion, every chapter of this book will help a novice who has no idea about the networking ecosystem in AWS to have a clear entry-level understanding of how networking works from one service to another. That is why we have spent a great deal of time touching on as many categories as possible and the most used services in AWS, to give insights and an overall view of the monitoring infrastructure in AWS and how Amazon CloudWatch is at the center of monitoring and also the observability of services within the AWS ecosystem.

Understanding the monitoring infrastructure in AWS will help you to achieve better configurations and management, and to secure your workloads running in AWS. This will also make implementing the best practices we mentioned in the *Best methods used in monitoring* section of this chapter much easier to imbibe in your organization and ensure systems are reliable and highly available.

Assessments

Chapter 1

1. The Reliability and Performance pillars
2. SMTP and SMPP
3. Proactive monitoring
4. A metric

Chapter 2

1. Amazon SNS
2. Event pattern
3. Reactive monitoring

Chapter 3

1. Logs
2. Dashboards
3. Metric filter
4. With a log group
5. IAM role

Chapter 4

1. CPU, memory, disk.

2. The unified agent collects both logs and metrics as a single solution, while the CloudWatch agent does not.

3. Amazon SNS.

4. A dashboard is a pictorial representation of a trend over time, while a metric is a specific indicator after logs have been aggregated.

Chapter 5

1. They host applications in the form of pods in the Kubernetes cluster.

2. Activate Container Insights for ECS and activate **Auto-configure CloudWatch Logs** in the ECS task definition.

3. They are both container orchestration tools.

4. No, there is no difference.

Chapter 6

1. DB load

2. DynamoDB

3. Use Amazon CloudWatch Contributor Insights

4. A wait.

Chapter 7

1. Function as a service

2. A Lambda function

3. AWS X-Ray tracing

4. Yes

Chapter 8

1. CloudWatch Log group

2. Loading or storage

3. Amazon S3

4. Number of shards of the stream

Chapter 9

1. Throughput utilization

2. Yes

3. Volume Disk Space

Chapter 10

1. VPC flow logs

2. CloudWatch Logs and Amazon S3

3. HTTP 2XXs

4. True

Packt.com

Subscribe to our online digital library for full access to over 7,000 books and videos, as well as industry leading tools to help you plan your personal development and advance your career. For more information, please visit our website.

Why subscribe?

- Spend less time learning and more time coding with practical eBooks and Videos from over 4,000 industry professionals

- Improve your learning with Skill Plans built especially for you

- Get a free eBook or video every month

- Fully searchable for easy access to vital information

- Copy and paste, print, and bookmark content

Did you know that Packt offers eBook versions of every book published, with PDF and ePub files available? You can upgrade to the eBook version at packt.com and as a print book customer, you are entitled to a discount on the eBook copy. Get in touch with us at customercare@packtpub.com for more details.

At www.packt.com, you can also read a collection of free technical articles, sign up for a range of free newsletters, and receive exclusive discounts and offers on Packt books and eBooks.

Other Books You May Enjoy

If you enjoyed this book, you may be interested in these other books by Packt:

Hands-On AWS Penetration Testing with Kali Linux

Kirit Sankar Gupta

ISBN: 978-1-78913-672-2

- Familiarize yourself with and pentest the most common external-facing AWS services

- Audit your own infrastructure and identify flaws, weaknesses, and loopholes

- Demonstrate the process of lateral and vertical movement through a partially compromised AWS account

- Maintain stealth and persistence within a compromised AWS account

Zabbix 5 IT Infrastructure Monitoring Cookbook

Nathan Liefting and Brian van Baekel

ISBN: 978-1-80020-223-8

- Explore the different types of monitoring available in Zabbix 5

- Find out how to build your own Zabbix templates

- Use Zabbix proxies for effective load balancing/scaling

- Work with custom integrations and the Zabbix API

- Set up triggers and alerting with Zabbix 5

- Maintain your Zabbix setup for scaling, backups, and upgrades

- Discover how to perform advanced Zabbix database management

Packt is searching for authors like you

If you're interested in becoming an author for Packt, please visit `authors.packtpub.com` and apply today. We have worked with thousands of developers and tech professionals, just like you, to help them share their insight with the global tech community. You can make a general application, apply for a specific hot topic that we are recruiting an author for, or submit your own idea.

Leave a review - let other readers know what you think

Please share your thoughts on this book with others by leaving a review on the site that you bought it from. If you purchased the book from Amazon, please leave us an honest review on this book's Amazon page. This is vital so that other potential readers can see and use your unbiased opinion to make purchasing decisions, we can understand what our customers think about our products, and our authors can see your feedback on the title that they have worked with Packt to create. It will only take a few minutes of your time, but is valuable to other potential customers, our authors, and Packt. Thank you!

Index

Index

W

www.ingramcontent.com/pod-product-compliance
Lightning Source LLC
LaVergne TN
LVHW081334050326
832903LV00024B/1157